I0831297

HENRY STUBBE
AND THE BEGINNINGS OF ISLAM

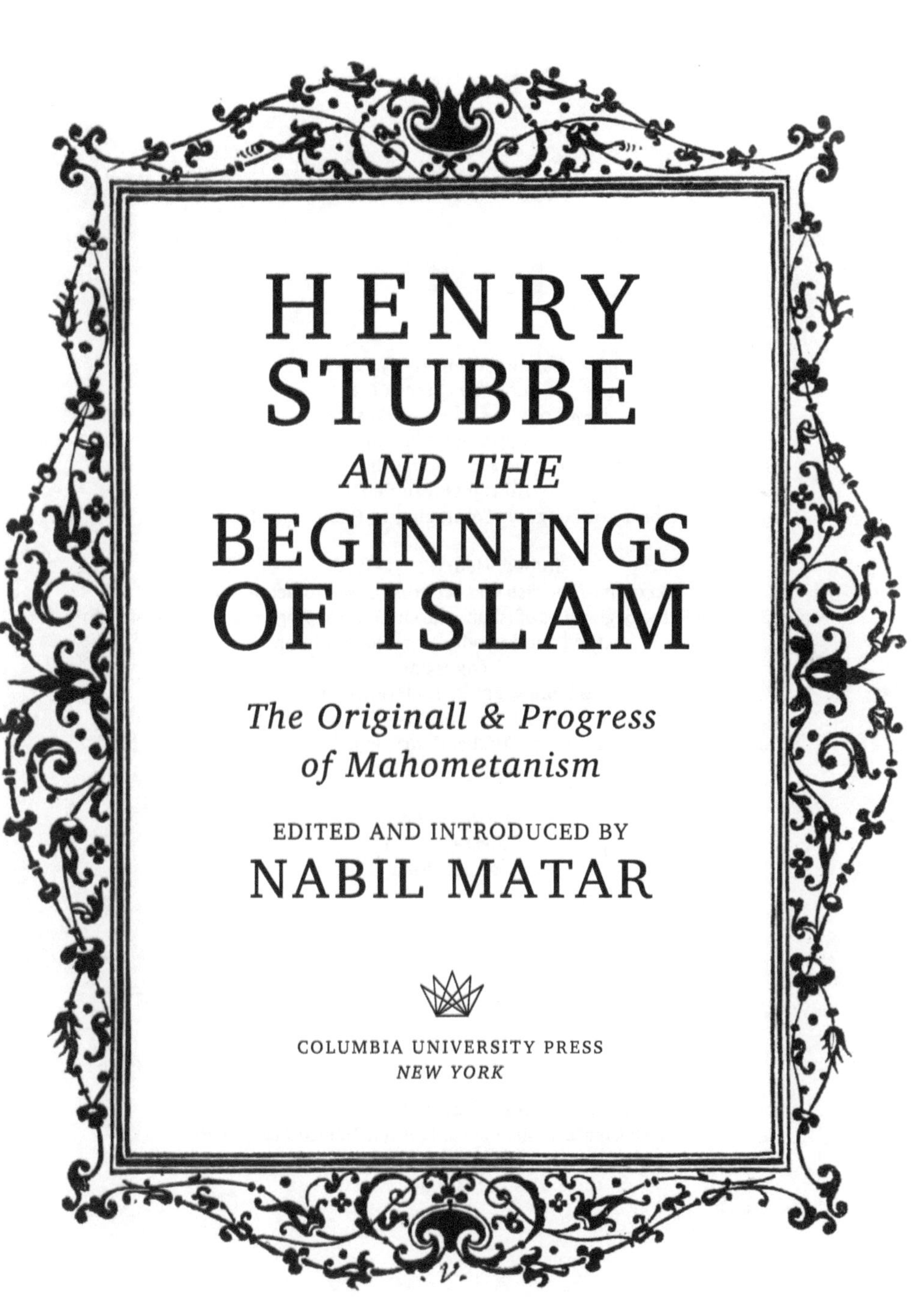

HENRY STUBBE AND THE BEGINNINGS OF ISLAM

The Originall & Progress of Mahometanism

EDITED AND INTRODUCED BY

NABIL MATAR

COLUMBIA UNIVERSITY PRESS
NEW YORK

Columbia University Press
Publishers Since 1893
New York Chichester, West Sussex
cup.columbia.edu

Library of Congress Cataloging-in-Publication Data

Stubbe, Henry, 1632–1676.
[Account of the rise and progress of Mahometanism]
Henry Stubbe and the beginnings of Islam : the Originall & progress of Mahometanism /
edited and introduced by Nabil Matar.
pages cm
Includes bibliographical references and index.
ISBN 978-0-231-15664-6 (cloth : alk. paper)—ISBN 978-0-231-52736-1 (e-book)
1. Islam—Early works to 1800. 2. Stubbe, Henry, 1632–1676. I. Matar, N. I. (Nabil I.),
1949– II. Title.

BP160.S7 2014
297.09—dc23
2013018042

Cover art: From *Historia Orientalis* (1660).
Andover-Harvard Theological Library, Harvard University.

Cover design: Milenda Nan Ok Lee

For Mohammad Asfour

نُورٌ عَلَى نُورٍ
يَهْدِي اللَّهُ لِنُورِهِ

Light upon light,
God guides to His light.

—QUR'ĀN 24:35 (KHALIDI'S TRANSLATION)

CONTENTS

ACKNOWLEDGMENTS

This project started as a result of incisive questions from two talented graduate students, both of whom have now completed their dissertations: Josh Mabie and Eric Carlson. In a course on "Britain and the Islamic Mediterranean," we read the 1911 edition of Henry Stubbe's treatise on Islam, but on a number of occasions I found myself unable to address adequately some of the issues they raised. When I visited England later that year, I decided to consult the manuscript versions of the treatise. I then realized the need for a new edition.

I was awarded a Grant-in-Aid from the University of Minnesota that allowed me to spend time at the British Library, the Senate Library of the University of London, and the Bodleian. To the staff at these libraries, I am deeply grateful. Closer to home, the staff of the James Ford Bell Library at the University of Minnesota have been most supportive: Dr. Marguerite Ragnow and Ms. Margaret Borg. So too were the ILL staff at Wilson Library. As always, the staff at the Houghton Library, Harvard University, some of whom I have known since my first visit in 1988, were most gracious.

I wish to thank Heather Krebs, a former graduate student, who typed the manuscripts. She faced a herculean task, which she completed with masterful accuracy. I also want to thank my tireless student assistant, Katie Sisneros, who helped in formatting and proofing as well as for preparing the index. I know it was not easy. I consulted many colleagues and friends to whom I am thankful: Professor Wadad Kadi (Arabic) who spent many hours with me; Professor Dominic Baker-Smith (Latin), Professor Philip Sellew (Greek), Professor Spencer Cole (Latin), Professor Marco Perale (Greek), and Mr. Gabriel Fuchs who focused on the longer Latin passages. To all: thank you. Any shortcomings that might remain are, of course, mine.

I am thankful to the Center for Early Modern History, director Sarah Chambers, at the University of Minnesota and the Center for Near Eastern

Studies at the University of Chicago for giving me the opportunity to present a lecture on my initial findings on Stubbe. I was honored by the UK arm of the Association of Muslim Social Scientists, director Anas Hajj Ali, and the Alwalid bin Talal Centre for Islamic Studies at the University of Cambridge, director Yasir Suleiman, with the Building Bridges Award, which afforded me another occasion to develop my thoughts in a lecture on Henry Stubbe.

On a personal note, I would like to thank the friends without whom I could not have completed this work: A. A. Baramki; Professor Muhammad Shaheen, University of Jordan, a deeply cherished friend, who met with me, in Amman and in Oxford, to offer suggestions and insights; Professor Jeanne Kilde, director of the Program of Religious Studies at the University of Minnesota, whose initiative and drive are ever an inspiration to me; and Professor Wadad Kadi, whose enduring friendship and vast scholarship have been my sustenance in the icy Minnesota "Polite." And from the British side of the pond, I would like to thank the many friends I have in London: Dina Matar and John Taysom for their wonderful hospitality; David Brooks, my Cambridge friend of yore; Samira Kawar, my student during my first teaching job at the University of Jordan in Amman, and her husband Yacoub Douani; Patrick Spottiswoode of the Globe Theatre, a dear friend and always an inspiration; Basim Ziadeh, friend from childhood in Beirut, and Riad Nourallah of AUB days.

As always, I remember Selim Kemal and Rudy Stoeckel, friends of Beirut, Cambridge, and Melbourne, Florida—towns of memory. And so too, the doe-eyed girl of the green.

And forever in the pictures around me in my study: Abraham and Hady, may the Lord ever shine His face on you . . . and forgive you the sarcasm you inflicted on me for wasting taxpayers' money on editing a seventeenth-century document; my sister Inaam, resisting retirement in Amman; Suheil Farouqui, a fellow traveler on the road to Jerusalem; GH always, always cherished and thanked; and, of course, Galina, *alḥabība*.

* * *

This book is dedicated to Mohammad Asfour.

It was his from the moment I started working on it.

With Mohammad, I shared the first office in my first job at the University of Jordan in 1976. Poet, translator, and teacher, Mohammad is unforgettable. I have met many of his former students in various parts of the world—at the University of Wisconsin, on a flight to Rabat, in the Reading Room of the British Library: there was always wonder in their eyes as we talked about him. I too had fallen under his spell: a man for whom language is sacred, and literature, both Arabic and English, an Ariadne's thread in the labyrinth of exile.

From him I learned about beauty and holiness, about Islamic devotion and Arabic prosody, about Byron and Jabra Ibrahim Jabra. And he continues to be a mentor: every so often, I pester him with questions and queries, and he responds, with grace and learning and illumination. As he approaches retirement, and with Um Firās by his side, I hope he will record his last journey from 'Ayn Ghazāl and the diaspora of Palestine.

HENRY STUBBE
AND THE BEGINNINGS OF ISLAM

INTRODUCTION

The "Copernican Revolution" of Henry Stubbe

UROPEAN MEDIEVAL representations of the Prophet Muḥammad and of the beginnings of Islam were uniformly negative, as Norman Daniel showed in his magisterial *Islam and the West: The Making of an Image* (1960). Although Nicholas of Cusa described the Prophet as merely a man in error (*Cribratio Alkorani*, ca. 1458–64), European writers always viewed Muḥammad and the Qur'ān from an oppositional perspective. John Tolan has shown that from Theodor Bibliander's *Machvmetis Sarracanorvm principis vita* (Basel, 1543)[1] to Humphrey Prideaux's *The true nature of imposture fully display'd in the life of Mahomet* (1697) there was not a single European text that attempted to present a historically accurate biography of the Prophet and of the beginnings of Islam.[2] Rather, and as the conflict among Christian denominations surged in Western Europe—Catholics, Lutherans/Protestants, Socinians, Deists, and others—writers dragged Muḥammad into the fray treating him as a forerunner of the Protestant heresy, an ally of the pope, a proto-Socinian, or an "atheist." Which is why Henry Stubbe (1632–76) is important: he was the "exception" to all early modern writers on Islam.[3]

This little-known physician who spent the last years of his life in between Stratford-upon-Avon and Bath undertook a Copernican Revolution (in Kant's use of the phrase) in the study of Islam. For Kant, the phrase served as a metaphor for the shift in the position of the observer that made possible a new astronomy and for him a new epistemology. In the study of Islam Stubbe moved away from Euro-Christian sources to the canon of Arabic histories and chronicles in Latin translation, instituting thereby a sharp methodological and historiographical break with the past. In just under sixty thousand words, Stubbe presented the first heavily annotated biography of the man who had given birth to "Islamism" as well as the first English description of ʿAli, the Prophet's cousin. But, Stubbe knew that it was the message in "Alkoran" that was of paramount importance: his encomium on Islam in the last pages of his treatise is unparalleled in early modern European writing.

In the seventeenth century, three Arabic histories about early Islam were translated into Latin: accounts by Jirjis ibn al-ʿAmīd al-Makīn, Saʿīd ibn al-Baṭrīq/Eutychius, and Gregorios Abū al-Faraj/Ibn al-ʿIbrī, all of which had relied on important Muslim historians such as Muḥammad ibn Jarīr al-Ṭabarī, ʿAbdallah ibnʿUmar al-Bayḍāwī, Muḥammad ibn ʿabd al-Karīm al-Shahrastānī, and others. A master of Greek and Latin, Stubbe consulted these translations closely and realized how sources indigenous to Islamic civilization could lead to a new understanding of contested history and a reassessment of the most misrepresented man in early modern European religious thought: the Prophet Muḥammad. These sources were widely available, having been published in the academic powerhouses of Oxford and Leiden, Paris and Basel. But among all the English writers about Islam and the "Mahometans" in the seventeenth century, from preachers to travelers, from theologians to comparative historians, only Stubbe consulted these sources to produce a detailed history of the beginnings of Islam, *The Originall & Progress of Mahometanism.*

Many were the readers who perused and copied Stubbe's treatise, as evidenced by the numerous manuscript versions of the treatise that have survived and the others that are known to have been lost. But, to date, all scholars who have written about Stubbe's treatise have relied on the Lahore 1911 edition of the work, *The Rise and Progress of Mahometanism,* published by Hafiz Mahmud Khan Shairani—with the exception of J. A. I. Champion's 2010 study. This edition was the composite of three "authors": the original text by Stubbe, "improvements" on the text by Charles Hornby in 1705, and the editorial excisions by Shairani of passages which were deemed "not polite." This mix of hands renders the edition unreliable. Only by focusing on the earliest complete manuscript of *The Rise and Progress of Mahometanism,* which I am renaming *The Originall & Progress of Mahometanism,* ca. 1701, will it be possible to examine the actual words, or close to the actual words, that Stubbe wrote. Because this manuscript is not an autograph, there can be no absolute certainty, but the sections that Charles Blount copied in 1678 and included in letters to Thomas Hobbes and to the earl of Rochester (which appeared in print in 1693 and 1695) and the three manuscript fragments that survive from the latter part of the century at the British Library all correspond exactly to this manuscript, with inevitable scribal variances.

A century before Edward Gibbon, Stubbe recognized how integrated "Muslim history [was] with that of the Roman and Byzantine empires."[4] Islam was not an appendage to Greco-Roman civilization, but a fresh start, "a revolucion" in world history (fol. 48). It was a religion that returned to the purity of monotheism that had been lost amidst the theological controversies of the "Jews Judaizing Arabians Judaizing Christians . . . Jacobites Nestorians Arrians Trinitarians Manichees Montanists Sabeans & Idolaters" (fol. 119).[5] In this respect the importance of Stubbe should not be underestimated: he was the first writer in English to use Arabic and non-Chalcedonian sources to develop a largely accurate interpretation of the beginnings of Islam and of the life of its founder. Although he fell into some of the errors and misrepresentations about Muḥammad that were endemic among European writers, he carefully referenced his sources to show where he had found his information. Toward the end of the treatise, and perhaps after further reading, Stubbe corrected some of his views and presented a heroic portrait of a "great prophet," thereby refuting the "foolish relations our authors give of their [Muslim] prophet and religion" (fol. 126). To a very large extent, Stubbe realized this goal in his treatise not by discovering new manuscripts or by learning new languages but by reading what was already available in print, in Latin, and in the libraries and bookstores. Thus his "Copernican Revolution."

THE LIFE OF HENRY STUBBE

Henry Stubbe was born on 28 February 1632 in Partney, Lincolnshire, to "anabaptistically inclin'd" parents, as his first biographer, Anthony Wood, recalled.[6] At the age of ten, and after fleeing with his mother from Tredagh, Ireland, in the wake of the Uprising (1641), he was admitted to Westminster School where he studied under Richard Busby. Through the patronage of Sir Henry Vane the younger, one of the leaders of the Independents, he matriculated at Christ Church, Oxford, in 1649, and, along with Humphrey Prideaux, future dean of Norwich, "presumably attended [Edward] Pococke's Arabic lectures."[7] After graduating BA in 1653, he joined up with the Cromwellian army in Scotland until 1655. On his return to England, he settled in Oxford, and in a number of letters to Thomas Hobbes he praised *Leviathan*, "so great a work," which he had "read all over." On 13 January 1657 he reported to Hobbes that he was dedicating four hours "each day to ye translation of ye Leviathan" into Latin.[8] With the help of John Owen, the Independent Dean of Christ Church (1651–58), Stubbe was appointed Second Keeper at the Bodleian Library, serving under Thomas Barlow. He remained in office "as a hired hand of Dr Owen" until 1659, when he was ejected, after which he moved to Stratford-upon-Avon "to practise the faculty of physic."[9]

By then Stubbe had become active in writing. His first letters and publications show him as a confrontational and rather pedantic man, with some interest in English literature, citing in the course of his treatises Abraham Cowley's poetry and the plays of Ben Jonson. He was, as Wood wrote in *Athenai Oxonienses* (1691–92), "the most noted Latinist and Grecian of his age."[10] In this early stage of his writing career, Stubbe did not show an interest in Islam, but, in 1659, upon disagreeing with William Prynne, the Presbyterian polemist, he ridiculed him for supporting monarchy and associated his ideas with practices of the Ottoman government: "I hope the Assembly of Lincolns-Inne will keep a Fast for the good success and prosperity of the Turke, that so they may have the best of Governments, a Monarchy."[11] Stubbe published other treatises in that year, revealing a knack for extensive citations from a wide array of sources. He had, as Wood explained, "a most prodigious memory."[12] Stubbe proved faithful to his patron, Sir Henry Vane, who was maligned in the dangerously transitional year of 1659 (he would be executed in June 1662) and wrote to defend him against the accusation of "Socinianism."[13]

After the Restoration Stubbe conformed to the Anglican establishment and became an ardent supporter of the Stuart king and of the Church of England. In 1661 he went to practice medicine in Jamaica, having secured the posting through the assistance of Sir Alexander Fraizer, the king's first physician.[14] After his return to England in 1665, he pursued his "practice in the Countrey" of Warwick, while keeping himself informed about the intellectual changes in the metropolis. Stubbe rejected the new scientific method promoted by the Royal Society because of its emphasis on utilitarian experimentation and its total disregard of historical learning, and he set out to refute the ideology that Thomas Sprat promulgated, in *History of the Royal Society* (1667), and which was taken up by Robert Boyle and Joseph Glanvill in the latter's *Plus Ultra* (1670). The result was a series of acrimonious exchanges that appeared in print in the late 1660s and early 1670s. "I was sensible of the injuries he [Glanvill] doth unto the dead," Stubbe wrote, "the affronts he puts upon the living, the contempt wherewith he decries the University Learning and those Studies by which Christianity hath been supported against the Arrians, the Jews, the Mahometans, and of late the Papists and Socinians."[15] Stubbe emphasized that the universities, with their historical traditions of knowledge, were crucial to science—contrary to the views of the Royal Society that saw the universities as antiquated. The "Utility of the Ancient and Established Method of Medicaments used in Physick," Stubbe asserted, revealed how much the "innovations" of the "Institution of the Royal Society" were really not innovations at all, but reworkings of past demonstrations. The desire to show that he was au courant with, although opposed to, the new "virtuosi" and his intense zeal to challenge them drove Stubbe to conduct experiments even on himself. Thus, "in January last 1669, I had another occasion to bleed . . . I took also some of the pure citrine Serum of my blood, which tasted not very salt."[16] He was not against the experimental method, he proclaimed, just against the skepticism it generated regarding the past.

In June 1670, Stubbe wrote to his friend N. N. how "during the late times, because I would joyn with no party in a Church, they imagined that I could be of no Religion."[17] Perhaps in his attempt to show that he *did* have religion, Stubbe combined his attacks on the Royal Society with a strong defense of the Anglican establishment and its theological appeal to the first "Three Creeds, and four general Councils, or thirty nine Articles."[18] Stubbe feared that the importance given by the Latitudinarian members of the society to reason in theological matters would expose England to Catholicism and "furnish the Spaniard with better and more advantageous Opportunities."[19] And so, he vehemently defended the "Monarchy and Religion of this land, the welfare of the Church or State" while continuing his attacks on Sprat, Glanvill and others for affronting him in their writings.[20] These attacks may help to explain why he was the butt of satire in Samuel Butler's "The Elephant in the Moon" (ca. 1671).[21]

In the course of his attacks Stubbe reminded his adversaries of Muslim contributions to learning. Instead of disposing with the knowledge and languages of the ancients, as the new scientists urged, "the King," wrote

Stubbe, "should erect certain Schools in all the principal Cities, wherein the Arabick tongue should be taught: that so by this means there may be such among his Subjects, as shall be able to Dispute with the Turks, Moors, and Persians."[22] Knowledge about the languages and heritage of other civilizations was needed in the defense and consolidation of England. That was why, continued Stubbe, medieval monks had fervently studied the "learning of the Sarracens"[23]—in order to refute them—a position that recalled the words of Alexander Ross in justifying his 1649 translation of the Qur'ān to English.[24]

When the Third Anglo-Dutch War (1672–74) broke out, Stubbe turned away from the Royal Society and its danger to attack the Dutch. Conscripted by Secretary of State Arlington to write in defense of the king's policy, Stubbe published a treatise showing how the Protestant Dutch had been more harmful to England than the Muslim North Africans. In *A Justification of the Present War against the United Netherlands* (1672) he stated: "If we look upon the number and quality of the injuries which we have received from the Dutch, the Turks of Algiers and Tunis are less offensive, and less perfidious. If we consider the courses by which the Dutch attacque us, the Algerines are the more supportable to an English spirit, since they act by force, and open piracy; what the Hollanders do by finess and deceipt."[25] To defend the king, Stubbe marshaled his usual flare for citations from learned tomes and presented arguments explaining and justifying the king's actions—not only in waging war on Holland but also in issuing the Declaration of Indulgence (both took place in March 1672).[26] The declaration generated so much opposition that the king had to withdraw it a year later, at which time Stubbe wrote a second treatise, *A further iustification of the present war against the United Netherlands illustrated with several sculptures* (early 1673). Stubbe denounced the "Sectaries" who were opposed to the declaration and turned to the history of the early church in search of quotations, allusions, and references that would justify the actions of his king.[27] He selected passages from the declaration and demonstrated how, in each passage, Charles II was following the "Declaration of Constantine the great, concerning a general Indulgence."[28] Stubbe highlighted the doctrinal confusions of early Christians and how important Constantine and Theodosius were in enforcing religious authority during times of fissure and heresy. The second part of the treatise was a vitriolic attack on Holland, in which Stubbe surveyed the history of anti-English Dutch activities dating back to the reign of Queen Elizabeth. In praising the courage and enterprise of English seamen, he described them as "our Legionaries, our Janizaries, and Mammelucks." [29]

While writing *Further iustification* and earlier preparing *An Epistolary Discourse Concerning Phlebotomy* for publication (1671), Stubbe started *The Originall & Progress of Mahometanism.* The reference in the latter treatise to Lancelot Addison's *West Barbary, or A Short Narrative of the Revolutions of the Kingdoms of Fez and Morocco* (Oxford, 1671) shows that Stubbe started writing after that date; and the reference to Wilhelm Schickard's *Jus regium hebraeorum. E tenerbris Rabbinicis erutum, & luci donatum*, which reappeared in 1674 (with heavy annotations, unlike the 1625 edition), suggests that he was still working on the treatise then. Islamic history was becoming part of his study, and in his attack on Andrew Marvell's *The Rehearsal Transpros'd* (1672) he referred in his opening to "Saracenical Histories" and rejected the allegation that "Mahomet" had had "two Companions, which clubb'ed with Him, in making the Alchoran."[30] Clearly, Stubbe had become steeped in Latin texts about Islam, for not only did he defend the Prophet, but in the opening of *Originall* he praised the (unnamed) man who had given rise to "Mahometanism":

> Nothing was more mild than his Speech nothing more courteous & obliging {than his carriage} he could dexterously accommodate himself to all Ages humours & degrees He knew how to pay his Submissions to the great without Servility and to bee complacent to the meaner Sort without abasing himself. He had a ready wit {a penetrating and discerning Judgemt} & such an Elocution as no Arabian before or since hath ever equaled when he pleased he could be facetious without prejudice to his Grandeur; he pfectly understood the Art of placing his favours aright he could distinguish betwixt the deserts the inclinations & the interests of men he could penetrate into their Genius's & intenciõns without employing vulgar Espialls or Seeming himself to mind any such thing.
>
> (Fol. 2)

After this opening, Stubbe moved to the two parts of his study of Islam. Part 1 focused on the beginnings of Christianity, from its messianic origins in Judaism and its subsequent doctrinal fissures to the century that saw the birth of Muḥammad (fols. 1-49). In writing this part,

Stubbe relied on the "higher criticism" of the Bible by the foremost exegetes of his century, both continental and English, and presented an alternative history of the "original and progress" of Christianity—one that differed markedly from the account in *Further iustification*. The parallels in style and references between *Further iustification* and *Originall* are clear, especially the long discussion of the Novatians, the Donatists, and the Arians, as well as some of the turns of phrases. Stubbe was working on the two treatises simultaneously, but with different goals in mind—perhaps confirming what Wood said about him: "So dexterous was his pen, whether pro or con, that few or none could equal, answer or come near him."[31] In *Originall* Stubbe turned the material about Constantine around and presented a devastating critique of Christian historiography in the centuries before the rise of Islam.

Similar critiques had been written by Anglican clerics about early Christian historiography, but always with the Church of Rome as target. The polarization between Anglicans and Catholics intensified during the Restoration over the place of reason and of authority in religion. Taking their lead from continental biblical scholars such as Isaac Casaubon, and form English polemists such as William Chillingworth, especially his influential *The Religion of Protestants* (1638), Anglicans emphasized the place of reason over the infallible authority of the pope. In such a context the study of church records and councils became central for Anglicans as they tried to prove the errors in Catholic claims. Thomas Traherne, a contemporary of Stubbe's (and also from Oxford, Brasenose College) published (anonymously) his *Roman Forgeries* in 1673 in which he criticized the claims of the Catholic Church to ecclesiastical preeminence, arguing that the first 420 years of the Christian Church had been reliably documented, until the subversions and forgeries of the papacy. In his work Traherne built on the foundations of formidable Anglican apologetics such as Bishop John Jewel's *Defence of the Apologie of the Churche of Englande* (1567) and Thomas James's *A Treatise of the Corruption of Scripture* (1611).

Stubbe was a rationalist, but not a Socinian,[32] and, unlike John Milton in *Of True Religion, Haeresie, Schism, Toleration* (1673), he was not interested in attacking "popery" much as he feared Catholic influence on the king. Instead, and armed with a rationalist/Hobbesian approach, he turned to examine the origins of Christian theology through the writings of the earliest church historians. His was not a theological but a historiographical battle, which is why he consulted the writings of Eusebius, Socrates, Zosimus, and other historians because they showed, in his view, how the Christianity of the first centuries so "degenerated into such a kind of paganism" (fol. 41) that it lost its original message. "All that is written contrary hereunto are palpable untruths" (fol. 33), he asserted, supported by the scholarship of the Dutch classicist, Gerard Vossius, who had discovered many a "forgery" in the records of early Christianity (fol. 44). While in *Further iustification* Stubbe praised Constantine, in *Originall,* and in direct opposition to Anglican sentiments in favor of the emperor and the veracity of early church councils (as expressed by Traherne and later by Andrew Marvell in the 1676 *A Short Historical Essay*), Stubbe described Constantine as a "Bastard" whose "Sword was his title" (fol. 32). The records of the councils, he stated, were completely unreliable, as Eusebius demonstrated (fol. 43). Roman imperial power, in the persons of Constantine and Theodosius, had consolidated Christianity by force, thereby diverting the Gospel message to the variety of sects and schisms that plagued the six centuries before the birth of Muḥammad:

> It may phaps seem strange that the generall descripcõn of the primitive Christians wch is here represented, should differ so much from the usuall Accts thereof wch are given by the Divines & Vulgar Historians, but in Answer hereunto I desire the Reader to consider first the grounds & proofs wch I go upon, and if the Authors be good the Citations true & indisputable, if the progress of Christianity be such as is conformable to the constant Course of human Affairs & great Revolucõns that then he would not oppose me, by discourses of Miraculous Accidents unimaginable effusions of the Holy Ghost & such like Harangues.
>
> (Fols. 42–43)

Having completed the first part of *Originall* (fols. 1–49), and using the same revisionist methodology, Stubbe turned to the second part—to study Islamic history in the manner he had studied early Christian history. This second part focused on Muḥammad and the revelation of Islam and it is in two sections:

a. The first section (fols. 49–107) includes chapters 3–7 in the University of London manuscript and corresponds to a fragment that has survived from the late seventeenth century: BL Sloane 1709. This fragment is a complete and separate pamphlet, with its own pagination, suggesting that it was written as a unit on its own.

b. The second section of the University of London manuscript, fols. 107–142, also survives in two fragments in BL Sloane 1786. Like BL Sloane 1709, these fragments are written in the same hand, on the same quality of paper, and stand as units on their own, each with its own title: fols. 107–113: "Concerning the Justice of the Mahometan Warrs & that Mahomet did not propagate his Doctrine by the Sword/with a vindication of Mahomett's Carriage towards the Christians"; fols. 114–128: "Concerning the Christian Additions"; and fols. 129–142: and "As to their opinions concerning God, purgatory, Judgmt & paradise they are these." In this section Stubbe relied heavily on the work of his friend and mentor Edward Pococke, who had been translating and commenting on Arabic histories for the previous twenty years. Heavily annotated with references to al-Makīn and Abū al-Faraj, , this second section focuses on the errors of "European Xtians" regarding the history of Islam (fol. 121). Importantly, and while the first section saw Stubbe including a few negative references to the Prophet, in this section Stubbe presents the Prophet and the revelation of Islam in wholly admiring terms: although his emphasis remained on the Prophet as a political and military leader, Stubbe showed how Muḥammad's actions had been determined by his historical context and by his goal of inspiring his followers towards empire. In so doing, Stubbe rebutted Euro-Christian errors about the Prophet and the miracles that were falsely ascribed to him: "Behold the simplicity of the Christians then who were deluded, and thought to delude by such fopperies as these" (fol. 122). In writing this part Stubbe often replaced *Mahometanism* with the term *Islam/Islamism* and *Mahometan/Mahometans* with *Moslemin.*[33]

While working on *Originall*, and in July 1672, Stubbe wrote but did not publish "An enquiry into the Supremacy spiritual of the Kings of England, occasioned by a proviso in the late Act of Parliament against conventicles."[34] Stubbe was serving as the king's publicist (and receiving handsome payments for his services), and he was clearly in total support of the king's policies.[35] But his opposition to Catholic influence on King Charles II was so intense that, after the passing of the Test Act and the removal of the duke of York as lord high admiral (June 1673), Stubbe published, anonymously in the *Paris Gazette,* a two-page attack on the marriage of the duke to the Catholic Mary of Modena (between 20 and 27 October 1673).[36] Like many of his Anglican compatriots, Stubbe feared Catholic power and, while remaining supportive of the royal and ecclesiastical establishments of the monarchy and the Anglican Church, he feared that the king's brother would beget Catholic children to inherit the throne from his heirless sibling.[37] As a result of this publication, on 30 October 1673, a warrant was issued to John Dawson "to take into custody Dr. Henry Stubbe for seditious discourses and printing and publishing unlicensed papers."[38] Anthony Wood explained that Stubbe was "hurried in the dark from one private prison to another, threatened with hanging, and was put to a great deal of charge."[39]

After his release, Stubbe quickly tried to ingratiate himself with the secretary of state and on 30 November 1673 he published a translation of Jaques Godefroy's *The History of the United Provinces of Achaia,* a third attack on the Dutch and a further defense of the king. The brush with the law might have alienated Stubbe from political involvement, for in the years that followed he dedicated himself to his medical practice and to the local scene. In 1674, he described in letters to the earl of Kent some of the ribaldries in Bath: The Duchess of Portsmouth "is frolicksom in the Bath shews her feet & leggs above water.[40] He also wrote about the wines of the spa city.[41] Meanwhile, he kept up his scholarship, visiting the Bodleian to consult books he did not own and meeting with Pococke, whom he often mentioned by name in *Originall.*[42] Wading into Christian and Islamic history to work on his treatise must have taken much of his time, but he continued living and working in Stratford-upon-Avon, in summer maintaining a practice in Bath. On 12 July 1676, while traveling from Bath to Bristol to care for a patient, having had a bit too much to drink, he fell off his horse and drowned. He was buried in St. Peter's and St. Paul's Church in Bath. Joseph Glanvill, his intellectual archenemy, who a few years earlier had described him as "this crackt Fop of W . . . rwick,"[43] gave, according to Wood, an "indifferent" funeral sermon. Not surprising, neither gravestone nor memorial has survived of Henry Stubbe in the abbey.[44] But there is one of Glanvill.

THE ORIGINALL & PROGRESS OF MAHOMETANISM

Stubbe has received well-deserved attention in studies of Islam in modern scholarship and has been recognized for the boldness of his thought.[45] P. M. Holt saw Stubbe's interest in Islam as a product of the mid-seventeenth-century civil wars, while James R. Jacob argued that *Originall* reflected the change in Restoration England that gave rise to a "secular conception of history" inspired by Hobbes.[46] Stubbe, added Jacob, wrote his treatise after he began to identify with the radical movement in English religious thought that included figures like John Milton, Andrew Marvell, Algernon Sidney, and Lord Shaftesbury. For Jacob, *Originall* was intended as a message to Charles II about proper governance at the same time that it could be viewed as the link between "radical Protestantism" and Deism.[47] Citing Jacob, Christopher Hill agreed, as did Justin A. I. Champion: the *Originall* is part of the "radical" religious developments that led to the "early English deists,"[48] and belongs in the trajectory that led to the Socinian tracts of the 1690s and to John Toland's *Nazarenus* (1718).[49] Humberto Garcia argued that the beginnings of the Enlightenment in England can be traced, in some measure, to Stubbe and his views on Islam.[50]

These views are cogent, but they do not explain Stubbe's fascination with the Prophet Muḥammad. Nor do they explain his attack on the sectaries whom Marvell had defended and his implicit alignment with Samuel Parker, the formidable Anglican conservative, whom Marvell had ridiculed in his *Rehearsal Transpros'd* (1672 and 1673). Neither is it clear how Stubbe's position regarding the Prophet could reflect the "religious and theological exuberance of the Interregnum" (Holt),[51] when the printing of the first English translation of the Qur'ān in 1649 caused an angry reaction from Interregnum authorities—along with the vicious attack on Muḥammad in the "Caveat" by Alexander Ross.[52] Nor why Stubbe's supposed "radicalism" extended to praising Islam: after all, Stubbe wrote in praise of Muḥammad in a manner that no other Restoration writer did—not even Milton. On the contrary, in *Paradise Lost*, Milton demonized Islam by comparing Satan to the Ottoman Sultan.[53] No other English writer who upheld politically "radical" views about English politics wrote about Islam and Muḥammad with the same admiration and scholarly erudition that Stubbe did, nor did any other writer, either in England or on the continent, establish a place for Islam in the historical sequence of monotheism as interpreted in the Qur'ān: from Abraham through "Ismael" to Muḥammad. By deliberately ignoring Isaac, Stubbe upheld the Muslim narrative of prophetic history.[54]

C. E. Bosworth argued that Stubbe's rejection of Trinitarianism stemmed from admiration of the Great Tew Circle, especially Lord Falkland and William Chillingworth, both of whom are mentioned in *Originall*.[55] Although they may not, as H. John McLachlan observed, "have been antitrinitarian in theology, their Latitudinarianism may be regarded as a step in the direction of Arianism and Socinianism."[56] Jacob and Champion concurred with Bosworth, confirming Stubbe's place within the rising trends of Socinianism, Deism, and Whiggism in the Restoration period. As Champion noted, Socinian tracts were widely available in the 1660s and '70s, and writers in the 1690s such as Arthur Bury, William Freke, and Stephen Nye identified "Unitarianism with monotheistic Islam."[57] But there is no evidence in any work that Stubbe admired Socinianism: actually, he attacked it from the time he defended Sir Henry Vane to shortly before he began writing *Originall*: "The Socinians multiply upon us," he complained in 1670.[58] That Stubbe would laboriously research a vast corpus of writings about Islam, that he would openly and unambiguously praise "Mahomet" and the Qur'ān, that he would elaborate on the role of 'Ali as the missionary of Islam, and that he would do all that to present Islam as a "standard against which to measure current Christian practice and the current conduct of Christian princes—and no doubt Charles II and the English church," as Jacob urges[59]—is unlikely. After all, Stubbe bluntly praised the Prophet as an able legislator, admired Muslim toleration of minorities, and defended the laws of the Qur'ān against usury and wine. Nor did Stubbe write an imaginary satire in the manner of later texts that used an Islamic mouthpiece to criticize contemporary Europe, such as Giovanni Paolo Marana's *Letters writ by a Turkish Spy* (1684–86) or Montesquieu's *Lettres persanes* (1721).[60] *Originall* is a work of meticulous historical revisionism, presenting "a thorough defence of their [Muslims] sentiments," as Thomas Magney wrote about the treatise just under half a century after Stubbe's death.[61]

Further, Stubbe's attitude toward Islam went beyond anything that even the Socinians proposed to the Moroccan ambassador in 1682. As the surviving account shows, the Socinian delegation did not praise the Qur'ān but rather wanted to show the Muslim visitor the common errors in the Bible and in the Qur'ān.[62] But Stubbe did not criticize Islam or the Qur'ān in his treatise. At the same time, had he written his treatise to advise Charles II, Stubbe would not have hesitated to state that openly. He was "a very bold man," as Wood confirmed, and "utter'd any thing that came into his mind, not only among his companions, but in public coffee-houses (of which he was a great frequenter) and would often speak his mind of particular persons, then accidentally present, without examining the company he was in."[63] He did not mince his words, nor did he appeal to the "rhetoric of subterfuge" or the "art of theological lying"[64] or treated Islam as "a beating stick with which to attack Christian revelation and the clerical establishment."[65] He wrote about Islam because he came to see Islam and the Prophet in a new light.

In regard to Deism: Stubbe's discussion of Islam led him to statements about religion that could have been taken from the pages of Lord Herbert of Cherbury's *De Veritate* (1624): "He taught his followers to abolish Idolatry every where And that all the world was obliged to the profession of these truths that there was one God, that he had no Associates, that there was a providence & a retribution hereafter proportionate to the good or evil Actions of Men" (fol. 108). But, no writer *before* Stubbe had argued for a "Unitarian-Islamic syncretism."[66] The first Deist and Socinian writers in England argued for a religious system based on reason: but they did not appeal to Islam as a model. And when Restoration Anglican theologians like Edward Stillingfleet, John Tillotson, Isaac Barrow, and Joseph Glanvill wrote to show that the Bible and "science" were compatible, not a single one of them praised Islam or Muḥammad. On the contrary, Barrow wrote a savage attack on the Prophet.[67] Perhaps most revealing of Stubbe's intellectual and theological position is the absence of reference in *Originall* to any of the aforementioned English theologians, nor, for that matter, to any Socinian writers.[68] Rather, his constant references were not to "radicals" but to his mentor at Christ Church, Edward Pococke, a nonradical of deep Anglican piety; to al-Makīn, Ibn al-Baṭrīq, and Abū al-Faraj; and to "Judicious Protestants" (fol. 45) like Isaac Casaubon, Joseph Scaliger, John Selden, Hugo Grotius, Johann Hottinger, Claudius Salmasius (of anti-Milton fame), and G. J. Vossius.[69] Had he been a generation younger, Stubbe might well have been part of the "republic of letters" that included many of those authors whose works he admired and cited.[70]

In 1678 Charles Blount, an avowed Deist, lifted pages from *Originall* and included them in two letters, one to Hobbes and the other to the earl of Rochester.[71] Significantly, in neither of these letters did Blount use any material from the Islamic sections of the treatise, nor did he allude to a "Unitarian-Islamic" association. At the end of the century, Humphrey Prideaux associated Islam with Deism and attacked them both; if he had Stubbe's treatise in mind, it is strange he did not mention it, since he was meticulous in referencing his sources.[72] Critics have associated Stubbe with the anti-Trinitarianism of Deism because of the treatise that appears after *Originall* in the 1701 University of London manuscript, *An Epistle from Achmet Benabdalla a Learned Moor concerning the Christian Religion*. This refutation of Trinitarian Christianity—which appeals for evidence to the Qur'ān and to the various doctrinal conflicts of European Christendom—was written in 1612 by "Ahmet Ben-Abdala" in Latin and addressed to the Prince of Orange who had hosted the Moroccan ambassador.[73] But the treatise was added in the manuscript after Stubbe's death; earlier Thomas Erpenius had thought of publishing it and John Selden had owned a copy of a Latin portion of the manuscript without them becoming accused of Deism.[74]

At the outset of the *Originall*, Stubbe presented the goal of his treatise: to study Islam in its historical context. To do so, he explained his methodology. There was always "a series of preceding causes which principally" contributed to change. History, he wrote, worked according to the laws of causality: "This is certain that when the previous dispositions intervene, a slight occasion oftentimes a meer casualty, opportunity taken hold of & wisely prosecuted, will produce those Revolutions which otherwise no human Sagacity or Courage could accomplish" (fol. 4). And so to understand Islam there was need to examine the Jewish and Christian background that gave rise to it. While other writers about Islam had been aware of that history, Johann Hottinger in particular, only Stubbe viewed that history as a heterodox cause to a monotheistic end.[75] As he explained, late Judaism developed expectations of a temporal Messiah to rule over Jew and Gentile, to which early Petrine Christianity adhered. But from Paul on and with Constantine and Theodosius, Christianity changed in regard to the belief in the Messiah, the theology of the sacraments, the role of the clergy, and the godhood of Christ. Christianity, wrote Stubbe, was corrupted by imperial power and diverted from the message expressed in the Acts of the Apostles, the only extant document that captured the ideals of the Christ movement. Such causes gave rise to Islam—not as anti-Christian, as European theologians viewed it, but as post-Christian.

Stubbe knew that such views were dangerous, but he was clearly growing angry with some of his Anglican compatriots who were waxing lyrical about the purity of the church: Thomas Traherne, Paul Rycaut, and others.[76] Stubbe emphasized that the Anglican Church, which he fervently defended, recognized the problems in the foundational documents of Christianity. These writings were "so depraved that the Church of England and generally the Protestants reject the authority of them and admit no general councils after that of Chalcedon under the Emperor Martianus." And, to make matters worse, there had never been a study of the earliest sources of Christianity: "I must add that the Church History of ye primitive times seems mainly deduced from the Latin & Greek writers who give no Acct. either of the Syriack or Judaizing Churches so that we hear no news of the latter till St. Jerom & Epiphanius came to represent them as Hereticks for adhering to the same Doctrine & Discipline wch St. Peter & St. James & all the Apostles (except Paul) had instructed them in" (fol. 44). And to those who would disagree with him, Stubbe answered: "what soever is alledged agt me must be out of suspected or spurious Writers partiall in their own case & ignorant either for the want of learning or want of books & Opportunities to be informed aright or a prejudicate opinion blinding their Judgmts: I conceive the Credit of what I write ought to seem most valid, because 'tis consonant to ye Acts of the Apostles & the reall existence of things" (fol. 43).

It is in the light of the extensive exposé of Christian historiography that Stubbe's discussion of Islam should be read. Islam was not a religious aberration or an erratic heresy, but part of the logic of history that had started with Judaism and Christianity. And it was a logic that Stubbe discovered after reading of Christian Arabic chronicles (in Latin translation).

ARABIC STUDIES IN ENGLAND

The seventeenth century witnessed an increase in the Arabic, and, to a lesser extent, Turkish and Persian, manuscripts that became available to English and continental writers.[77] The first catalogue of the Bodleian

Library in 1605 included only a few works by Averroes and Avicenna,[78] and in 1615 the Arabist William Bedwell complained that the only copy of the Qur'ān he could consult "was so badly imprinted, that in verie many places, I was constrained to diuine and guesse."[79] By mid-1630s, however, and as Samuel Hartlib mentioned in his *Ephemerides*, the "world" of Arabic manuscripts had been "brought thither," that is, to Oxford.[80] The change occurred during the tenure of William Laud as archbishop of Canterbury and vice-chancellor of Oxford. Laud encouraged the purchase of Eastern manuscripts for the Bodleian and established a chair of Arabic in 1636. From 1655 to 1670 the first professor of Arabic, Edward Pococke Sr., was able to train "almost single-handedly a new generation of Arabists" at the university.[81] Pococke, who died in 1691, was at the center of a group of English thinkers who wrote about (and against) Islam. He was the student of William Bedwell (d. 1632) and Matthias Pasor (d. 1658); the friend of John Gregory (d. 1646), John Selden (d. 1654, whose collection of oriental manuscript augmented the Oxford collection after his death), and John Greaves (d. 1652); and the teacher of Henry Stubbe (d. 1676), John Locke (d. 1704), Humphrey Prideaux (d. 1724), and Samuel Clarke (d. 1729). His *Specimen* also influenced the French orientalist Richard Simon (d. 1712).

The Laudian oriental collection and the disciplines that were developed to study it showed Britons, including Stubbe, what the swarthy "Moors" and the "Mahometan Turks" and sword-wielding "Saracens" had produced: a vast civilization that had adopted and adapted the same Greco-Latin legacy that Britons claimed as their own classical patrimony. Archbishop Laud, although not a scholar himself, recognized that there was a "great deale of Learning and that very fit and necessary to be knowne,"[82] a view upheld by Pococke: "the Progress" that the Arabs had made "in ingenious Studies," he wrote, "was so great, that they hardly came behind the Greeks themselves."[83] In the polyglot Bible prepared by Brian Walton in the mid-1650s, there was praise for the intellectual legacy of the Arabs in "Marocum, Gessum, Septae, Hobbedae, Constantinae, Tuneteum, Tripoli, Alexandria, Alcairo, Basor, & Cusa in quibus millia studiocorum omnium facultarum"/in which there were thousands eager to learn every discipline. Not only did the libraries in those cities contain Arabic books, wrote Walton, but Greek and Latin, too, that had been translated into Arabic.[84] The importance of Arabic could not be ignored—which explains the attraction to the language and its output not only in

Britain but also on the continent, ranging from Thomas Erpenius's use of Arabic to write to Bedwell—and signing his name, Touma ibn Erpin—to the three-thousand-page *Lexicon Arabico-Latinum* by his Dutch compatriot Jacob Golius in 1653.[85]

Earlier, in 1645, the Maronite priest, Abraham Ecchellensis/Ibrahīm al-Ḥaqilānī, published his *Concilii Nicaeni Praefatio* in which he showed how Arabic texts had preserved much that had been lost in Latin and Greek and that the "Oriental tradition is much stronger" than the Western one regarding accuracy in church records and history.[86] Al-Ḥaqilānī corrected the errors of scholars ranging from Nicholas of Cusa to Cardinal Bellarmin who, ignorant of Arabic, had mistakenly understood a number of Qur'ānic verses as urging Muslims to worship the Prophet.[87] Like his fellow Maronites, Jibrā'īl al-Ṣuhyūnī/Gabriel Sionita and Yūḥanna al-Ḥaṣrūnī/John Hesronita, al-Ḥaqilānī introduced Arabic writings about Islam to Christian European readers. Such emphasis on the value of the Arabic legacy was confirmed by an Egyptian Copt by the name of "Yusuf al-Misri al-Gibti" who coedited, and published in 1672 through the Sheldonian press in Oxford, a huge tome of early church council resolutions. Stubbe referred to al-Gibti in *Originall* (fol. 116).[88]

The Christian Arabic writers were a great discovery to Stubbe. "It is certain," Stubbe wrote, "that the Christians which lived under the Mahometans, as Elmacin & others, do mention Mahomet wth great respect as Mahomet of glorious Memory, and Mahumetes sup quo pax & benedictio"—unlike the European "others" who see in him the "Antechrist" (fol. 118). Stubbe determined that the study of the beginnings of Islam should be conducted through sources written in the language of Islam and by writers belonging to the world of Islam. But, for a non-Arabic reader, there were no Latin translations of Islamic history and theology by Muslim authors. Although there were numerous geographical, alchemical, and medical treatises by Muslim writers that were available in Arabic and in Latin translation, there were no oriental sources on the Prophet Muḥammad available in Latin other than the chronicles by the Christian Arabic authors. These writers described the prophetic calling of Muḥammad without the kind of vituperation that dominated medieval and early modern Euro-Christian writings. While an uninformed writer like Samuel Purchas could well believe that a "Christian Arabian" would attack the "words and Phrases" of the Qur'ān,[89] Stubbe realized that the Christian Arabic writers had no reason to calumniate Muḥammad who was a "great Honorer of Isa so he [Muḥammad] alwaies express'd a great Reverence for them, And 'tis concerning them that he Sayes that Isa their prophet shall save them in the last day" (fol. 114) Since Muḥammad respected Christ, the Christians living among the Muslims respected Muḥammad, who in turn respected them. "That the Arabian Xtians were men of just Strict deportm[t] appears from hence, that Mahomet Saith of them that one might safely intrust them wth any sume of money they would restore it again" (fol. 114–15).[90]

And so Stubbe turned to these Christian Arabic authors, all of whom drew on a non-Latin tradition of Christian history and, in two cases, non-Chalcedonian. These authors were the following—in the order of their seventeenth-century appearance in print:

Jibrā'īl al-Ṣuhyūnī/Gabriel Sionita

Sionita (1577–1648) was a Maronite priest from Lebanon who had studied in Rome at the Maronite College (est. 1584), and later moved to France. Together with a fellow Maronite, Yūḥanna al-Ḥaṣrūnī (d. 1626), he translated the abridged geography of al-Idrīsī (d. 1166) which had been published in Arabic in Rome (1592). Their translation appeared in Paris in 1619, confusedly entitled *Geographia nubiensis*.[91] They then added a treatise, "De Nonnvllis Orientalivm Vrbibvs, Nec non indigenarvm Religione ac moribus tractatus brevis," of sixteen short chapters about oriental religions and mores as well as about cities such as Baghdad, Damascus, "De Bochara Avicenna patria," Mecca and Medina, along with their native Lebanon and its Maronite patriarchate. They relied, as they stated, on a number of Muslim scholars, notably Muḥammad ibn Qāsim (whom Stubbe often mentions). They included descriptions of the theology and culture of Islam: thus the chapters on the "origo, fraus, dominium, sepulchrum, vxores, liberi, socij"/origin, fraud, rule, tomb, wives, children, allies of Muḥammad, on the Jacobite and Nestorian heresies in the east (and the Greek "schisma"), and on the funerary rites of Muslims and Christians.[92]

Sionita and Hesronita's description of Muḥammad was hostile: perhaps it could not have been otherwise, given that their book was published in Paris under royal auspices, "Summa Priuilegij."[93] But the two authors expressed great pride in the Arabic language and the intellectual legacy that had been developed throughout Islamic history, in "philosophiae, Medicinae, Astrologiae, legum, [and] Rhetorices."[94] They recorded the names of many great historical figures who had flourished and written in Arabic. What is significant is that they mixed Muslim with Christian Arabic writers without distinguishing them. Thus there were Muslims such as "philosophi nobilissimi, Auerroes, Algazeles, Abū-Becr, Alfarabius" as well as Christians, such as "Abu-Zaid Ben-Honain, qui Euclidem in Arabicam linguam translutit, & Thabet Ben-Corra, qui eundem Euclidem à, multis mendis correxit, atque commentariis anno ab Hegyra 282 illustrauit"/who [corrected?] many mistakes from this same Euclid and showed in his commentaries it was the 282nd year after the Hijra. The Lebanese authors presented the two groups of writers as part of the intellectual legacy to which they belonged, and which they were eager to present to their European coreligionists.[95] Two decades later, in 1641, and in line with the Maronites' eagerness to present Arabic learning to European readers, Ibrahim al-Ḥaqilāni translated and published in Paris *Synopsis propositorum sapientiae Arabum philosophorum.*[96] He dedicated the book to Cardinal Richelieu.

In 1630 Sionita translated from Arabic into Latin a short text that had been brought to Europe by the Capuchin Pacifique Scaliger: *al-'Ahd wa-l-shurūṭ al-latī sharra'ahā Muḥammad rasūl Allah li-ahl al-milla al-nuṣrāniyya/Testamentum et pactiones initae inter Mohamedem et Christianae fidei cultores* (Paris, 1630, reprinted in 1638 and 1655).[97] It consisted of treaties between the early Muslim armies and the Christians of the Byzantine East. Interestingly, in his translation Sionita used the phrase "Mahomedem Apostolum Dei"/Muḥammad the Apostle of God (which was removed by the printer from the title page), and he opened with "Mahomedes à Deo missus ad omnes homines erudientos"/Muḥammad sent by God to instruct all mankind. Nevertheless, the treaties were not about the Prophet, but about the history of Islamic protection of Christians during the early conquests, a protection that had allowed for the continuity of Christian society in the Islamic polity. Stubbe, who mentioned Sionita in the *Originall,* specifically referred to those treaties because they supported the view that Islam did not spread by the sword and that Muḥammad had made a place for the Jews and the Christians within the bounds of his "dominion": "There is extant a Compact or League betwixt Mahomet & the Xtians, published in France by Gabriel Sconita & reprinted by Johannes Fabricius a Dantzicker, wch. is by him afirmed to be mostAuthentick, & mention'd by Selden tho Grotius takes it to be but a figment of the Xtians, that they might gain favour wth the Moselmen" (fol. 110). Significantly, Stubbe did not accept the authenticity of the treaties, judging them "Suppositious" (which scholars also question today).[98] But he saw that they confirmed the spirit expressed in the Qur'ān which contained "Sundry passages . . . wherein he [Muḥammad] permits the unbelievers to hold their own religion, & declares that every of them [*sic*] Jew Xtian or other might bee Saved if he hold that there was one God Creator, a day of Judgem^{t}.. & lived justly & uprightly" (fol. 110). Notwithstanding the dubious history of those treaties, Stubbe wanted his English readers to consult them, which is why he directed them to the English translation in Paul Rycaut's "Relacion of the Turkish Governm^{t} l. 2, c.2" (fol. 110). Like his mentor Pococke, Stubbe admired Sionita (whom Pococke had met in Paris),[99] and he relied heavily on al-Idrīsī's geography for information about Arabia.[100] But Sionita and Hesronita remained less useful to his project than other Christian Arabic writers who had belonged to non-Catholic backgrounds: al-Makīn, who was a Copt, Ibn al-Baṭrīq, who was a Melkite, and Abū al-Faraj, who was a Jacobite. Importantly for Stubbe, these writers had been part of Islamic society in the medieval East, and it was in the Eastern traditions of Christianity, which had developed their own and differing theologies, that Stubbe met with a view of Muḥammad that was found nowhere else in Western Christian thought. Specifically, from al-Makīn and Abū al-Faraj Stubbe was able to compile an account of the last ten years in the life of the Prophet—the first ever in English to present the battles, strategies, and negotiations of Muḥammad, with considerable admiration.

Jirjis ibn al-'Amīd al-Makīn

Al-Makīn (ca. 1205–73) was the author of *Tārīkh al-Muslimīn*/History of the Muslims, which had been translated into Latin by Thomas Erpenius, the Dutch orientalist (who had been introduced to Arabic studies by William Bedwell), and published in 1625 in Leiden as *Historia Saracenica*, the "first historical work in Arabic to be published in Europe."[101] Al-Makīn wrote a history of the world, starting with the creation, and ending with the accession to power of the Mamluk sultan of Egypt, Baybars, in 1260. In the Latin translation Erpenius did not include the parts preceding the life of the Prophet Muḥammad and began his text with his birth,[102] giving the subtitle (which is not al-Makīn's) as *Res Gestae Mvslimorvm, a inde Mvhammede primo Imperij & Religionis Muslimicae auctore*. Al-Makīn stated at the outset that he followed the account of the Prophet by al-Ṭabarī, the ninth-century historian whose *Tārīkh al-rusul wa-l-mulūk*/History of Messengers and Kings was, and remains, one of the most important histories of early Islam. As Pococke wrote, al-Ṭabarī was *thiqat fī naqlihi wa tārīkhihi*/an authority in his historical writings.[103] What is striking is that al-Makīn's section on the Prophet is not very long, but it was intensively quoted by Stubbe, as also by Pococke, John Gregory, and Johann Hottinger.[104] Al-Makīn's work was a standard reference among scholars from Oxford to Basel.

Erpenius opened his translation of al-Makīn's account by keeping the Islamic invocation, "In nomine Dei misericordia miseratoris" an opening that Christian Arabic writers sometimes used.[105] Adopting the words from Islam, al-Makīn found no problem in proclaiming with his fellow Arabic-speaking Muslims the name of God, the merciful, the compassionate. Al-Makīn then turned in the first chapter to the "Primus Muslimorum Imperator"/the first emperor of the Muslims, with Erpenius oddly translating the plural *umarā'* as the singular "Imperator," a word that has no Arabic root, about "Muhammed Abūlcasimus, gloriose memorie"/of glorious memory, a close but not literal translation of *ṣalla Allah 'alayhi wa sallam* (Muḥammad was known as Abū Qāsim). Al-Makīn continued with information about the life of the Prophet, emphasizing famous events mentioned in al-Ṭabarī about "nativitatem ejus, genealogiam, & res gestas, donee fugit Medinam: deinde autem bella ejus, & victorias, omnemque fortunam, donee é vita excessit"/his nativity, genealogy, and other events leading to his flight from Mecca: then his wars and victories, and all the fortunes of his life, until his death.[106] It was Muḥammad, according to al-Ṭabarī, and al-Makīn repeated unreservedly, who first revealed the religion of Islam/*azhara dīn al-Islam:* "Religionem Islamisimi . . . primum manifestavit & observavit." Notwithstanding his Christian faith, al-Makīn carefully described the prophetic calling of Muḥammad, confirming how Khadīja, the Prophet's wife, had been first to accept his prophethood, "Prima in prophetiam ejus credidit Chadiga"/Khadīja was the first to credit him with prophecy.

Al-Makīn used the Hijri calendar, and only sometimes the Coptic calendar (starting in AD 284), and he took the side of the "Arabs" as he described their wars with the Byzantines. Such commitment on the part of al-Makīn to Islamic history did not surprise Stubbe: al-Makīn had been "Secretary of State to one of their [Muslim] Princes" (fol. 110), and early in his life he had commanded Muslim armies in Egypt and Syria. Al-Makīn confirmed for Stubbe that the Prophet "was, God's prayer and peace on him well mannered, gentle in speech. He visited his companions as they visited him, and he kissed their faces as they kissed his. He consoled the weak and praised the strong and was compassionate to the poor, and whoever asked him for anything, received what the Prophet could give him, or received a helpful word."[107] Of the Arabic Christian writers, al-Makīn furnished Stubbe with the longest, and most "Islamic," perspective on the Prophet. Towards the end of *Originall* where Stubbe turned to a year-by-year life of the Prophet after the Hijra, he followed al-Makīn's chronology and description (as did Pococke and Hottinger, too).

Very important for Stubbe was the history of the Christian community during the early years of Islam. Al-Makīn emphasized how favorable the Prophet was to the Christians of Arabia who came to see him: "A dignitary from among the Christians came to him [the Prophet], so he stood up to welcome and host him. They asked him about that [his action] to which he replied 'Treat well the Copts of Egypt, for you have relatives from among them' [since one of his wives was a Copt]. And he said, 'He who mistreats a *dhimmī* will be punished on the day of judgment.' And he said, 'He who hurts a *dhimmī* hurts me.'"[108] The Arabic text missed a few prepositions in the printing, which may explain why the translation into Latin omitted some words. Also the Latin added some marginalia that did not appear in the Arabic, although they served to emphasize Muḥammad's protectiveness of Christians: "Affectus Muhamadis erga Christianos." In his *Originall*, Stubbe echoed those views about the treatment of Christians, because he found the information about the Prophet's openness to Christians (and to Jews) very important in the context of his presentation of Islam:

> Thus Mahomet Ben Achmed expounds him, Elmomin who collected his History of the Saracens out of the best Mahometan Writers and was himself Secretary of State to one of their Princes, avowed that Mahomet did give protecciõn & Security to the Pagans Magicians & Jews & Xtians also. wch swore fealty to him & paid him yearly tribute,

> Moreover that he Sent Omar to the Xtians to assure them that they should live Securely under his dominion. And that he would esteem their lives as the lives of his Moslemin & of their Goods as the goods of those others.
>
> (Fol. 110)

A page earlier, Stubbe quoted the whole Pact of 'Umar which confirmed for him a point he repeated often in his treatise: that Islam accepted other religious communities and did not try to forcibly convert or expel those communities. It was a point that the next Christian Arabic writer whom he consulted repeated: Ibn al-Baṭrīq.

Aftīshyus/Sa'īd ibn al-Baṭrīq/Eutychius

Ibn al-Baṭrīq (877–940) was the author of annals of the Church of Alexandria, *Kitāb al-Tārīkh al-Majmū'*. A short selection about the history of the Alexandrian patriarchs had been translated by John Selden and published in a bilingual Arabic and Latin text, with copious notes, in London in 1642 (the first substantial Arabic printing in England).[109] Selden, "the chief of learned men reputed in this land," as John Milton described him in *Areopagitica* (1644), urged his friend Pococke to translate the whole text because it was "considered by learned Men abroad [Erpenius and Casaubon] as a very useful Work."[110] Pococke did not agree since he viewed the history as unreliable; still, he went ahead and in 1654 produced a translation of *Eutychii Patriarchae Alexandrini Annalium*, followed by another edition with the title *Nazm al-Jawhar/Contextio gemmarum, sive, Eutychii patriarchae Alexandrini annales* (Oxford, 1656).[111] Another Oxford edition appeared in 1658/59.[112]

Sa'īd ibn al-Baṭrīq was an Egyptian Melkite and patriarch of Alexandria. Disagreeing with Pococke, Stubbe viewed him as a "Historian of good Credit" (fol. 31), perhaps echoing Selden, who had described Ibn al-Baṭrīq as the "Egyptian Bede."[113] Ibn al-Baṭrīq's history covered the time from Adam to AD 938, with specific focus on the Christian Eastern (in his case, Egyptian) communities and their encounters with the expanding empires of the Persians, the Byzantines, and the Muslims. Although he had little to say about the Prophet Muḥammad—but always added words of praise whenever he mentioned him—he started the history of the rise of Islam with reference to the migration to Yathrib/Medina, correctly recognizing the historical decisiveness of that event. He summarized the lives of the first four caliphs and later dynasties, focusing in great detail on the actions of the second caliph 'Umar, since it was during his reign that pivotal contacts with Christians occurred.

Ibn al-Baṭrīq described the many theological controversies that had bedeviled Christian history. After all, as the brief biography stated, he had lived at a time of much "dissidia"/conflicts.[114] He then described the confrontations between the Monophysites and the Melkites and the plots and collusions of bishops and patriarchs as they vied for ecclesiastical office and doctrinal supremacy. Stubbe quoted him: "Ismael Ibn Ali a Mahometan Historian, that at the Nicene Council in the 20th year of the Raign of Constantine there were assembled 2048. Bishops out of wch he Chose 318. . . . It is granted by ye Orientall Historians of the Church that Such a Number of Bishops was sumoned as the Mahometans specify, So Saith Eutychius & Josephus an Egyptian Presbyter in his preface to the Arabick version of the Councils" (fol. 116). In his attempt to learn about the beginning of Islam, Stubbe was turning to historians other than those recognized in the Western Latin legacy. The fact that those historians were Christians of the Arabic tradition gave him ammunition for his argument: that the forgeries on which some church doctrines had been based can be exposed by the Christian historians who had lived among the Muslims. Ibn al-Baṭrīq showed how the divisions, disputations, and conflicts among the various Christian communities were resolved by Constantine's imperial authority, resulting in the alienation of the non-Melkite Christians from the centralizing power of the Constantinople-based patriarchate.[115] The history of Ibn al-Baṭrīq showed Stubbe the Christian doctrinal confusions that preceded, and explained, the rise of Islam—a chief argument in *Originall*.

Ibn al-Baṭrīq presented Stubbe with a historiography that emphasized the continuing distinctiveness of the Christians in the context of the rise and expansion of Islam. The Egyptian writer saw Christianity within the continuum of the Islamic empires (Umayyad and Abbasid)—so much so that in his writing he adopted numerous phrases and images from the Arabic of the Qur'ān.[116] Very importantly, Stubbe found in Ibn al-Baṭrīq historical descriptions about how Christians interacted with the early Muslim conquerors: Ibn al-Baṭrīq emphasized how the Byzantines fought against the Arabs, while other Christians, including the Copts, did not.[117]

Muslim-Christian relations had been more accommodating than the battles that Stubbe witnessed during the mid-seventeenth-century civil wars in England, Scotland, and Ireland: which is why he must have paused at Ibn al-Baṭrīq's account about the peace that "Chaledo Ebn Walid"/Khālid ibn al-Walīd granted to Damascus and how much the Muslim leader tried to put an end to bloodshed.[118] Most striking for Stubbe would have been the meeting between the Caliph 'Umar and the patriarch of Jerusalem, Sofronius, and the subsequent treaty of peace: "In the Name of God Mercifull & gracious, from Omar ye Son of Alchittabi to the Inhabitants of the City Elia Security & protection is granted as to their psons Children Wives Estates. & all their Churches that they bee neither destroyed alienated nor prohibited the Xtians to resort to" (fol. 109).[119]

Ibn al-Baṭrīq presented Stubbe with information about Islamic protection of Christians and their religious holy places, institutions, and traditions. The history of Islamic conquest had set the tone for accepting the Christians and granting them "securitate ipsis & pace pacta"/security to these very people and an agreed-upon peace,[120] and although violations occurred, as Ibn al-Baṭrīq bitterly noted, Christian life continued—as the thirteenth-century Christmas sermon published in Arabic and in Latin in 1656 showed. The beautiful Arabic and the rhyming prose of the "Homile in Natalem Chrsiti" by "Petre Sancto, Catholico, Patriarcha. D. Elia Tertio, vulgo dicta Ibn Hadit" was lost on Stubbe, but the translation conveyed a deep emotional intensity on the part of the celebrant and his congregation—all of whom were living in the midst of the Islamic polity.[121]

Gregorios Abū al-Faraj

Abū al-Faraj (1226–86), author of *Tārīkh mukhtaṣar al-duwal/A Short History of Dynasties*, was so respected in his Muslim society that although "Christianus erat," wrote Edward Pococke, "à quo tamen didicerunt multi è Muslemorum eximiè doctis"/although he was a Christian, many of the *fuḍalā' al-Muslimīn*/the dignitaries of the Muslims revered his work.[122] He was of "the Sect of the Jacobites," wrote Humphrey Prideaux in 1697, "an Author of eminent note in the East, as well among Mahometans as Christians."[123] From Gregorios/Abū al-Faraj/Ibn al'Ibri/Bar

Hebraeus, Edward Pococke had published a translation of thirty pages in 1650: *Specimen historiae Arabvm: sive, Gregorii Abul Farajii Malatiensis, de Origine & Moribus Arabum* (Oxford), to which he added over two hundred pages of dense notes, producing a scholarly compendium about early Islam. Over a decade later, Pococke translated the whole book, *Historia compendiosa dynastiarvm authore Gregorio Abul-Pharajio* (Oxford, 1663), which was reproduced in 1672 under the title of *Historia Orientalis: Authore Gregorio Abul-Pharajio* (Oxford).[124]

Abū al-Faraj included a historically balanced description of the life of the Prophet Muḥammad, confirming for Stubbe the traditional Islamic narrative about birth, parentage, marriage, flight, and consolidation of the Islamic polity. Abū al-Faraj lived in Aleppo for some time, supported in his bid for the patriarchate by the Damascus-based al-Mālik al-Nāṣir. In 1258 Hulago attacked Aleppo, and so Abū al-Faraj was sent to implore him to spare the city. Hulago did not heed him. After witnessing the horrors of conquerors, he, like the other Christian Arabic writers, realized how benevolent Islamic rule had been and therefore, in his history, conveyed a respectful view of Muḥammad, "Author Legis Islamitica Mohammed Ebn Abdallah."[125] And so, like al-Makīn, he opened his volume with the Islamic invocation, "In nomine Dei Miseratoris Misericordes" and then, as he recounted the life of the Prophet, he mentioned the famous episode from the *Sīra*/biography about the monk Bahīrā, who declared that the boy Muḥammad would be famous all around the world: "In the future, he said, this boy will enjoy greatness, and his fame will spread in east and west, for when he arrived here, a cloud covered him with its shade."[126] Quite striking a few lines later were the words that Abū al-Faraj used regarding the prophetic revelation: "*azhara al-da'wa*,"[127]/"prophetae munus sibi arrogavit"—the same verb that had been used by al-Makīn, "*azhara*."[128] Two pages later Abū al-Faraj cited the words of Abū Sufyān to 'Abbās after Muḥammad's entry into conquered Mecca in 630. Abū Sufyān, the erstwhile enemy, converted to Islam in order to save his life, and when he saw the armies of Muḥammad he turned to the Prophet's uncle, 'Abbās, who had also initially opposed him and told him: "'Your nephew has become a great king.' To which the uncle replied, 'Be quiet [*wayḥak*], it is Prophecy'/'Imo vero, Prophetia est.' And he replied, yes. Respondit ille, 'Esto igitur.'"[129]

Like the other writers, Abū al-Faraj did not question the prophetic role of Muḥammad. After all, Muḥammad was nearly taken by his followers to be buried in Jerusalem, "locum scil.in quo sepulti essent Prophetae"/ where prophets are buried.[130] This Arabic admission, coupled with the history of inter-Christian rivalries which Abū al-Faraj described, produced in Stubbe the conviction that the Christianity which Muḥammad encountered had been corrupted and corrupt: that is why Stubbe compared the Qurayshites to the Sadducees (fol. 69), and the early Muslim victims of Qurayshite persecution to the early Christian martyrs. As Jesus sought to "reform" Judaism (a verb that Stubbe used consistently), so did Muḥammad seek to correct the errors of the Jews and the Christians.[131] And to protect them: "the Christians who had been so persecuted by Cosros & finding their Condition very uncertain among the Arabians according to the humours or interests of the Government were very Glad of his [Muḥammad] rise & magnified his undertaking" (fol. 66).

No other seventeenth-century writer about Islam or about the Prophet Muḥammad used the Arabic Christian writings in the informative manner that Stubbe did. Neither great poets like Milton or Dryden, nor great theologians like Barrow, Baxter, Tillotson, nor travel writers like Rycaut and Maundrell, nor historians of comparative religion like Pagitt and Ross were willing to give credit to the Arabic historians—even though their works had been edited, translated, and published. On the contrary, even those who are known to have read the Arabic/Latin sources persisted in their hostility to Islam. Thomas Smith, who read Ibn al-Baṭrīq and Abū al-Faraj, attacked Islam violently in his *Remarks upon the manners, religion and government of the Turks* (London, 1678; Latin versions in 1672 and 1674); Lancelot Addison, an Anglican clergyman, who wrote about Morocco after serving as chaplain in Tangier, and who mentioned al-Makīin and Abū al-Faraj, produced a vicious biography of the Prophet in 1679, as did Humphrey Prideaux, bishop of Durham, in 1697, whose *The True Nature of Imposture fully display'd in the Life of Mahomet* (London, 1697) was a vitriolic attack on the Prophet, notwithstanding Prideaux's reading and quoting of the Arabic writers.

The Arabic/Latin texts demonstrate that there was a scholarly body of writings in the seventeenth century in England and on the continent that diverged markedly from the negative representation of Muḥammad and Islam. These writings could have played a significant role in disaggregating hostile representations and in furnishing new information based on fresh scholarship. But only Henry Stubbe turned to those texts that drew "on the narration of the Mahometans or Arabick Xtians" and not on "the European Xtians" (fol. 121) and rewrote the history of Islam. By giving credence to the Christian Arab writers, Stubbe brought them to the center of Islamic-Christian history, making them indispensable interlocutors who challenged Western historiography and the Western canon.

ʿĪSA: THE QUR'ĀNIC JESUS

At the end of *Originall* there is a crossed out paragraph in which Stubbe showed how God could not have expected believers to subscribe to such an "impossible" doctrine of "Father the Son & the Holy Spirit" (fol. 142). Stubbe was thinking in terms of the Qur'ānic Jesus whom he met in numerous texts against Islam. But as was his wont, Stubbe selected from these attacks the information that supported his point of view: that Jesus was historically closer to the Qur'ānic portrait than to the theological doctrine that had developed around him in the Christian church. In this context of an anti-Trinitarian Jesus, the originality of Stubbe becomes striking: while his contemporary John Milton was writing his *De Doctrina Christiana* and invoking Christian history in his defense of a non-incarnational Jesus, and while Socinians appealed to "reason," Stubbe turned to Islamic sources for support.

One writer whom Stubbe read carefully in regard to the figure of Jesus in the Qur'ān was Levinus Warner and his *Compendium Historicum Eorum quae Mahummednai de Christo* (1648).[132] Warner wrote to challenge the Muslim view of Christ (the title continues, *Et praecipuis aliquot religionis Christianae capitibus tradiderunt*/They relate in particular chapters some things [about] Christian religious practice), but still, he gave a detailed description of the "Muslim" Jesus: the meaning of his name, the virginity of his mother, his disciples/*al-ḥuwariyyūn*, his prophetic lineage from Abraham, and the conundrum of his execution—all from passages in the Qur'ān. Using an Arabic text of the Qur'ān (alongside a Latin translation), and focusing on the verses that dealt with Jesus and the *naṣārā*/Christians, Warner "amass'd abundance of Testimonys of some Mahometan Doctors, who make honourable mention of our Lord Jesus Christ," as the Dutch orientalist, Adrian Reeland, explained over half a century later.[133]

In his address to the reader, Warner stated that although the Qur'ān rejected the Christology of Jesus, it did not reject his prophetic/messianic role in history. Warner did not accept the refutations of the divinity of Jesus that appear in the Qur'ān and in other Muslim sources, but in presenting those refutations he emphasized how the Qur'ān still recognized that Jesus was "natus non sit, nisi solo Dei verbo"/was not born except by the word of God alone. Warner also linked the annunciation to Mary that appears in the Sura of 'Imrān ("ô Maria, Deus tibi annunciate VERBUM suum: nomen eius Christus"/O Mary, God announces to you His word, whose name is Christ) to the first verse of the Gospel of John, "In principio erat verbum/In the beginning was the word."[134] Throughout his short treatise Warner added various stories from the vast compendium of the Hadith about the ascetical piety of Jesus.[135] The Muslims had been "blind" to the doctrine of the incarnation, but they had many "vestiges" of truth regarding the prophetic role of Christ. It is from Warner, whom he mentions specifically, that Stubbe borrowed some of the sayings and proverbs of Jesus in the *Originall*.

Stubbe noted the high regard accorded to Jesus in the Qur'ān, and perhaps because he wanted to distance himself from the Nicene Jesus, he used the Qur'ānic name, 'Īsa, throughout his treatise: "(So they call Jesus Christ & So I shall name him in the subsequent story)" (fol. 59). At no point did Stubbe use the name Jesus. For a scholar who was quite familiar with the apocryphal literature about Jesus in the Christian tradition, it may well be that the Hadith stories confirmed his suspicions: that the Jesus of the Arabian tradition, who found his way into the prophetic revelation in Mecca and Medina and subsequently into Islamic piety, was the nondivine figure venerated by the Christian Arabs at the time of the Prophet Muḥammad. That is why, Stubbe believed, Muḥammad continued the teachings of Jesus and why the Qur'ān confirmed that "Isa was his predecessor [Muḥammad's] & taught ye same doctrine" (fol. 120). At the same time, Jesus spoke in language that invokes the Qur'ān: at the end of an invocation by 'Īsa ibn Maryam that Selden reproduced in his edition of Eutychius, Jesus appeals to God in words that are Islamic in their resonance: "Neque praesice mihi eum qui non miserebitur mei, Pro misericordia tua, O Miserantissime miserescentium"/Do not send against me those who are not merciful to me, you who are most merciful and compassionate.[136] Since Muḥammad did not bring a new revelation, and since the Qur'ān confirmed the original teachings of Jesus, then, concluded Stubbe, it was "but Justice to stile him a Xtian" (fol. 120).

In the vast corpus of Hadith about ʿĪsa, from the eighth century on, the unwavering emphasis of the tradition is on the poverty of Jesus, his humility and contempt of the world, his celibacy and love of God—the same Jesus whom Stubbe advocated.[137] Quite striking in this context of the Islamic ʿĪsa is Stubbe's summary of a story that recalls Chaucer's "Pardoner's Tale" about the three men who found a treasure and in their greed killed each other for it. Jesus commented at the end: "Behold how these three suffered by it these are deceased & left behind what they thought to bee owners of woe unto him that seeks riches in this world" (fol. 117). Stubbe found this story in another text by Warner: *Proverbiorum et sententiarum Persicarum Centuria collecta.*[138] Even more striking is that it is the same story about Jesus that al-Ḥasan al-Yūsi, a contemporary jurist in Morocco (1631–1691), used.[139] The same Jesus was in the Maghrib and in Stratford-upon-Avon—and in much of Islamic piety. It is very unlikely that Stubbe knew much about the image of Jesus in contemporary Islam other than what he read in Latin translation, but it is significant that all the stories about Jesus he included in his treatise came from the Islamic tradition, with very few references to the Gospels.

THE PROPHET MUḤAMMAD

So how does the Prophet Muḥammad appear in the *Originall*?[140] Stubbe presented the first historical biography of the Prophet in English, based on the Qur'ān and on "the formal words in wch ye Mehometans express themselves" (fol. 127), very likely meaning the Hadith and the biography (all of which had been excerpted and discussed in the works of Selden, Pococke, Hottinger, and others). It was the first account of Muḥammad in England that was chronologically presented and not theologically argued. Stubbe ignored the hostile literary and dramatic representations of Muḥammad in European writings and concluded his treatise with a year-by-year description of events until the death and burial of the Prophet. Influenced by Hobbes and the secular view of history (as Jacob noted), Stubbe showed that Muḥammad and the beginnings of Islam should be contextualized in Arabia's sixth/seventh-century religions and societies: thus his emphasis on continuity between many

Judaic and Islamic teachings and on the fact that the military victories of Muḥammad and the consolidation of the new faith were a result of intelligent and inspired leadership, as had been the case with the Hebrew prophets. Stubbe showed that Islam made perfect sense as a religion: it was not the "scourge of God" to sinful Christians, but a continuation of revelation, a monotheism that prevailed over polytheism as a result of the Prophet's tenacity, the "heavenly wisdom" of the revelation (fol. 70), the support of the four successors, especially his cousin 'Ali, and the perseverance of the "Moslemin."

From the outset, Stubbe was interested in examining how the Prophet, "a fiercely opposed" man of low social standing ("mean estate," fol. 1), was able to transform the Arabs from tribes to empire through the power of revelation. Stubbe wanted his English readers to view the Prophet in the manner in which he had been seen by Arab Christians, who had deeply respected him. That is why the Christian Arabic writers became for Stubbe the measure of truth: whatever they did not mention, he did not accept. None of them, for instance, ever mentioned the frequently repeated "Fable" that Muḥammad had been inspired by a pigeon that he claimed as the "Holy Ghost" (fol. 121). Following Pococke, who in his notes to *Specimen* had rejected this allegation, or the other allegation about Muḥammad's tomb being suspended in midair, Stubbe denounced such credulity in European writers. He also added his own insights: no pigeon, he explained, could have been trained to perch near Muḥammad's ear without rousing the suspicion of his followers and detractors. What clinched Stubbe's "empirical" refutation of this allegation, however, was that no "Christian of the Arabians mention it" (the pigeon) (fol. 121).

Stubbe was highly selective in his information. Although he carefully read the universal history of Marcus Boxhornius (published 1652), for instance, he picked what he thought fitting, ignoring the derogatory material that was always included in European texts about Muḥammad. Some of these denigrations included references to Muḥammad as a camel driver, poor and illiterate: "homo pauper & mercaturam exercens cum camelis," wrote Boxhornius.[141] In regard to the last, Stubbe reminded his readers of the humble backgrounds of many of the Hebrew prophets and of Jesus and his carpentry. He emphasized also how the Prophet had been theologically and intellectually versatile by mentioning the journeys of Muḥammad, all the way to Egypt and Spain, regions that had not been associated with the Prophet during his lifetime.[142] Given such travel and exposure, Muḥammad was not as outlandish a man as he appeared in the "great untruths" of Euro-Christian sources. Rather, added Stubbe, he was like any of the "Nobles of Venice or Genoa" (fol. 57),[143] a merchant and a traveler with acute observation. For Stubbe, these Renaissance cities were not much different from the cities of Arabia: Sionita had described Mecca as "vrbs Arabiae Matrix nobilissima,"[144] while Erpenius had observed in his 1613 oration on the dignity of the Arabic language that Mecca was comparable to Amsterdam "Meccam, Amsterdami nostri magnitudine emporium."[145] Stubbe repeated the analogy by Erpenius.

In following this line of argument, Stubbe was using the method that his contemporary Edward Stillingfleet had used in historicizing the Prophet Moses. In *Origines Sacrae or, A rational account of the grounds of Christian faith, as to the truth and divine authority of the Scriptures, and the matters therein contained* (1662), the Anglican divine wrote against the skeptics who were raising questions whether a man as uncouth and unexposed as Moses could have written the Pentateuch. In chapter 2 of the second book, Stillingfleet examined the early education of Moses, emphasizing the latter's mastery of "Mathematical, Natural, Divine, and Moral learning of Egypt, their Political wisdom most considerable." Although there is no scriptural information to support this view, Stillingfleet emphasized that Moses was a historian and a law-giver, thereby proving the "certainty" of his writings, and the divine "truth of Scripture."[146] Stillingfleet confronted the detractors who rejected the Mosaic authorship of the Scriptures in the same way that Stubbe argued against those who attacked Muḥammad's role in the Qur'ān, and, as Stillingfleet did not doubt that the Pentateuch was the divine Scripture written by Moses, neither did Stubbe doubt that the Qur'ān consisted of "Surats" which "the angel Gabriel presently" brought him, as he had earlier brought them to "Edris Noah Abraham Ismaell Moses Isa" (fols. 100, 84).

It is in this context of approximating Muḥammad with Moses that Stubbe's challenge to the illiteracy of the Prophet should be read. From the start, Muslim exegetes had appealed to the illiteracy of the Prophet in confirmation of the divine revelation of the Qur'ān. Stubbe mentioned this view, emphasizing that the Arabians believed him to be "Nabian Ommian, that is the illiterate prophet" (fol. 123). But Stubbe knew that European authors always used this reference to illiteracy as proof of the falsity of "Alcoran": since Muḥammad was illiterate, writers argued, he could not but have sought help in formulating his revelation from local

Jews and Christians. Since "the Author himself being no Linguist or Scholar, nay, not able to read or write," wrote Alexander Ross in 1649, Muḥammad could not but have sought help from the Nestorian monk Sergius in formulating his "lyes and sensless follies."[147] Because Muḥammad was "illiterate," wrote Sir William Temple contemporaneously with Stubbe, he produced "a wild Fanatick Rhapsody of his [Muḥammad's] Visions or Dreams."[148] It did not help that very few men of those who attacked the Qur'ān could read it in Arabic, but rather relied on the poor Latin translation by Robert of Ketton (in the twelfth century), the poorer translation into French by André du Ryer (in 1647), and the poorest of all translations, to English by Alexander Ross in 1649, which Stubbe denounced (fol. 139).[149]

Nor could Stubbe read Arabic. But he was intent on refuting such accusations. And so, to turn the tables on the detractors, Stubbe argued for a literate and cultured Prophet. He did so by showing his readers that in Muslim exegesis the adjective *umiyy* could refer not only to illiteracy but also to Mecca, mother of the villages, "*ommal koras*" (fol. 123). He learned this information from the careful discussion by Pococke (which he summarized).[150] But, whereas Pococke was the philologist searching for alternative meanings to *umiyy,* Stubbe was the polemist. Stubbe knew that illiteracy was a sine qua non in Muslim historiography, and thus, he continued, notwithstanding the Prophet's literacy, the Qur'ān was still a revelation from God. He recalled the words in the translation of the Sūra of Yūsuf/ Joseph by Erpenius earlier in the century: "per verbum Dei intelligent suam quae Coranum ipsis dicitur, & quàm Muhamed ijs persuasit coelitus ad se demissam"[151]/"by the word of God they understand their own [biblia/book], which they call the Coran and which Muḥammad persuaded them had been sent down to him from heaven." Also, in Pococke's *Porta Mosis,* Stubbe came across a reference to al-Ghazalī's discussion of Muḥammad's "*luminis prophetici*"/*nūr al-nubuwwa*/light of prophecy.[152] Stubbe concluded that, whatever the level of the Prophet's literacy, it remained separate from authorship because the Qur'ān was "inimitable," a word that he repeated twice in the treatise (fols. 100, 138). It was a word that recalled the description of the Qur'ān by Abū al-Faraj, "eloquentissimi," and a doctrine that was upheld by all Muslims.[153] All the early companions of the Prophet, confirmed Stubbe, believed the "Coran" to be "derived from God" and full of "heavenly wisdom" (fols. 61, 70). Toward the end of the manuscript, Stubbe affirmed that for

Muslims only what was mentioned in "the Alcoran" was foundational to Islam (fol. 140) because the Qur'ān was a "Standing Miracle" (fol. 141).

The three BL Sloane fragments are especially important in this context because they show a transformation in Stubbe's view of the Prophet. It is quite possible that after Stubbe finished the first fragment (BL Sloane 1709, fols. 94r–115r) he circulated it among readers, who objected to his largely favorable view of the Prophet. Although he had mentioned some of the medieval falsities about Muḥammad, Stubbe had still presented an admiring portrait. So, and not untypical of Subbe, he wrote the second two fragments (BL Sloane 1786, fols. 181r–185r and 186r–190r) in response to those readers where he confronted them with a totally positive view. These latter fragments show Stubbe in an argumentative mode, sometimes reminding readers that he had already mentioned some of the discussion points earlier. Mostly, he was eager to show his readers a more accurate view of the Prophet from what he had earlier written.

The Prophet in BL Sloane 1709

Without having access to Arabic primary sources that would furnish a more accurate view, Stubbe made some mistakes in this fragment, such as claiming a Qur'ānic origin for a dialogue between Muḥammad and a Jew (fols. 81–82), which was mentioned in many of the texts he read, [154] or treating Abū Bakr as the Prophet's uncle. Eager to present a "secular" view of the Prophet, in the manner he viewed other prophets, Stubbe emphasized the personal initiative of Muḥammad and his astuteness of "designe" (fols. 63, 64, 66). But he mentioned that the Prophet had concocted prophecy (fol. 60), "intitling God and the angel Gabriel to his dictates" (fol. 65); on another occasion, he wrote of "venery" (fol. 63) , although a scribe could have made a mistake in this particular case.[155] Such views were not uncommon among European orientalists: even the learned Hottinger, whose study of the Prophet's history was both detailed and extensive, called Muḥammad, on every page of the printed text, the "pseudopr.." Stubbe was not immune to such views, and in this fragment there is a sense that he was still searching for a full interpretation of the Prophet. Chiefly, however, Stubbe was trying to approach Muḥammad as a historical figure: his interest was more in the religious and military achievement than in the prophetic background. What he wanted to show his readers was that Muḥammad's actions could be perfectly understood from a historical perspective: the Prophet had been a great strategist, warrior, and negotiator, whose success lay in harnessing the power of revelation to create the Islamic polity.

The Prophet in BL Sloane 1786

Stubbe continued searching and, in the two fragments which conclude *Originall*, he arrived at his final view of Islam. He started by demolishing the widely held belief that Islam spread its message by the sword by referring to the Christian Arabic writers who had left important documents about Islamic history. He also brought in stories that demonstrated Islamic reverence to Jesus and he defended Muḥammad against accusations of sensuality, emphasizing the "stoical" element in Islam, as in Christianity (fol. 134). In these fragments Stubbe gives the impression that he had a list of all the criticisms that had been leveled at him—and he was refuting them, one after another. He praised Muḥammad for opposing usury, wine, and divination, and he discussed the thorny issue of the Prophet's miracles, which were commonly ridiculed in contemporary European writings. While some believed those miracles, so much so that Abū al-Faraj referred to them,[156] Stubbe emphasized that the Qur'ān did not confirm them and that many Muslims rejected them because the only miracle that was to be credited to the Prophet was the Qur'ān (fols. 140–141). Earlier, Stubbe made the case for Muḥammad as a legislator superior to Moses (fol. 136) and praised him in the highest terms that a Christian writer in the seventeenth century could: in his piety before God, Muḥammad was like the historical (not theological) Jesus, for he, Muḥammad, told Christians "that such as beleived in Isa ought to live according to his pcepts with great humility piety & unconcernedness for ye pomp and Vanities of this world" (fol. 115). Stubbe then introduced a number of sayings by Jesus from the Hadith which had been preached to Christians by the Prophet (fol. 117). Perhaps thinking of this analogy between Jesus and Muḥammad, where the latter confirmed the teaching of the former, Stubbe described Muḥammad toward the end of the treatise as "a great prophet" (fol. 137)—the same phrase that described Jesus in the Gospel of Luke 7:16. No English writer had ever made that analogy—twice (fol. 61).

Nor had any writer praised the Qur'ān as did Stubbe. A contemporary such as Richard Baxter was willing to concede that "God hath made use of Mahumet as a great Scourge of Idolaters of the World," but he had produced "an Alcoran" that was "a Rhapsody of Nonsence and Confusion."[157] Stubbe moved beyond such invective to open praise, and, having learned from Pococke that the Qur'ān was revealed in "Arabic verse," he used the only word available to him in English, "poem," as a translation of "surat."[158] But, the "poem" was not "Nonsence"; rather, affirmed Stubbe, "God by Mahomet took a better Course by leaving to Mankind one lasting Miracle, the truth whereof should in all ages bee Satisfactory & Convincing" (fol. 138). Cognizant of the criticisms that European Christian writers leveled against the Qur'ān, he asserted: "I have often reflected upon the Excepcōns made by the Xtians ag^{t} t the Alcoran & find them to bee no other than what may be argued wth ye same strength against our bible. And what the Christians say for themselves will fully Justify the Alcoran" (fol. 139).

Interestingly, Stubbe paraphrased various verses from the Qur'ān and sometimes integrated them into his text:

> The Alcoran, a transcendent miracle, & wch is more one that is permanent, from generation to generation. Nor is there any lasting Miracle of ye prophet, excepting that whereunto he appealed, challenging all the Wits of Arabia (&Arabia did then abound wth thousands whose chief study was eloquence & poetry) to make one Chapter or more that might compare therewith & thereby demonstrated to the most incredulous, the truth of his prophesy. And God Said concerning it, that if all Men & Angels should combine to write any thing like it, they should fail in their enterprize.
>
> (Fols. 138–139)

Although Stubbe was meticulous in his recording his sources, he did not mention that the last sentence was a Qur'ānic verse: 17:88. His readers, thus, would have taken the Qur'ānic assertion as his own conviction And it was a conviction on which Stubbe elaborated. Having read Pococke's translation of passages from al-Ghazali's *Tarjamat 'qīdat ahl al-sunna*,[159] he found no qualms in presenting that creed in his treaties: it is in the Qur'ān that God is revealed, His oneness, omnipotence, and omniscience; the power of God over all the creation; the prophetic continuity in His messengers to humankind; reward and punishment; and the salvation of the damned (apocatastasis):

> That God is one God that there is none other that he hath no equall no Son nor Associate. That his Eternity hath neither beginning nor end that 'tis impossible to explain properly his Attributes and yt no intellect can comprehend the Extent of his Dominion. That contemplative Men may conjecture at his being by the daily occurents on earth, but never understand his Essence. That ye Heavens are his Throne, the Earth his footstool, but that the Governmt. of both is no trouble to him: That he is Omnipotent Omniscient Omnipresent, who sits upon the Universall Throne by his Essence, & by his Understanding penetrates into all things: That his providence disposeth of all Affairs below, neither doth any thing fall out not the Corn grow not the Grass wither but according to the Decrees of his eternall pdestination That whatsoever Man doth ascribe to him or imagine to bee in him it is eternall, & those attributes do not argue any Composition or istinction [of] {in} his being: That all things in this World good or evill befall us according to his Will: that the beginnings progress & Conclusion of all Emergencies depend absolutely upon him: and that he determined from all Eternity whatsoever should come to pass, That his knowledge extends to the deepest Secrets, That nothing happens agt or not according to his pleasure, that in all Matters to think to Will to do depends upon him. That the Souls of Men are imortall, That those who are pserved by Faith & the intercession of the Apostles of God, Moses Isa Mahomet from Sin) do upon death live in happyness untill ye resurrection & day of Judgemt that those who are more or less wicked, must in the Grave in a kind of Purgatory undrgo some torments until the last day and there wth more or less difficulty they shall be Saved, but that nothing of Evil how little soever shall escape unpunished nor any thing of good how small soever pass unrewarded.
>
> This is the Sum of the Mahometan Religion.
>
> (Fol. 129)

There is nothing comparable to Stubbe's breadth regarding Islam in any contemporary English or European text. While he made mistakes and sometimes slipped hostile remarks about the Prophet, he was careful about his presentation of Islamic revelation as an expression of absolute monotheism.

"LET US THEN FANCY THE GALLANT ALY"

Stubbe's reading of the Arabic histories showed the active role that the first four caliphs played in the consolidation of Islam. Although he mentioned Abū Bakr, the first caliph, on a number of occasions, especially his role in ensuring the compilation of the Qur'ān, it was 'Ali who caught Stubbe's attention as the best preacher of Islam. Muḥammad was the Prophet and 'Ali represented the piety and the determination that the Qur'ān inspired.

Stubbe's description of 'Ali is both fascinating and unusual: fascinating because Stubbe dramatized the activities of 'Ali during the initial stages of Islam's development, a dramatization that recalls the 'Ali of the Morisco warrior saga of the sixteenth century.[160] Stubbe was also unusual because he described the Prophet's cousin without associating him with Persia and its tradition of Shiʿism—the theological and political locus for 'Ali. Pococke included some notes about Shiʿism and the concept of the imamate in his notes to *Specimen,* and in the *Present State of the Ottoman Empire* (1670) Paul Rycaut wrote about "*Mahomet* and *Hali,* that is, the Turk and the Persian."[161] But Stubbe ignored such references which dominated English plays, chronicles, and travelogues as he ignored the supposed rivalry in prophetic calling that some writers claimed between the two cousins.[162] Actually, Stubbe's 'Ali united Muslims—and ignited in them the spirit of religious unity to fight their enemies: the Byzantines and the Sassanids. 'Ali was not the divider between Turk and Persian, but the pan-Islamist calling on all Muslims to confront those who had subjugated them: "lett us not live devided under more petty princes then we have tribes lett us all unite into one monarchy as we are all of one language and one parentage we are all ageien's all Ismaellites the Same Hegira will suite with all the Same Crescents is our comon Standard" (fol. 86).

An important influence on Stubbe's view of 'Ali was Pococke, who had found in 'Ali "a man of such account with that impostor [Mahomet], not only for his valour, but knowledge too, that he was wont to declare, that if all the learning of the Arabians were destroyed, it might be found again in ‘Ali, as in a living library.”[163] Earlier, Sionita had also praised ‘Ali, “simul cum Mohamede Moslemannica lege fuit imbutus, quam ob causam saepe dicere solebat, ego sum primus Moslemannus” / ‘Ali was instructed in Muslim law with Muḥammad, for which reason he was accustomed to say often, ‘I am the first Muslim.’[164] And also al-Makīn:

> Averfabatur mundana, ac Deum valde timebat: multus erat in dandis eleemosynis: justus, atq; humilis, defensor veræ religionis; acutus valde, & multũ pollens eruditione, quippe speculartivis scientiis & practicis instructus: audax & audcaciâ celebris, liberalis, optimæ indolis & naturæ./He distanced himself from the world, feared God, just and humble, defender of the true faith, learned and perceptive, well instructed in practical and scientific knowledge, brave and famous for his bravery, generous, good natured.[165]

Abū al-Faraj mentioned the story about ‘Ali carrying the gates of Khaybar,[166] while Hottinger listed the miracles associated with ‘Ali: “ei multa miracula tribuunt.”[167] In 1651 the work of Ibn al-Rāhib was published in Latin in Paris by Hesronita. Ibn al-Rāhib, another Jacobite Arabic writer of the thirteenth century (a contemporary of al-Makīn), wrote a history that was translated as *Chronicon Orientale*. In describing the rise of Islam, after having written about the Rūm and others, Ibn al-Rāhib presented a chronology of events, starting with the migration of the Prophet, but with only a few words about Muḥammad. Although Ibn al-Rāhib was noncommittal about Muḥammad, he praised Abū Bakr as a pious ascetic, renouncing worldly pleasures and taking from the treasury only three dirhams per day. ‘Ali, however, received the highest praise; he was a man contemptuous of worldly things, dedicated to the free bestowal of alms, and a fierce advocate of his religion.[168]

This image of ‘Ali holding the world in contempt was repeated by Stubbe: “Aly . . . had a contempt for the world it’s glory & pomp, he feared God much gave many Alms” (fol. 60). But the ‘Ali of the *Originall* is much more than the model of a God-fearing man. Stubbe turned for information about ‘Ali to Adam Olearius, who had traveled between 1633–1639 to Moscow/Russia and Isfahan/Persia as part of a commercial mission. During his travels Olearius learned about the meanings and histories of Shi‘ite rituals, especially “Auschur, or solemn Feast, in memory of Haly, their great Saint and Patron,"[169] which he described with a high degree of accuracy. Because Olearius had read al-Makīn, he drew a line of demarcation between the historical 'Ali and the 'Ali of Persian veneration—a line that Stubbe also observed. "Aly," wrote Olearius, "did not change anything in the Alcoran, and though he gave several Interpretations to the words of Mahomet, and explicated the sense of his Law, yet did he submit to his Authority, where it was clear, and where the Text admitted no explication, in so much that this occasion'd no change in the Religion."[170] In similar vein, Stubbe confirmed 'Ali as a fellow fighter with Muḥammad against the idolaters. Even the Turks, noted Olearius, acknowledged 'Ali "a near Kinsman of Mahomet's, that he is truly an Imam, or Saint, and that he led a very exemplary life; and particularly that he was valiant."[171]

'Ali also came to Stubbe's attention through his proverbs in the collection of his works by al-Sharīf al-Raḍī (AD 970–1015), later known as *Nahj al-Balāgha*. The proverbs are in the hundreds, and in 1629 Jacob Golius published a selection of them in Arabic without a Latin translation: *Shadhra min kalām 'al-'Arab ayy ba'ḍ amthāl 'Ali al-khalīfa/Proverbia quaedam Alis, imperatoris Muslimici*. Golius treated the proverbs as moralistic aphorisms, without theological content, and so he presented them to readers as part of the wisdom of the "imperator" of Araby. His publication may have been instrumental in alerting Pococke to the importance of 'Ali. As the 1740 biography of Pococke by Leonard Twells shows, the Oxford Arabist became deeply interested in the proverbs: "The book, which he first undertook to read on, was the Proverbs of Ali, the fourth Emperor of the Saracens, and the cousin german and son-in-law of Mahomet: a man of such account with that impostor, not only for his valour, but knowledge too, that he was wont to declare, that if all the learning of the Arabians were destroyed, it might be found again in Ali, as in a living library."[172] Pococke translated many proverbs, and, soon after his appointment to the chair of Arabic at Oxford in 1636, he lectured on them[173]—although he did not publish the translation, nor did another later translator, Thomas Smith.[174] But a large number of these proverbs were included by Hottinger in *Historia Orientalis* under headings such as piety, humility, patience, justice, and others.[175] Stubbe knew Hottinger's work well and may have been thinking of him when he referred to the proverbs in his manuscript: "Mahometan sayings having some of them ascribed unto Aly" (BL Harleian 1876, fol. 133).

Stubbe realized that 'Ali, unlike Muḥammad, whose prophetic revelation could prove objectionable to his readers, would not provoke a knee-jerk reaction from worried Christians. Stubbe thus turned to 'Ali as a "neutral" medium by which to present Islam. In the rather long speeches that Stubbe put in the mouth of 'Ali in *Originall*, the echoes of the proverbs ring clear: If you prefer the next world to this one, you win; friendliness in a face is a second beauty; reliance on God is enough; the ornament of men is their civility; belligerence in a man will destroy him; fear of God clears the heart; the best wealth is that which is spent for God; and many others. 'Ali became Stubbe's mouthpiece of Islam: where Muḥammad was the political and prophetic leader, 'Ali was the commentator and teacher. He was the pious observer who accepted the revelation to his cousin and eloquently propagated it.

'Ali continued to attract orientalists long after Stubbe's death. In 1717, a selection of 'Ali's proverbs was translated and published by the professor of Arabic at Cambridge, Simon Ockley: *Sentences of Ali Son-in-Law of Mahomet* (London). Ockley had great admiration for the Arabic legacy and repeatedly denounced his countrymen for their ignorance of that legacy. "What we here present the Reader with," he wrote in his preface to the translation, "is a little Collection of Wise Sentences, calculated for the Direction of a Man's Conduct in Affairs of the greatest Consideration, and are of the same Nature as the Proverbs, and Ecclesisasticus. / / They are called the Sentences of Ali the Son of Abu Taleb. The whole Book is, as near as I can guess, not much less than our New Testament." As an Arabic scholar, however, Ockley was aware that 'Ali had not been the author of all the proverbs. Still, he explained, the proverbs are important because even if 'Ali had just collected them, he was a contemporary of the Prophet Muḥammad. He concluded: "The Sentences are full, and to the Purpose: They breathe a Spirit of pure Devotion, Strictness of Life, and express the greatest Gravity, and a most profound Experience in all the Affairs of Human Life. . . . There is enough [in the Sentences], even in this little Handful, to vindicate, in the Judgment of any Man of Sense, the poor injured Arabians, from the Imputation of that gross Ignorance fastned upon them by Modern Novices."[176]

It was an imputation that Stubbe had rejected in his *Originall*, and, in presenting a devout, heroic, committed, and decisive 'Ali, Stubbe showed his admiration for the man most closely associated with the Prophet Muḥammad and the rise of Islam. 'Ali's was a piety that continued to be admired by English orientalists: George Sale, in his commentary on Sura 76, mentioned the abstinence and poverty of 'Ali, who did not have enough provisions at home to fulfill a vow to God after his children, Hasan and Hussayn, were cured of sickness.[177] Edward Gibbon, impressed with Ockley's translation, wrote that 'Ali "united the qualifications of a poet, a soldier, and a saint: his wisdom still breathes in a collection of moral and religious sayings; and every antagonist, in the combats of the tongue or of the sword, was subdued by his eloquence and valour."[178] Their views were in line with the writings of Henry Stubbe, the first English writer to "fancy Aly."

ISLAM AND EMPIRE

Many Euro-Christians who visited, or did not visit, the Ottoman Empire wrote about the plight of the Christian minorities and how they were living in fear and ignorance; others expressed hostility, describing the Eastern Christians as intellectually and theologically superstitious, which is why they needed to be converted to Protestantism or Catholicism.[179] Stubbe quoted from Grotius's *De Veritate Religionis Christianae* a long passage about the deplorable conditions of the Eastern Christians under "Mahomet [who had] propagated his Doctrine by the Sword" (fols. 115–116), but he did not use the London 1632 English translation perhaps because the frontispiece showed a "Turke" with a sword in his hand. The caption read: "The Turke stands with his sword in his hand, by which he defends his Religion, that sprang from Mahomet, a false Prophet, foretold in general by Christ, Mat. 24:5-24 also a halfe Moone." The author of the preface to the 1649 translation of the Qur'ān had also invoked this treatise for exactly the same reason: that Islam was a religion of the sword.[180] But, unlike the author of the preface, Stubbe did not turn for his information about Eastern Christians to theologians, but to travelers such as Adam Olearius, Paul Rycaut, and Henry Blount, all of whom included descriptions of the Christian populations of the Persian and Ottoman empires in their works.[181] Stubbe thus repudiated Grotius (who had not traveled east) by introducing into the discourse about Eastern Christians an unusual contrast: between the condition of the American Indians under the Iberians, and of other slaves whom "wee keep," and the condition of Christians under Muslim rule.

Stubbe did not need to elaborate on the plight of the Indians or the slaves under the Spaniards; such knowledge had become widely familiar in England.[182] It was usual to compare the tyranny of the Spaniards "towards the poore Indians who neuer offend them" with the tyranny of the Turks towards all "those fall into their hands."[183] Stubbe differed, and instead he contrasted the plight of the Indians with the "Musarabick Christians"/Arabized Christians under Muslim rule in Spain, "who alwaies lived quietly & Safely under them & others in their other Kingdoms & Dominions, An inviolate Justice being preserved towards them, and tho' the rich & potent Nobility & Rulers were destroyed or reduced to nothing wch was don to prevent future Rebellions." Not only did Muslims protect Christians at the time of the early conquests by the caliphs, but also in current times, as confirmed by one of the greatest scholars of Europe, Joseph Scaliger: "Yet 'tis observed by Scaliger," continued Stubbe, "& 'tis an assured truth that the vulgar Greeks live in a better Condiciõn undr the Turk at present then they did under their own Emperors when there were perpetuall Murders practiced on their Princes & tyranny on their people, But they are now Secure from Injury if they pay their Taxes" (fols. 109–10).[184] Such protection, as well as Muslim concern for Christian well-being, was not, Stubbe realized, a matter of Muslim whim but of binding Qur'ānic law. John Selden, whose *De Jure Naturale et Gentium* he often cited, praised Qur'ānic theology, which promised mercy and reward for the Christians: "mercedem autem ibi memoratam nuncupat ille . . . compensationes operum suorum."[185] Stubbe concluded with a view that proved prophetic: "& 'tis more the interest of ye princes & Nobles then of the people at present wch keeps all Europe from submitting to the Turks" (fol. 110). Contemporary Christian communities in Europe were being attracted to Islam, and, just a few years after Stubbe's death, some Protestant groups supported the Turks in their attack on Vienna (1683).

The Arab and Ottoman Empires had been spread by war and the sword, but, unlike the European empires, which had also spread by war and the sword, they had not forcibly converted the native populations. Rather they had protected them. Stubbe recognized that his was the age of empires and that England might just be starting to think in such terms, especially after the celebration of England's future glory in John Dryden's *Annus Mirabilis* (1667). Christian and Muslim, Spanish and Ottoman and Persian—all had built, and were continuing to expand, empires. But where the Christian empires enslaved and deculturalized the conquered populations, the Ottoman Muslims did not. Although slavery was practiced by all empires and all religions, at least Muslims did not enslave fellow Muslims, and "the successors" of the early European empires, presumably the English, should not be casting the first stone since they deliberately prevented Indians from finding Christ in order to keep them as slaves. Though "the principles of the Xtians seem to condemn Slavery, yet in Portugall & other places, it is frequently practiced and perhaps the Xtian Laws & Customs ag^{t}. such usage had no higher rise then Ecclesiasticall & civil policy, which the successors have indiscretely (& not out of Conscience duly inform'd) retain'd still" (fol. 113).

Stubbe learned that the acceptance on the part of Muslims of the religious Other was an ongoing practice. In Olearius he read about Armenian Christians in the Persian Empire of the 1630s—about patriarchs and congregations, all enjoying freedom to trade, pray, and increase, walking in processions with bishops parading their crosses and banners and wearing "Pontifical Robes; with Wax-Candles in their hands."[186] Acceptance was also a matter of commonality of belief: Muslim rulers shared with their Christian subjects the expectation of the return of 'Īsa—a messianic finale that must have resonated with the eschatological and millenarian excitement of Britons during the civil wars. Pococke, ever Stubbe's mentor, described the signs of the end in Islamic eschatology and noted that the final moment would witness "Descensus Jesu in terram . . . apud turrim albam ad partẽ Damasci orientalem"/the descent of Jesus to earth near the white minaret east of Damascus.[187] It was perhaps that Islamic openness to Christ/Christians that, Stubbe observed, made European princes willing to join forces with Muslim armies and to invade Christian regions. Religion, observed Stubbe sardonically in *Further iustification* had never been a divisive factor when it came to the advancement of empire. "How often," he asked rhetorically, "did the Emperours of Constantinople, the Kings of Spain and France, contract for the assistance of the Saracens against Christians?"[188] It was hypocritical to trade and cooperate with Muslims and then denounce their religion, or to praise their "government" but decry "Mahometanism," as Robert South preached in his 1660 London sermon, "Ecclesiastical Policy the Best Policy: or Religion the Best Reason of State."

It is tempting to treat Stubbe's *Originall* as a continuation of the letter exchange with John Locke. After reading Stubbe's *Essay in Defence of the*

Good Old Cause (1659), Locke wrote Stubbe a letter in which he expressed "admiration" for the "strength and vigour" of the style, but complained about the extent to which Stubbe was willing to go in advocating toleration (in this case for the Quakers). At that point in time, Locke still believed that religious differences in the state would result in anarchy and violence.[189] It may well be that in *Originall* Stubbe was addressing Locke, and other proponents of toleration, as Christopher Hill argues, by writing the history of Muḥammad, a wise legislator, who had established an empire with absolute toleration.[190] Whether Locke read Stubbe's treatise or not is not known, but it is significant that, thirty years after disagreeing with Stubbe over toleration, he wrote his *Letter on Toleration,* which became one of the cornerstones of the Enlightenment. In the *Letter,* and in the sequels, Locke argued for the toleration and endenization of Muslims in the Stuart monarchy—for granting Muslims (and Jews and pagans) the same status that Stubbe had so admired about Muḥammad's toleration of Christians and Jews.[191]

* * *

Stubbe read what others read about Islam, but he was selective in what he adopted from the works of scholars, all of whom, including Selden, Hottinger, and Pococke, were negative in their views about Muḥammad.[192] Although he himself had fallen prey to some misinformation about Muḥammad in the early stages of writing his treatise, and although he inherited a dramatic, theological, and poetic legacy of relentless bigotry toward Islam, Stubbe was able to change his views and present, for the first time in English, a well-documented history.

Stubbe showed how long-held bigotries could be overcome by consulting indigenous sources, thereby decentering the historiographical perspective. It may well be that Stubbe shifted away from the Eurocentric sources of knowledge about Islam because he was not a clergyman. In the seventeenth century, experts on the Christian and Islamic East, with its various languages and religious communities, were ordained clergymen, educated at Oxford or Cambridge, and restricted in their writings by their (Anglican) church allegiance.[193] Stubbe was a physician, and in his last years he seemed to have been a successful one. And so, as he treated the maladies of patients, he turned to treat the malady of ignorance which he diagnosed, as he would have a disease, through careful examination of symptoms. On many occasions in the treatise, Stubbe used his medical knowledge to support his arguments: for him, the historian, like the physician, was to rely on research: and as the treatment of diseases did not discriminate on the basis of culture or geography, so the treatment of history. As he pored over the tomes of English Edward Pococke, Swiss Johann Hottinger and Isaac Casaubon, French Claudius Salmasius, English John Selden, Dutch Thomas Erpenius, and the chronicles of al-Makīn, ibn al-Batrīq, and Abū al-Faraj, Stubbe became the physician trying to find the cure for the disease of ignorance. It is no coincidence that the *Panarion* of Epiphanius, that fifth-century compendium of pre-Islamic Jewish and Christian heresies, which Stubbe constantly cited, was subtitled *Contra octoginta haereses opus, Panarium, sive Arcula, aut Capsula medica appelatum*/the Medicine Chest [panarion] against Heresies.

Henry Stubbe belongs to that century in English and continental history when Arab-Islamic manuscripts made an impact on European thought. They were collected, edited, translated, and integrated into early modern intellectual activity, sometimes accepted, sometimes rejected, and sometimes adapted into discussions of biblical history, philosophy, philology, law, geography, and mathematics. But the Arabic/Latin histories of al-Makīn, Ibn al-Baṭrīq, and Abū al-Faraj were the first published sources about Islam to become available to non-Arabic readers in Western Europe. All previous information about Islam had derived from Greek and Latin sources, which is why these indigenous Arabic texts presented a view of Islam that was different from everything before them. Still, no English theologian or playwright, poet or Sunday preacher, translator or chronicler of world religions turned to them for an alternative view of Muḥammad and Islam in the manner Stubbe did. Perhaps it was difficult to do so: Britons of Stubbe's generation had experienced civil wars of fierce religious polarization, massacre, and desecration, and during the Restoration period the "Great Persecution" was inflicted on the nonconformists, with draconian laws curtailing mobility, education, and livelihood. A few years after Stubbe's death, England was gripped by the hysteria of the Popish Plot and the intimidation, false accusation, torture, and execution of Catholics. In 1682 three witches were burned.

Early modern English society was still caught in religious and denominational exclusivity and violence. It would have been very unlikely that "Mahometanism" or "Mahometans" could have been treated differently, which helps to explain why *The Originall & Progress of Mahometanism* was not published—although it was read and copied and, among a few, Charles Hornby for one, it was admired. But it had been a very controversial project: as the text shows, Stubbe repeatedly defended himself by introducing his first-person voice against readers among whom he circulated the manuscript. He was not dogmatic in his views, and recognized the limitations of his sources and of his knowledge: he made a number of historical and factual mistakes, only because his sources made those mistakes. In order to deal with the vast diversity of information in his sources, he often presented multiple views in a series of conjectures and then, to make a determination, he appealed to his medical knowledge (as in the case of the Prophet's alleged epilepsy); invoked logic and common sense, especially against "Christian fables"; and showed how many of the features of Islam denounced by his contemporaries – such as polygamy, militarism, and the literalism of the joys of the afterlife – were present in the history of Judaism and Christianity (fols. 111–114). Although Stubbe viewed Muslims as erring in "the manner than in the object of their devotion" (fol. 127), he recognized Islam as a religion and a polity that had been inspired by a prophetic legislator, who, with his cousin, began an empire the sun of which was "no sooner . . . elevated above ye horizon but it was in its meridian" (fol. 107).

But in Restoration England there was not yet a place for a positive and historically accurate presentation of the beginnings of Islam. Henry Stubbe was alone among his contemporaries who found in the Arabic/ Latin sources a compelling historical alternative to misrepresentation—thus his "Copernican Revolution" about the "great prophet" of Islam (fol. 137).

THE PRINTED AND MANUSCRIPT SOURCES

Editorial Policy

HE *ORIGINALL* SURVIVES in fragments as well as in toto. Although the text was not printed until 1911, three excerpts had appeared in print in 1693 and 1695, in letters by Charles Blount to the earl of Rochester (published twice), and to Thomas Hobbes.

MATERIAL COPIED AND PRINTED BY CHARLES BLOUNT

December 1678 and 1693: letter from Blount to Thomas Hobbes ("Arrians") appeared in Charles Blount's *The Oracles of Reason* (London, 1693), 97–105. The letter corresponds to fols. 38–41 in University of London MS 537. The letter is reproduced in Thomas Hobbes, *The Correspondence*, ed. Noel Malcolm (Oxford, 1994), 2:759–763.

December 1678 and 1693: letter from Blount to the earl of Rochester ("republic") appeared in *The Oracles of Reason*, 157–166, and in Charles Blount's *Miscellaneous Works* (1695), 158–168. The letter corresponds to fols. 3–8 in University of London MS 537. The letter is reproduced in Jeremy Treglown, *The Letters of John Wilmot, Earl of Rochester* (Oxford, 1980), 206–213.

Blount sometimes made alterations in punctuation, word order, and omission of biblical references. Where differences suggest change of meaning, they are listed in the notes that follow.

MANUSCRIPTS

Late Seventeenth Century. British Library Sloane 1709 and Sloane 1786

The first fragment in BL Sloane 1709, fols. 94r–115r, corresponds to fols. 48–107 in MS 537 of the Senate Library, University of London. This fragment contains the unit on "The hist. of the Saracens & of Mahomet." The writer/scribe used folded papers and wrote on four-page clusters. He then numbered them 1–12. This pagination suggests an autonomous unit. The second fragment in BL Sloane 1786, fols. 186r–190r, corresponds to fols. 107–118 in MS 537 and contains the unit "Concerning the Justice of ye Mahometan Warrs." Like the previous fragment, this unit appears as autonomous. The third fragment in Sloane 1786, fols. 181r–185v, corresponds to fols. 130–142 in MS 537. This fragment begins in the middle of a sentence because the preceding folios have been lost; the first surviving folio has "fol. 3" at the top left-hand side of the page. It includes the chief part of "concerning God, purgatory, Judgement & paradise." This fragment appears at the end of MS 537 and was written at a later stage—since Stubbe refers in it to his previous discussion of "Aly."

All three Sloane fragments are by the same hand, written densely on the same kind of folios, and with frequent marginalia. In comparing this hand with the hand in the letters to Hobbes (BL Letters from Stubbe to Hobbes, MS 32553, fol. 5 and fol. 25v), most probably by Stubbe himself, it is clear that the two are not the same.

While it is difficult to speculate about the time or place in which Stubbe wrote the material in the fragments, he must have worked on it when he had access to books that he did not own in his library—or at least were not listed in BL Sloane 35, the posthumous inventory of his books. The units relied heavily on Erpenius's translation of al-Makīn (1625) and Pococke's *Specimen* (1650): neither of these appears in the inventory. But others do appear: Hottinger's *Historia Orientalis* (1651), *Geographia Nubiensis* (1619), and works by Selden and Salmasius.

1701, University of London, Senate House Library, MS 537

Complete manuscript, University of London, 537. Since this manuscript is edited in this volume, I requested from the Senate House Library information about its provenance. Ms. Tansy Barton kindly sent me the following paragraph:

> This MS. bears the bookplate of the Rev. John Disney, D.D., of The Hyde, Ingatestone Essex. Items 1559, 1562, and 1564 disposed of with other property of Disney's at Sotheby's in April 1817 were all versions of this same work, but none corresponds with the present MS. Two manuscripts at least in the British Museum, Harl. 1876 and 6189, contain longer versions of the main text of MS. 537, but neither includes the letter. "An account of the life of Mahomet . . . from an MS. copied by Charles Hornby of the Pipe Office in 1705", was edited and published by Hafiz Mahmud Khan Shairani in 1911. It would seem therefore that MS. 537 is the earliest dated MS. copy of this text to survive. The gift of New College, Hampstead, 1960.

There was no further information on its provenance.

The inner leaf of the manuscript includes reference to "Charles Hornby" and "January 3rd 1701." See Champion's 2010 study for information about Hornby.

Two hands appear in this manuscript of the treatise. There is another treatise that follows upon Stubbe's with new pagination and in a different and very elegant hand.

Hand A: this hand is of the scribe who copied the whole manuscript. The scribe abbreviated words ("Xtians" for "Christians"), was inconsistent in spelling (spelling "Islamism," "Islanisme," and "Islamisme"), and was not familiar with the terminology he was copying—thus wrote "Reblah" instead of what must have been "Keblah"/*qibla*. He copied mechanically and did not pay attention to meaning: thus "fund a Mentall" (fol. 74). The scribe paid little attention to new sentences, capitalizations, or other stylistic or syntactical markers. There are duplications of words, some blank spaces, and many mistakes in subject-verb agreement. There are numerous mistakes in the Latin passages, and the Greek words are sometimes illegible. Still, the scribe made some corrections, either inserting them above the lines, or adding them in the margins. Some of the corrections were significant: for instance, in fol. 28, the scribe corrected "Jews" to "Gentiles"—by deleting the first word and writing the second above it; fol. 30, "rights" is corrected to "rites."

Hand B: this hand added chapter divisions and titles, as if preparing the manuscript for publication. This hand also indicated the sections that Charles Blount had copied and made page references to another (lost) manuscript. The publication of the Blount letters in 1693 and 1695 shows that although Blount had copied from another version of the manuscript with its own stylistic variants, the text was taken from Stubbe's *Originall.*

Toward the end of the manuscript there were references to folio numbers, written in Hand A, next to specific paragraphs or sections. It is not clear what the purpose was—unless they indicated passages that were to be copied in, or were copied from, another manuscript.

This manuscript does not include the heavy marginal notes of the Sloane fragments. But the scribe either used the Sloane manuscripts or the Sloane scribe and this scribe were using the same (lost) manuscript/s. The difference between this manuscript and the Sloane manuscripts is that this manuscript contracts sentences and sometimes omits whole sentences or phrases. Occasionally, the scribe of MS 537 corrects egregious mistakes: Sloane 1709 fol. 115r writes that it was the will of Muḥammad "yt Moslemin should be deceived"; this manuscript corrects the sentence that it was the will of Muḥammad that "the Moslemin should be undeceived" (fol. 106). What suggests a link between this manuscript and the two Sloane fragments is the following:

1. Many of the stylistic features of the Sloane manuscripts appear unchanged in this manuscript, such as the opening and closing of parentheses for exactly the same (but not all) sentences.
2. On some occasions the Sloane scribe writes a word and then deletes it to replace it with another. MS 537 does not include the deleted word, but copies the replacement word that appears in Sloane.
3. On numerous occasions, the scribe of the Sloane manuscripts and this manuscript start paragraphs at the same point.
4. The Sloane fragments include extensive comments in the margin—some of which appear as part of the text in this manuscript.
5. Transliterations of Arabic words/names are the same in Sloane and in this manuscript.

6. The scribe of this manuscript did not know Greek and either copied what he saw or left blank spaces where Greek appears in later manuscripts. His Latin was as erratic in spelling and punctuation as the English.

This manuscript ends on fol. 142. It is followed by a new paragraph that is not completed and is crossed out.

The organization of the material in this manuscript is as follows (there is no title):

Fols. 1–48: History of Christianity
Fols. 48–56: "Chap 3. A Brief Account of Arabia & the Saracens/The History of the Saracens & of Mahomet."
Fols. 56–65: "Chap 4. The Transactions from the birth of Mahomet to his Flight from Mecca."
Fols. 65–91: "Chap 5. Mahomet's Conduct at Medina the Embassy of Aly to the Agarens & Saracens."
Fols. 91–101: "Chap VI. The Return of Aly & the Wars of Mahomet."
Fols. 101–107: "Chap VII Mahomet's last Pilgrimage his Death & Burial."
Fols. 107–113: "Concerning the Justice of the Mahometan Warrs & that Mahomet did not propagate his Doctrine by the Sword/with a vindication of Mahometts Carriage towards the Christians."
Fols. 114–128: "Concerning the Christian Additions."
Fols. 129–142: "As to their opinions concerning God, purgatory, Judgmt & paradise they are these."

Early Eighteenth Century (?), British Library Harleian 1876

Complete manuscript, BL Harleian 1876 ("The Life of Mahomet" on spine). The Sloane scribe of BL 1709 and 1786 and the scribe of this manuscript were copying from the same manuscript, or the scribe of this manuscript was using the Sloane fragments along with another manuscript to produce a complete copy of *Originall*. The marginalia of references and notes are the same in this manuscript as in the BL Sloane fragments. But this manuscript "improves" on both the BL fragments and the University of London manuscript. One example will suffice.

University of London MS 537, fol. 47:

It appears by Pauls carriage Acts 23.6. that he did Act by Somwhat like to Judging In his proceedings, how else could he cry Christianity assuring each of them singly that he was in the truth, and that afterwards when Paul was dead, each of 'em ptended his Religion to bee the true Religion derived from Paul whence arose great Feuds amongst them.

BL Harleian 1876, fols. 64–65:

It appears by Paul's carry age, Acts 23.6. that he did act by somewhat like unto Jugling in his proceedings. How else could he cry there, He was a Pharisee, & called in question of the hope of the Resurrection of the Dead? And in his Preaching unto the Jews, he became as a Jew, that he might gain the Jews; to them that were under the Law, as under the Law, that he might gain them that are under the Law; to them that are without Law, as without Law, (being not without Law to God, but under the Law to Christ, that he might gain them that are without Law; To the weak, he became as weak, & became all things to all men, that he might by all means save some. 1 Cor. 9.20, 21. This behavior of Paul, though it multiplied the number of Christians, yet it did lay the foundation of perpetual Schisms & Heresys; for they would not relinquish, as erroneous or evil, those Tenets or Usages, which he without reprehension indulged them in, & complyed actually with himself. When he had layd in them his Foundation, That Jesus was the Messiah, he permitted any Superstition, in Wood, Hay or Stubble, any variety of Doctrines, not ending in direct Idolatry; assuring his Confidents, that notwithstanding this they might be saved, 1 Cor 3. 11, 12, 13, 14, 15. And who knows how sincere, or how complacential he was in his Writing, whose Deportment otherwise <65> was thus related? I remember a Mahometan Story of Achmed Ben Edris, that Paul instructed Three Princes in Religion, & taught each of them a different Christianity, assuring each of them singly, that he was in the Truth;* & that afterwards when Paul was dead, each of them pretended his Religion derived from Paul, whence arose great Feuds amongst them.

This manuscript is similar to University of London MS 537 in that words that were changed in the last dated manuscript (BL Harleian 6189,

7 July 1718) are not changed in this manuscript or in MS 537. For instance, MS 537 has "criminal" (fol. 19), which appears in BL Harleian 1876, but in BL Harleian 6189 the word is changed to "Ceremoniall" and a different hand adds in the margin: "Criminal . . . d over it Ceremonial" (fol. 33) suggesting that the scribe of BL Harleian 6189 was using a manuscript that had changed "criminal" to "ceremonial." At the same time, MS 537 includes words and sentences that are in BL Harleian 1876 but not in BL Harleian 6189. Sometimes the Sloane scribe starts a marginal comment, but then deletes or discontinues it (fol. 186r "This practice of his," which appears in full in BL Harleian 1876).

The scribe of this manuscript started by adding the references to the sources at the time of copying the manuscript. But then, on fol. 22, he stopped and later returned to add the references, along with longer comments, in a smaller script. He then went over the manuscript again and made a few additions: fol. 42: "Dr Pococke, histo. Arab. P. 212, 313" after "Pococke" the word "specim." is added above the line (see also fols. 46, 48, 49). Whether the comments were Stubbe's cannot be determined, but there is no reason not to think they were his. It would not have been easy for someone else—a scribe, for instance—to locate the page and chapter references. At the same time, and in all his publications, Stubbe added precise references to his sources.

Both the BL Sloane fragments and BL Harleian 1876 include marginalia referring to the sources, although a small number is missing from Sloane. But when both scribes record a reference, it is exactly the same title, chapter, and page. Neither manuscript introduces a different page or chapter, but on a few occasions BL Harleian 1876 enters a reference the BL Sloane fragments do not—perhaps suggesting a hasty or careless Sloane scribe; after all, the folios in BL Sloane 1709 and 1786 are tightly packed, unlike BL Harleian 1876, which is written in a clear and beautiful hand, with wide line spaces, in a manuscript dedicated solely to *Originall* (unlike the BL Sloane fragments, which are included among other manuscripts; Sloane 1709 consists of "Miscellaneous Pieces").

In some cases what appears as marginalia in BL Harleian 1876 appears in brackets within the text in BL Sloane (cf. BL Sloane fol. 187r and BL Harleian fol. 225). The titles in BL Sloane and BL Harleian are the same: "Concerning the Christian Additions" (Sloane 1786 fol. 187v and Harleian fol. 230). But it is interesting to note the titles of the unit from Grotius:

BL Sloane 1709, fol. 188r: "Grotius de veritate relig. Christ. 1.6. cum notis"
University of London MS 537, fol. 115: "Grot. De Veritate Rel. Christianae lib.6"
BL Harleian1876, fol. 207 "Grotius de veritat. Relig.Christian. lib.6. cum notis

Was "cum notis" forgotten or did the scribe use another manuscript?

The title and the organization of the material in this manuscript are as follows:

"An Account of the Life of Mahomet" [title]
Fols. 1–55 (the unit on Christian history)
Fol. 55 "The History of ye Saracens and of Mahomet"
Blank folio
Fols. 57–100: "A generall Preface to the account of the originall & progress of Mahometanisme"
Blank folios
Fols. 103–193: "The History of the Saracens and of Mahomet"
Blank folio
Fols. 195–203: "Concerning the justice of the Mahometan wars & that Mahomet did not propagate his doctrine by the sword"
Blank folio
Fols. 205–210: "Concerning the Christians Additions"

1705. Bodleian MS Eng. Misc. c. 309

Complete manuscript, Bodleian MS Eng. Misc. c. 309. This manuscript was used by Shairani, although he re-arranged its chapters in his printed edition. It is the longest of all existing manuscripts, as it was rewritten and heavily "improved" by Hornby, who relied on a lost manuscript.[1]

It is likely that Hornby wanted to publish this manuscript by Stubbe, whose name he mentions on the title page as the "supposed" author. Evidently, the manuscript was circulating, but there was no definite knowledge about its author. Hornby wrote elegantly, gave clear and separate titles of chapters, but he did not include the annotations that appeared in the BL Sloane and the Harleian 1876 manuscripts. Another hand entered few of the references in bolder ink, more in the first than in the second part of the treatise; toward the end there is barely any reference.

Hornby "improved" the text by consulting further sources and adding material—but he did not contradict Stubbe's views, nor the general tenor about Muḥammad or Islam. One comparison of entries from University of London MS 537, BL Harleian 6189, and Oxford MS Eng.. Misc. c. 309 will suffice to show the range of intrusion on the part of Hornby. He introduced a reference to John Gregory M.A. 1631, also of Christ Church, Oxford, which does not appear in the other manuscripts:

MS 537 UNIVERSITY OF LONDON, SENATE HOUSE LIBRARY

> I do not find any understanding Author who doth controvert the Elegancy of the Alcoran, & it hath this advantage over the Xtian Bible, that being a poem, there is a greater Liberty allowed to fiction figurative expressions & Allegories then is allow'd of in prose also defects in Chronology & Errors in History are here tolerable, tho' for my part I beleive that many of the incoherencies & Chronologicall & Historical defaults are voluntary, partly because the vulgar being prepossessed wth them (in many cases this is evident to have dissented thereform would have been prejudicial to his Aims the universall Credit of the Errors being likely to overbear ye reall truth of things, partly because it was a received tradition among the Jews & Judaizing Xtians (& 'tis now made use of as an Apology for our Scripture that the Spirit of God in the prophets is not confined to the Gramatical Rules ordinary Methods.

MSS BL HARLEIAN 6189 AND BL HARLEIAN 1876

> I do not find any understanding author who doth controvert [fol. 301 in BL Harleian 6189] the Elegancy of the Alcoran; And it hath this advantage over the Christian Bible, that being a Poem, there is greater liberty allowed for fiction, figurative expression and Allegories, than is allowed of in prose. Also defects in Chronology, and Errors in History are here tolerable: though for my part, I believe that many of the incoherences and Chronological or Historical defaults *were voluntary*: partly because the vulgar being prepossesed with

them, (in many cases this is evident) to have [fol. BL 96 Harleian 1876] dissented therefrom, would have been prejudicial to his Aim, the universal credit of the Errors being likely to overbear the real truth of things; partly because it was a received Tradition amongst the Jews, and Judaizing Christians, and 'tis now made use of as an Apology for our Scripture, that the Spirit of God in the Prophets, is not confined to Grammatical Rules or ordinary methods:

MS OXFORD ENG. MISC. C. 309 AND BL HARLEIAN 6189; ADDITIONS IN THE OXFORD MANUSCRIPT ARE IN BOLD; THE ITALICIZIED PASSAGES ARE IN BL HARLEIAN 6189

¶ **The truth is** I do not find any understanding author who doth controvert [fol. 301 in Harleian 6189] the Elegancy of the Alcoran, **it being generally esteemed as the standard of the Arabian Language and Eloquence, but they raise great exceptions against it for incoherency & confusion Errors in History &** [fol. 138 in Oxford Eng. Misc. c. 309] **chronology and charge it with numberless trifles fables and absurdities.**

The late learned Mr. John Gregory in the preface to his works has this passage. "I was (says he) asked once by an able and understanding man whether the Alcoran as it is of it's self had so much in it as to work any thing upon a rational belief: I said yes. Thus much only I required that the believer should be brought up first under the engagement of that book. That which is everywhere called Religion hath more of Interest and the strong impressions of Education, then perhaps we consider otherwise for the book it's self it is taken for the greater part out of our Scripture, and would not appear altogether so ill if it were look'd upon in it's own Text, or through a good Translation."

We see this learned Man had not so ill an opinion of the Alcoran, and we shall likewise find upon examination that those who have most diligently perused that and the other books of the Mahometans, have abated much of the general prejudices of the Christians against that Religion and it's Author and entertained more favourable thoughts of both, then others whose aversion is kept up by their ignorance. If we look upon the Alcoran with the same indifferency as upon any other book we shall find that *And* it hath this advantage

> over the Christian Bible, that being a Poem, there is greater liberty allowed for fiction[, **Parables**], figurative expression and Allegories, than is allowed of in prose. Also defects in Chronology, and Errors in History are here tolerable: though for my part, I believe that many of the incoherences and Chronological or Historical defaults [**are here tolerable, tho' I believe most of those we call so Mahomet grounded upon the ancient Accounts in the Books of the Arabians or the general Traditions among them, and upon the Apocryphal books of the Jews and heretical Christians**] *were voluntary: partly because the vulgar being prepossesed with them,* (in many cases this is evident) [**which being respectively received as Authentic by those of the several Religions and the vulgar prepossessed with them,**] to have dissented therefrom, would have been prejudicial to his Aim, the universal credit of the Errors being likely to overbear the real truth of things; [**Many of the mistakes and incoherencies therein might be voluntary**] *partly* because it was a received Tradition amongst the Jews, and [fol. 139 in Oxford Eng. Misc. C. 309t] Judaizing Christians, and 'tis now made use of as an Apology for our Scripture, that the Spirit of God in the Prophets, is not confined to Grammatical Rules or ordinary methods.

Gregory lived a short life, and his work appeared posthumously—and then went through numerous editions, attesting to the popularity of his polylinguistic research.[2] That Hornby brought him into his improvement shows to what degree Stubbe was following in the scholarship about Muḥammad and Islam that emanated from Christ Church, the college founded by Cardinal Wolsey where the first chair of Hebrew had been established.[3]

This manuscript formed the basis of the Shairani edition. But Shairani edited out passages of which he did not approve..

The title and the organization of the material in the manuscript are as follows:

"An Account of the Rise and Progress of Mahometanism with the life of Mahomet and a vindication of him and his Religion from the Calumnies of the Christians Supposed to be Written by Dr. Stubb Copied by C.H. Anno Dni 1705 With some variations and additions" [title, on a separate sheet]

The Contents [on two separate pages]

1718. British Library Harleian 6189

Complete manuscript: British Library Harleian 6189 ("History of Mahometanism" on spine). The date is given at the end of the manuscript in the same hand that transcribed the whole text: 7 July 1718. As noted previously, the scribe was using a manuscript that included corrections. On several occasions, the scribe referred to those corrections: "These words were underlined by the Corrector" (fol. 34); "Interlined by the corrector of the Or.[iginal]" (fol. 35) . These notes by the scribe point to a different set of manuscripts that were not available to the copyists in cluster introduced heretofore.

Hornby and the copyist of this manuscript must have used similar versions of the *Originall*. The word "Metaphysicks" appears in BL Harleian 1876 (fol. 42), but in University of London MS 537 and in this manuscript the word is "Mathematicks" (fols. 35 and 60 respectively), which is the same as in Hornby (fol. 60). On other occasions the scribe used the same word/s that appear in MS 537 and BL Harleian 1876: thus "revolutions" appears in BL Harleian 1876 (fol. 47), but in this manuscript it appears as "Resolutions" (fol. 66). There are passages in University of London MS 537 and in BL Harleian 1876 that do not appear in this manuscript. Was the scribe of this manuscript "editing" out passages, as for instance in the description of Muhammad, which is omitted from the beginning of this manuscript?

> He had a ready Wit, & such an Elocution as no Arabian before or since hath ever equalled: whensoever He pleased He could be facetious without prejudice to his Grandeur; He perfectly understood the Art of placing his favours aright. He could distinguish betwixt the deserts, the inclinations, & the interests of Men, He could penetrate into their Genius's & Intentions, without employing vulgar [3] espialls, or seeming Himself to mind any such thing: In fine, such was his whole deportment, so was his naturall freedome tempered with a befitting reservedness, that He instructed others not to importune him with unbecoming proposalls, but never suffered any to understand what it was, to be denyed.
>
> (BL Harleian 1876, Fols. 2–3)

The title and the organization of the material in this manuscript are as follows:

"The Rise and Progress of Mahometanism" [title]
Fols. 1–78: "The Rise and Progress of Mahometanism"
Fols. 78–216: "Of Mahomet and the Saracens"
Fols. 216–230: "Concerning the Justice of Mahometan Wars and that Mahomet did not propagate his Doctrine by the Sword"
Fols. 230–240: "Additions Concerning the Christians"
Fols. 240–308: "A generall preface to the account of the Original of Mahomentanism Progress"

Lost Manuscripts

In University of London MS 537 and in BL Harleian 6189 the scribes make reference to manuscripts they were using. These manuscripts are presumed lost. Hand B, in the former manuscript, mentions a "blew book" (fol. 113). There may well have been other manuscripts of Stubbe's treatise.

Final Remarks

Based on these manuscripts, it is possible to venture the following clusters:

BL Sloane, University of London MS 537 and BL Harleian 1876
Oxford MS Eng. Misc. c 309 and BL Harleian 6189

There are no two manuscripts that are alike. Each scribe deleted, added, and rewrote passages in his own style, at the same time that he left other passages unchanged.

The two manuscripts that are closest to each other are BL Sloane and University of London MS 537.

The other manuscripts exhibit significant differences: as shown, BL Harleian 6189 has a different sequence of chapters from Bodleian MS Eng. Misc. C 309 at the same time that the latter deletes/excludes passages that appear in University of London MS 537 and in BL Harleian 6189.

THE PRESENT EDITION

The present edition is a modernized version of the earliest complete version of *Originall*: University of London MS 537. My goal is to make Stubbe's text as accessible as possible to today's reader while preserving its seventeenth-century syntax and style.

I have regulated all spelling in accordance with current usage (American). Also, I changed "then" to "than" (when appropriate); "their" to "there," expanded ampersands and contractions ("enthron'd" to "enthroned," "'tis" to "it is"), added or removed punctuation, introduced or removed capitalization, closed parentheses, removed double letters ("originall" to "original" and "ff" to "f"), and introduced new paragraph divisions. I have indented speeches and long quotations and added inverted commas to statements. I also regularized the spelling of place names that the scribe confused: "Pallestine," "palestine," "Palestine" and others. I also modernized them to correspond to today's geographical usage: thus "Affrick" becomes "Africa," and others.

I have not deleted or added words, even when the sense is unclear.

In the case of Latin and Greek phrases and passages: it is unlikely that in the original version of the manuscript by Stubbe, who was a master of those languages, there would have been mistakes in spelling. The scribe, however, made a vast amount of mistakes. I have corrected those mistakes by quoting the original Greek and Latin sources Stubbe consulted.

In the case of Arabic names and phrases: Stubbe knew no Arabic and therefore could not determine the accurate spelling of words. Relying on the works of numerous Arabists and scholars, he was confused by their different spellings of the same words. In frustration, he sometimes listed the variants: "the Caab Alccab Caaba Kabe Cabea" (MS 537, fol. 53). The scribe must have been equally confused, and so in the manuscript the same word is sometimes spelled differently, even on the same page. There are, however, words that are always spelled the same: "Medina," "Zamzam," "Omar," and "Edris." And there are names that are spelled consistently the same, but then are changed for a few pages, after which the old spelling is resumed ("Ismael" and "Ismaell").

On the first occurrence of words or names with variants, I have listed the variants in the note. In order to make the text as accessible as possible, I have chosen the spelling that is closest to today's pronunciation and used it throughout the edition. In the case of names that appear infrequently, I have retained the originals and explained them in the notes.

I have left unchanged but italicized all the Arabic words, names, and phrases that Stubbe transliterated. These transliterations are significant for the following reasons:

1. In some cases the transliteration shows the exact source from which Stubbe borrowed it. Most of his transliterations of names and phrases came from Pococke, Hottinger, and Selden.

2. Words such as *Musulman* and *Moslemin*; *Coran* and *Alkoran*; *Islamism, Islanism,* and *Islamisme* and other variants: by bringing names and titles from the Latin texts into his treatise, Stubbe may have introduced them into English for the first time.

3. In specific cases, Stubbe deliberately kept the Arabic nomenclature to emphasize the Islamic context. While he used "Abraham" and "David" and other biblical/Hebrew names in their English form, he used "Ismael,"

rather than Ishmael, and "Isa" rather than Jesus (even though his sources used "Jesu"),[4] and "Edris" rather than Enoch (or alongside). Further, he sometimes used the Arabic word where an English word would have been quite satisfactory: *sallah* and a few others.

I have included reference to the marginalia made by the two hands on the manuscript, as well as all significant variants and notes from the Sloane fragments and BL Harleian 1876 and 6189. In my notes I have corrected and elaborated on the sources mentioned in the marginalia

The transcript of MS 537 is available through Columbia University Press.

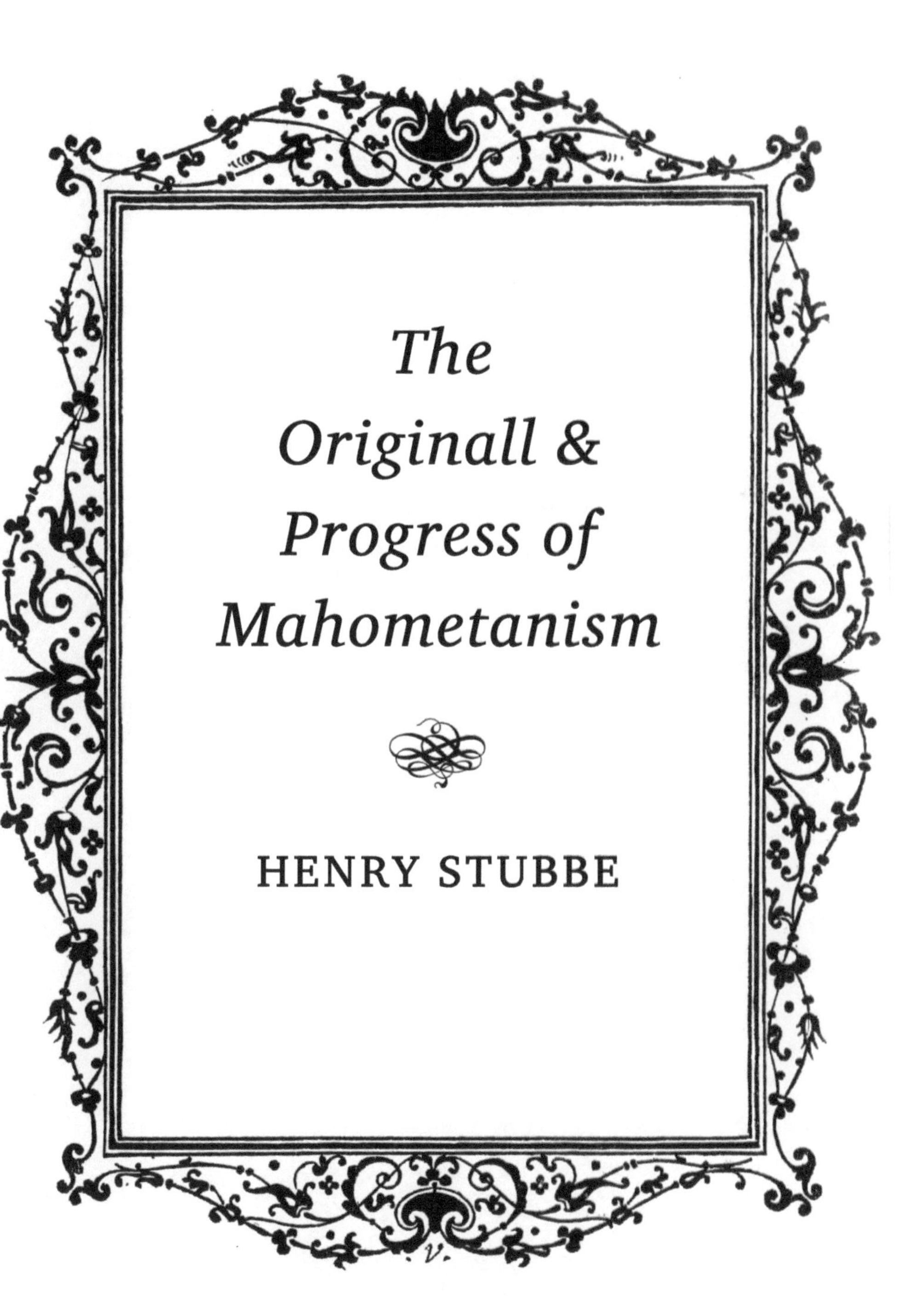

The Originall & Progress of Mahometanism

HENRY STUBBE

TABLE OF CONTENTS

Folios refer to the pagination in the University of London Senate House manuscript. In the text itself they appear in bold between pointed brackets.

INTEND TO WRITE of one of the greatest transactions the world hath ever yet been acquainted with: "The Original and Progress of Mahometanism," wherein a new religion was introduced into the world to the desolation, in a manner, of paganism, Judaism and Christianity, which hath now maintained itself above a thousand years and has increased its extent and proselytes over more than a fifth part of the known earth. Whereas Judaism, including all its colonies, was never equal thereunto, nor perhaps Christianity itself, if we consider the condition of it either before Constantine, or even to the days of Theodosius (during all which time as the senate of Rome so the greatest part of the empire were pagans), or afterwards, when uniformity was settled.[1] But the inundation of the Arian Goths and the general irreligion, impiety, and division into sects, some whereof were idolaters, do not permit me to think that true and fervent Christianity was so far diffused as Mahometanism is at present.[2]

The same narration includes in it the rise of an empire greater than any of the four so famed monarchies, erected in a barren poor country in the midst of two potent princes, one reigning over the Eastern Christians, the other over the Persians: and all this to be brought about in the compass of a few years by a man of a mean estate, fiercely opposed, and slenderly befriended.[3]

By this time your curiosity prompts you to search after the physiognomy of this extraordinary person. This great soul was lodged in a body of a middle size: he was no giant nor did his stature equal that of an Almain Cimber whose bulk amazed the old Romans.[4] He had a large head, a brown **<2>** complexion but fresh color, his beard long and black but not gray, a grave aspect wherein the awfulness of majesty seemed to be tempered with admirable sweetness which at once imprinted in the beholders respect, reverence, and love. His eyes were quick and sparkling. He had very handsome legs, an incomparable mien, easy motion and every action of his had a grace so peculiar that it was impossible to see him with indifference. The Arabians compare him to the purest streams of some river gently gliding along, which arrest and delight the eyes of every approaching passenger. [5]

Nothing was more mild than his speech, nothing more courteous and obliging than his carriage. He could dexterously accommodate himself to all ages, humors and degrees.[6] He knew how to pay his submissions to the great without servility and to be complacent to the meaner sort without abasing himself. He had a ready wit, a penetrating and discerning judgment and such an elocution as no Arabian before or since hath ever equaled. When he pleased he could be facetious without prejudice to his grandeur: he perfectly understood the art of placing his favors aright. He could distinguish betwixt the deserts, the inclinations, and the interests of men; he could penetrate into their geniuses and intentions without employing vulgar espials or seeming himself to mind any such thing.

In fine, such was his whole deportment.

So was his natural freedom tempered with a befitting reservedness as instructed others not to importune him with unbecoming proposals, but never suffered any to understand what it was to be denied. Besides all those embellishments and qualifications, he had a great strength and agility of body, an indefatigable industry, an undaunted courage such as never forsook him in the greatest dangers. He was much addicted to ride the best and most warlike horses, **<3>** and since every action of great men is remarkable and often carries a presage of future accidents, I shall relate one. He being once mounted on a brave but unruly courser, his friends desired him to forsake his back; but whether it were that he duly apprehended his own skill and abilities, or his great spirit thought it more fitting to contemn than acknowledge a danger into which he had rashly engaged himself, he denied the request, adding that it became the timorous and effeminate to have their horses exactly managed for them: that a generous and true Arab could not be surprised with an untamed steed, that the intractableness of his horse added to his pleasure, as a storm delights an intelligent pilot since it gives him an occasion to discover that skill which could not be manifested otherwise, and rewards the danger and trouble by an accession of glory.

Behold the character of that man who hath gained so much upon the esteem of one part of the world and filled the rest with astonishment.

But to discover the means by which he achieved those great things is a matter of more difficulty, and in order thereto you must consider what it was that disposed the people to such a change and what gave beginning thereunto. Prudent persons distinguish cautiously betwixt those two circumstances and know that the bravest actions do frequently miscarry under very happy pretenses or beginnings, in case the antecedent causes be not proportionate to the design.[7] Never any republic did dwindle into a monarchy or any kingdom alter into an aristocracy or commonweal without a series of preceding causes which principally contributed thereto.[8] Never had Caesar established himself, nor Brutus erected a senate: and if you inquire why the first Brutus could expel Tarquin and the second could not overthrow Augustus and Antony;[9] why Lycurgus, **<4>** Solon, and others could establish those governments which others have in vain attempted to settle in Genoa, Florence and other places, you will find it to arise from hence:[10] that some considering those antecedent causes which secretly and securely incline to a change took the advantage thereof, whilst the others did only regard the speciousness or justice of their pretensions without a mature examination of what was principally to be observed.[11] This is certain: that when the previous dispositions intervene, a slight occasion, oftentimes a mere casualty, opportunity taken hold of and wisely prosecuted, will produce those revolutions which otherwise no human sagacity or courage could accomplish.[12]

I cannot find any authentic ground to believe that the sects among the Jews were more ancient than the days of the Maccabees, but arose after that Antiochus had subdued Jerusalem and reduced the generality of the Jews to paganism; and (the better to confirm his conquests) erected there an academy, placing the Pythagorean, Platonic, and Epicurean philosophers there. This I conceive to have been the original of the Pharisees, Sadducees, and Essenes.[13] Though afterwards, when the Maccabees had made an edict against and anathematized all that taught their children the Greek philosophy, one party did honest their tenets by entitling them to Sadoc and Baithos, and the others from a Cabbala derived from Eleazar and Moses successively.[14]

The introduction of those sects and of that Cabbala occasioned that exposition of the prophecy of Jacob (Genesis 49:20): "The scepter shall not depart from Judah nor a lawgiver from between his feet until Shiloh come, and unto him shall the gathering of the people be."[15] From whence they did according to that fantastical Cabbala imagine that when so ever the scepter should depart from Judah and the dominion thereof cease, that then there should arise a Messiah of the line of David (this was no general opinion: for how then could any have imagined Herod the Great to have been the Messiah; and how could Josephus fix that character upon Vespasian) who should <5> restore the empire and glory of Israel, and all nations should bow and submit to his scepter?[16]

I do not read that the Jews harbored any such exposition during the captivity under Nebuchadnezzar; albeit that the scepter so departed at that time from the tribe of Judah and house of David that it never was resettled therein. After their return to Jerusalem, no such thing is spoken of when Antiochus Epiphanes subdued them, profaned their temple, destroyed their laws and rites, and left them nothing of a scepter or lawgiver—during all which time, although they had the same prophecies and scripture, there is no news of any expected Messiah.[17] But after that, the curiosity of the rabbis involved them in the pursuance of mystical numbers, and Pythagorically or Cabbalistically to explain them, according to the Gematria.[18] Then was discovered that Shiloh and Messiah consisted of letters which make up the same numerals, and therefore a mysterious promise of a redeemer was insinuated thereby. And the prophecy of Balaam (Numbers 24:17) concerning a star out of Jacob and a scepter rising out of Israel with a multitude of other predictions (which the condition of their nation made them otherwise to despair of) must be fulfilled under this Messiah.

I name no other prophesies because either they are general and indefinitely expressed as to the time of their accomplishment, or else inexplicable for obscurity and uncertain as to authority, as the weeks of Daniel, which book the Jews reckon among their *hagiographa* or sacred (but not canonical) books.[19] And also this prophesy had a contradictory one (Jeremiah 22:30), where it is said of Coniah, no man of his seed shall prosper, sitting upon the throne of David and ruling any more in Judah. And Ezekiel 22:26–27: "Thus saith the Lord God: Remove the diadem, and take off the crown: this shall not be the same: exalt him that is low, and abase him that is high. I will overturn, overturn, overturn it, and it shall be no more, until he come whose right it is; and I will give it him."

The aforesaid obscure prophecy, which did not take effect at first until the reign of David, and which suffered such a variety <6> of interruptions, seems to have fallen under this interpretation in the days of Herod the Great, whom the Jews so hated for his usurpation upon the Maccabee Levitical family and his general cruelties; he was particularly detested by the Cabbalistical Pharisees. That to keep up their rancor against him and his lineage, and to alienate the people from him, I could easily imagine this to have been a contrivance, wither perhaps was Herod displeased with the interpretation of the prophesy after that the Herodians had accommodated it to him and made him the Messiah, who after their conquest and ignominy under Pompey,[20] had restored the Jews to a great reputation and strength, rebuilt the temple, and found some who could deduce his pedigree from the thigh of Jacob, as directly as David and Solomon. This sense of the prophecy being inculcated into the people, and all those Jews or strangers or proselytes, which resorted to Jerusalem at the great festivals from Alexandria, Antioch, Babylon, and all those parts where the Jews had any colonies, there was an universal expectation of the Messiah to come (I except the Herodians) which continued amongst them ever after and possesses the Jews (our Jews are but the remains of the Pharisees) to this day.[21]

Their impatience for his appearance seems to have been less under Herod the Great (there being no mention of false Messiahs then), perhaps because the prophecy was not so clear and convincing whilst Herod was king since the scepter and legislative power seemed to be still in Judea. Though swayed by an Idumean proselyte, the priesthood continued, the temple flourished, and there was a prince of the Sanhedrin, Rabbi Hillel of the lineage of David.[22] But ten years after the birth of Christ, when Archelaus was banished to Vienna,[23] and Judea reduced into the form of a province, the scepter seemed then to be entirely departed from Judah. The kingdom was now become a part of the government of Syria and ruled by a procurator, who taxed them severely. Then the sense of their miseries made the people more credulous, and whether they more easily believed what they earnestly desired might happen, or that the malcontents did the more frequently and diligently insinuate into the multitude that opinion, there arose then sundry false Messiahs, and the world was big with expectation raised by the Jews in every country who had used the intelligence <7> from their common metropolis (Jerusalem) that the great prince was coming who should reestablish the Jewish monarchy and bring peace and happiness to all the earth.[24]

Those circumstances made way for the reception of Christ, and the miracles he did (miracles were the only demonstration to the Jews, Mark 8:11). Convincing the people that he was the Messiah, they never stayed till he should declare himself to be so (I think he never directly told any so but the woman of Samaria, John 4:26) or evince his genealogy from David. For though some mean persons called him the Son of David, and the populace by that title did cry "Hosanna" unto him, yet did he acquiesce in terming himself the Son of Man, but esteemed him a prophet Elias, Jeremiah, and even the Messiah. And when he made his cavalcade upon an asinego, they cried him up as the descendant of King David. But his untimely apprehension and death, together with his neglect to improve that inclination of the people to make him king, did allay the affections of the Jews towards him, disappoint all their hopes, and so exasperated them that they, who had been a part of his retinue in that intrado of his, called for his execution and adjudged him by common suffrage to be crucified.[25] His disciples fled; the apostles distrusted and sufficiently testified their unbelief by not crediting his resurrection. After that he was risen again, and they, assured thereof, they assume their former hopes of a temporal Messiah, and the last question they propose to him is: "Lord, wilt thou at this time restore the Kingdom to Israel" (Acts 1:6).

After his assumption into heaven, they attend in Jerusalem the coming of the Holy Ghost which seized in them and gave them the gift of tongues for a season: whereby they preached to the Jews, Elamites, Parthians, Alexandrians et cetera (those Salmasius shows not to be absolute strangers, natives of those countries, but Jews planted there) as also the proselytes.[26] Those surprised with the miracles of the cloven tongues and gift of languages, being possessed with the desire and hopes of a Messiah, and being there ascertained by Peter that Jesus whom Pilate had crucified was the Lord and Christ (Acts 2:36), were to the number of three thousand immediately baptized in his name. And such as were to depart, when they came to their colonies, did divulge the **<8>** tidings and engage other Jews and proselytes to the same belief, the apostles themselves going about and also ordaining others to preach the glad tidings of a Messiah come who, though dead, was risen again (according to the obscure prediction of David) for the salvation of Israel, and whose second appearance would perfect the happiness of all nations, as well Jews as Gentiles.[27]

That we may the better understand the way whereby those glad tidings were spread, it is requisite to be informed of the condition of the Jews in those days. It will not injure any relation if I translate a piece of a letter written by Agrippa, a king in Jewry (though not of Jerusalem), to Caius Caligula on behalf of the holy city, and published by Philo in his embassy to the emperor:

> Jerusalem is the metropolis not only of the country of Judea, but of many other places, by reason of the colonies translated thence at several times, either in adjacent territories, as Egypt, Phoenicia, Syria, Caelo-Syria, or those more remote, as Pamphylia, Cilicia, most parts of Asia as far as Bithynia, and the inmost parts of Pontus. Nor is Europe exempt from this jurisdiction, the Jews being planted in Thessalia, Boetia, Macedonia, Etolia, Attica, Argos, Corinth, throughout Peloponnesus, especially in the principal parts of that isthmus. Nor is the continent only replenished with this nation: they have settled themselves in the chiefest isles as Euboea, Cyprus, and Crete. I mention not those beyond Euphrates, every place where the soil is rich, except a small part of Babylon and some parcels in other principalities inhabited by Jews.[28]

To illustrate this further, let us consider the number and interest of the Jews at Alexandria. What the glory and power of the Alexandrian and Egyptian Jews was, it is easy to understand out of Josephus and Philo. They were exceeding numerous there, the chiefest dignitaries, as well military as civil, were vested in them. They had a peculiar temple built for them at Heliopolis and Onias.[29] For their High Priest (though deserted before the time of Christ), they had always their distinct ruler under the Egyptian kings, chosen by themselves out of their senate to rule them for life, being **<9>** styled 'Αλαβάρχης, Γενάρχης, 'Εθνάρχης[30] And you may easily guess at their splendor and number by this relation of the rabbi: he that has not seen the cathedral church (or chief synagogue) at Alexandria never saw the real glory of Israel. It was like a royal palace: there were two porticos by which to enter into it; there were in it seventy chairs adorned with gold and jewels according to the number of the elders; and a wooden pulpit in the midst thereof, wherein stood the bishop of the synagogue.[31] And when the law was read after the pronouncing of every benediction, a sign was given by the shaking of a handkerchief for the people to say "Amen." They did not there sit promiscuously, but men of several ranks and professions did sit in distinct places. There were once so many Jews there that the multitude was double to what went first out of Egypt.[32]

In the next place, let us consider the multitude at Babylon and the neighboring territories, of those which went up with Ezra, Nehemiah, and Zorobabel. The number was but small, and those consisting of two tribes principally Judah and Benjamin with four orders only of the priests and Levites. Josephus[33] informs us that the rest of the multitude of Israelites chose rather to remain in the Babylonian territories, wherefore only two tribes are to be found in Asia and Europe subjected to the Roman Empire. The other ten tribes continue beyond Euphrates until this day, being an infinite people not to be numbered.[34]

This account, how ten tribes remained, ought not to seem strange to those who consider how St. James writes his catholic epistle to the twelve tribes which were scattered abroad;[35] nor to them which believe that the seventy-two interpreters of the Bible were chosen out of the twelve tribes,[36] or who give any credit to the itinerary of Benjamin Tudelensis, a Jew who met with many of those Israelites that were captivated by Salmonasar in Media and other neighboring countries.[37] Many of the Israelites fled[38] into Judea also removed thence with the Levites upon the schism, and the rest continued in the dominions of Ashur till Nebuchadnezzar **<10>** brought the Jews into the like captivity and scattered them all over his dominions, which comprised one hundred and twenty-seven provinces (Esther 8:9). And it is not to be doubted but the interest of the Jews was very great there about the time of Christ, since at the time of Benjamin's travels about five hundred years ago, they had so great a power and jurisdiction there, since they could be contradistinguished from the Palestine Jews, have their own Targum and Talmud, and their republics and universities in *Soria*, Pumbeditha and Nehardea continuing till the times of Theodosius, Arcadius, and Honorius, besides an infinity of synagogues and a reverence universally to the rulers, equivalent to what was shown unto the Christian bishops and clergy.[39]

All those came up frequently to the great festivals at Jerusalem, as Salmasius shows out of Acts 2:9, where the old Jews from the place of their residence are called Parthians, Medes, Elamites.[40] And besides this inestimable number of Jews, there was a multitude of proselytes whom they continually converted to entire Judaism. For not only Abraham but all the Jews did perpetually endeavor to draw others to their religion.[41] Idumeans were made proselytes in the days of Hyrcanus; in the Babylonian Empire, many of the nations turned Jews (Esther 8:17). The Talmudists reckon upon Nero, Cæsar, and Antoninus Pius as proselytes.[42] But to evince their number better, let us learn from Salmasius that the originary Jews did never use the Septuagint in their synagogues, but that was made use of by the proselyte Jews and their posterity at Alexandria and elsewhere. The Hellenists, mentioned in the Acts, were no other; and the deacons elected there to provide for the widows were of that number, and being a proselyte of Antioch.[43] That they were Jewish proselytes appears from hence: that the gospel had not then been preached to the Gentiles.

How diligent the Pharisees were to engage new converts the gospel tells us, and to descend so after ages, which is of some importance to the subsequent discourse. Dio Cassius tells us that in the time of Adrian when Bar Kokhba acted the Messiah, many nations joined with that imposter and the Jews; so that the whole world was in a commotion, which cannot be understood of any but entire proselytes.[44] For the Jews would not have mingled with others. And after that, under the Christian emperors, our codes and ecclesiastical constitutions inform us that they retained the custom of inveigling proselytes. This being the condition of the Jews, and all the nation, however dispersed, **<11>** being prepared aforehand to entertain any tidings of a Messiah who should advance the throne of David to an universal monarchy, it is not to be wondered that Christianity was so soon spread over the whole earth.[45]

But wherein consisted this primitive Christianity which was there diffused? Certainly, the principal tenet which gained upon the spirits of all men was the doctrine of the coming of the Messiah. And it is evident that this was the fundamental article, from whence the Christians had at first their name in Antioch,[46] and which they propagated everywhere as the sum of their religion: that Jesus who was crucified was the true Messiah, that he was risen again, and would return in glory to restore Israel and establish truth and peace throughout the earth.

The first part is apparent from these texts.[47] The second seems demonstrated hence: that not only the Jews but the[48] Christians were millenaries and did believe and expect the temporal reign of the Messiah and the union of the Jews and Gentiles under one most happy monarchy. Not one of the two first ages did dissent from this opinion; they which opposed it never quoted any for themselves before Dionysius Alexandrinus who lived at least 250 years after Christ. Of this opinion was Justin Martyr and (as he says) all Christians that were exactly Orthodox; Irenæus sets it down directly for a tradition and relates the very words which Christ used when he taught the doctrine.

And if this tenet were not an universal tradition in the most primitive times, I profess I know not what article of our faith will be found to be such upon the most diligent research.

This doctrine was taught by the consent of the most eminent Fathers of the first ages without any opposition from their contemporaries, and was delivered by them not as doctors but as witnesses, not as their own opinion but as apostolic tradition.[49] This tenet has been so fully handled by Dr. Mead (not to mention some others) that I might have declined the allegation of those impartial and able witnesses—the Lord Falkland and Mr. Chillingworth.[50] These were the principal tenets of those that were the first Christians, and from whence they were denominated. As to the subordinate doctrinals, they were no other than these: that the Messiah being already come, and since his ascension, being upon his return, in order to the recollection of Israel, the reestablishing of that kingdom and uniting of all nations under one scepter, a scepter of righteousness and truth; that all persons ought to prepare themselves for this holy kingdom of the Messiah and of heaven, and to relinquish all idolatry and wickedness, to repent **<12>** of their sins unfeignedly, and to submit to those laws under the obedience whereof God had concluded mankind though in sundry manners,[51] there being one obligation upon the Jews and entire proselytes, and another upon the rest of men, who were not under that dispensation but subjected to the seven commandments of Noah, and, by due observing thereof, might render themselves capable of a portion in the future life and be sufficiently qualified for the kingdom of Christ on earth: it being the custom of the Jews always to make proselytes where so ever they lived. And if they prevailed not so far, at least to reduce them from idolatry and Gentilism to the observation of that law of nature which they esteemed all the progeny of Noah and such as were not of the Jewish profession to be obliged to.[52]

It is no wonder if upon the persuasion that the Messiah were born, and returning again in glory, that some became apostles and others evangelists and teachers, both to Jews and Gentiles. The partition wall and distinction was to be taken away when all the world should become subjects to the same prince, who should extend his favors first to the Jews and then to the Gentiles, the greatest prerogatives and privileges appertaining to the Jews as the peculiar people and children of the promise.[53]

We find in the first churches a distinction between Christians that were Jews and entire proselytes and those that were Gentiles or uncircumcised. The first had their apostles, all except Paul being of that number, and of Peter it is particularly said that he had the apostleship of the Jews committed to him, as Paul was charged with that of the Gentiles (Galatians 2:9). And of those which were scattered upon the persecution as far as Phoenicia, Cyprus, and Antioch, they preached to the Jews only (Acts 11:19), though amongst the Jews there we find this distinction: that some of them being entire proselytes, but not understanding Hebrew nor reverencing that holy language so much as the originary Jews, they spoke Greek and used the Septuagint in their synagogues. Those are the Grecians spoken of (Acts 11:20) as Salmasius well observes.[54] And such were the churches in Jerusalem to whom the apostles appointed deacons, all proselytes. Of them that preached to the Gentiles, some taught them the necessity of circumcision and becoming entire proselytes: thus did Peter (Galatians 2:14) and others (Acts 15:2), and even Paul circumcised Timothy though the son of a gentile father (Acts 16:3). Sixteen bishops of Jerusalem were successively circumcised, saith Sulpicius Severus; and even those who derived their pedigree so as to show they were of the kindred of Christ, called *deposyini*, were always of the circumcision **<13>** (Eusebeus, *Ecclesiastica Historia* liber 1, caput 7).[55]

From hence we may frame to ourselves a prospect of the primitive judaizing church, since it is certain that they were zealous as to the Mosaical Law (Acts 21) and lived in a perfect conformity to the legal rites. It is not to be doubted but their religion and doctrinals varied much from ours: such a sacrament as we make baptism to be, they had none, the Jewish baptism extending only to proselytes when newly made and their present family, not successive posterity—except we take it in a general sense for washing, as Luke 11:38. And so they might baptize either arbitrarily upon some great occasion, as at the preaching of John, or out of respect to legal or superstitious Pharisaical uncleanness. To this alludes the apostle when he tells the Hebrews of the doctrine of baptism (Hebrews 6:2). They that were circumcised resorted at usual times to the public temple service (Acts 3.1): they paid vows, offered sacrifices, and walked orderly, keeping the law, and yet were believers (Acts 21:20) et cetera. And there is not any sign that they were separated from the other

Jews or were accounted heretics upon any other account than that they held Jesus to be the Messiah and taught in his name (Acts 14:17–18).

As to that other sacrament of the Lord's Supper, neither did they use that otherwise than Christ had done, as a Judaical rite used either at the Passover or constantly at meals, the cup of blessing being then distributed by the master of the household, and the bread broken and distributed. The use of red wine, the breaking of the bread formally, and the distributing of it, the very names and rites are the same which were usual among the Jews. Nor was this ever done in the Jewish synagogues but at home. And so it is recorded they continued daily in the temple and, breaking bread at their own houses, did eat their meat with gladness and singleness of heart (Acts 2:46). It is very probable that they added to the usual benediction of the bread and wine some commemorations in honor of the Messiah, which was no innovation or schismatical act since every rabbi might enlarge the synagogue worship or private devotion of his disciples in that manner. And it was usual for them so to do, wherefore this could give no distaste. And if we may believe that they imitated Christ in the celebration of his Last Supper, as that we may (for what was read of the Lord was delivered unto them (1 Corinthians 11:23), we must believe that all the ceremonies of the Jews were entirely retained by them at such time, seeing that in the evangelists we find nothing done in the Lord's Supper but what the Jewish rituals prescribe. **<14>**

Scaliger avows it:"Ea omnia quae Evangelio traduntur, in ritibus Judaeorum sine ulla discrepantia eodem modo praecepta esse,"[56] with whom doth Buxtorf and those that are most versed in the rabbinical learning agree.[57] But that they did never believe Christ to be the natural son of God by eternal generation,[58] or any tenet depending thereon, or prayed unto him, or believed the Holy Ghost, or the trinity of persons in one deity, is as evident as it is that the Jews and they did expect no such Messiah, and the introducing such doctrines would have been capital among them as tending to blasphemy and polytheism. It was blasphemy adjudged in Christ to say that he should sit at the right hand of power—that power being esteemed an incommunicable attribute of God. And so suffered Stephen (Acts 7:56–57) though Jesus did not upon the adjuration of Caiaphas say that he was Christ the Son of God (Matthew 26:63), and albeit it is manifest that the term "Son of God" was not unusual amongst the Jews so that they bestowed it on men, yet did they not import thereby any real divinity in the person (nor did Caiaphas in this adjuration mean so), but an extraordinary perfection lodged in humanity and hyperbolically expressed.

Neither is to be believed that they conceived that Christ's death had put an end to the ceremonial law as consisting of types and fading shadows since they obstinately retained them so long after. And, which is most considerable, during this time they were instructed and governed by the apostles and their immediate successors. Such was the condition of the Judaizing Christians amongst which it is further remarkable that as the Jews originally did use the Hebrew Bible in their synagogues (howsoever that they expounded it in Syriac and Chaldean as they do now in Spanish, Italian, and according to the language which the auditory best understands), and the proselytes did follow the Septuagint and had a Greek liturgy, so it happened in Christianity: the Jewish converts did use the Hebrew Bible, and others adhered to the Septuagint, and as they hated each other before by reason of the use of the Septuagint, so they seem to have retained the same passion and animosity under the gospel. And the murmuring of the Greeks (Acts 6:1) perhaps derived its beginning from hence—the Hebrews not relieving the widows of those others, whereupon the **<15>** Hellenist proselytes had seven deacons chosen out of their number to attend to that care.[59]

The Hellenists did relate miracles concerning their version and feigned a tale of seventy cells in which each translator finished his version, and upon comparing, they were found to be the same word for word. But the Jews say that darkness was upon the face of the earth in the time of Ptolemy when that translation was made and in the month of Thebeth kept a fast to testify their sorrow and resentments for it.[60] And though the Hellenists did reside in Judea or resort thither from Alexandria and Antioch, yet they held synagogues distinct from those of the Hebrews. Thus we have the synagogue of the Libertines, of the Cyrenians, Alexandrians, et cetera (Acts 6:9). Such were the Jewish synagogues of which Justin Martyr and Tertullian speak, in which the Septuagint was read;[61] such was that in Cæsarea the Metropolis of Judea, whereof we read in the Hierosolymitan Talmud that Rabbi Levi went to Cæsarea, and hearing them reading the lesson in Greek, he would have hindered them, but Rabbi Jesse was angry and said: "Must not he read at all who cannot read Hebrew? Let him read in any language that he understands and he discharges his duty."[62]

This distinction of synagogues upon the same account was introduced amongst the Christians. For though the Hellenists and Gentiles did use the Septuagint and Greek service, the Hebrews did not so, nor used they the same gospels with the other. Such were the Nazarenes who lived at Cæsarea Borea, and elsewhere, who used the Hebrew Bible and either a gospel peculiar called Evangeluim Nazareorum or Evangeluim Secundum Hebraeos or at least the Gospel of Matthew written in Hebrew, but with that discrepancy from the others, that the church hath rejected it as apocryphal, sophisticated, with sundry fables and otherwise corrupted.[63] But the Nazarenes and Ebionites, the remains of the Judaizing churches, did repute that as the only authentic **<16>** gospel, as Epiphanius relates.[64]

And from hence I conceive arose that division whereby some declared themselves to be of the synagogues of Paul, others of Apollo, and others of Cephas. The apostle of the circumcision did retain the Jewish rites, the Hebrew Scriptures and Hebrew Gospel (according to what descended to the Nazarenes at Pella Borea, et cetera) with a regimen exactly Judaical.[65] But Apollo, being an Alexandrian Jew (or rather Jewish proselyte), as one would guess by his name, used (no doubt) the Septuagint and such books as composed the canon at Alexandria, and in all probability did introduce in his synagogues a conformity with the Alexandrians' rites and government, adding thereunto that Jesus was Christ which is all that I find he preached (Acts 18:28). But Paul who dealt with the Gentiles and did not reduce them under the Judaical law and circumcision, nor enforced them to any uniformity, but became all things unto all (by way of condescension) that he might gain them to Christ, whence his synagogues or churches must needs have varied exceedingly from those erected by Peter and Apollo, which gave occasion to the distinction at Corinth, some being of Paul, some of Apollo, and some of Cephas (1 Corinthians 1:12).[66]

From hence, if one will frame unto himself a prospect of the first Christianity, he must imagine to himself distinct synagogues of the original Jews and Hellenist proselytes none of those subordinate to the same governors, but as independent as were the Jewish synagogues everywhere, each synagogue having its peculiar bishop or angel of the church and ruling presbyters which are termed in the civil law and by the Jews *archisynagogi* and *presbyteri*, though perhaps the *nasi* or patriarch at Jerusalem might have one universal superintendency over them as he had a power to exact money from all the Jewish synagogues in the **<17>** east and west. The officers which were sent to gather his *aurum coronarium* or tax were called "Apostles."[67] And in imitation thereof did Christ institute his apostles.

The whole constitution of the primitive clergy relates to the Jewish synagogue not to the hierarchy. The presbyters were not priests but laymen set apart to their office by imposition of hands: no temples, no altars, no sacrifices were known in those days, the name of priest unheard of then.[68] Before the destruction of the temple at Jerusalem, the said apostles did go forth and collect the said money as shekels paid to the temple which was afterward converted into *aurum coronarium*. In the subsequent ages, there is mention of the *patriarchi minores* to whom the Theodosian Code gives the title of *spectabiles* (as the other grand patriarchs are styled *illustres* and *clarissimi*), as also *primates*.[69] There is also mention of the *hieres* whose office is not known now except it relate to the *cohen* now in use among the Jews.

How ancient are the lesser patriarchs (who seemed to have ruled over the *archisynagogi* and presbyters of particular synagogues) I cannot tell.[70] But since all learned men do now agree that the Christian Church was governed according to the pattern of the Jewish synagogue, there can be little doubt but that every officer of the Christian synagogues resembled those of the others as well in office as name; and that as they retained the rites and customs of the Jewish synagogue in all other things (as to structure), not building their synagogues east and west but west and east so that the coming in was at the east and they prayed to the west (so is Saint Peter's Church, built now at Rome), in **<18>** observing the Sabbath, paschal, circumcision et cetera—so they did in their government. And it is observable that, even at this day, though the Jewish synagogues agree in the substance of their service, yet for the particulars thereof, there is a great discrepancy amongst them in several countries, and so there was in the primitive times amongst the Christians.[71]

It is very possible also that the Judaizing Christians were at first subordinate to the Jewish patriarch and primates, having none of their own, before the Jews were animated against them and anathematized them as they were at first called by one common denomination of Jews. And some of them frequented the Jewish synagogues, the tenet of Christianity rendering them only *mimes* or heretics not separatists (as St. Jerome says), and they continued to do so in his time, through all the synagogues of the eastern Jews.[72]

We may further collect out of the different sects of the Jews (some of every one whereof embraced Christianity) the differences to have been as great in the Christian synagogues as in those of the Jews where the Sadducees, Essenes, Pharisees and Samaritans made sects.[73] Each retained their opinions mixed with the doctrine of the Messiah. And here came those Judaizing sects of which such a number is recounted by Epiphanius.[74] We may also imagine a great diversity betwixt the Jews living in the land of promise and those which lived out of it: for the Jews did not take themselves (nor do now) to be obliged to the Mosaical **<19>** rites, much less any temple worship, out of Palestine. The criminal laws have no coercive power out of these bounds,[75] the Paschal Lamb is not slain in any other country, all ground besides that holy Canaan is too impure and profane for such services and rites, though they did by authority of their rabbis frame to themselves many succedaneous rites and retain circumcision, the Judaical doctrines, and an opinion of their particular holiness above the Gentiles.[76] Of these Judaizing Christians or believing Jews (being reckoned not as heretics but good Christians) doth Origen speak as continuing to his time as the Gentiles that were converted to the belief of the Messiah, though Paul were the apostle of the uncircumcision and did not reduce them under the Mosaical Law and rites.[77] Yet being originally an Hebrew, it is easy to observe that in the settling of the church government, and in the penalty of excommunication, he did introduce in their church several Judaical constitutions, and also accommodated the pagan ceremonies frequently thereunto.

The intromission of the Gentiles by baptism was no Jewish rite in proselytes of the uncircumcision and can only be looked on as a particular washing from uncleanness such as was that of John Baptist or in imitation of that pagan rite so frequently used in case of enormous sins to wash them away by bathing in a river to which the poet Ovid alludes: "Ah nimium faciles, qui tristia crimina caedis/ fluminea tolli posse putatis aqua! Sed tamen, antiqui ne nescius ordinis erres," Tristia, liber 2. And Virgil: "Tu genitor, cape sacra manu patriosque penatis; me bello e tanto digressum et caede recenti attrectare nefas, donec me flumine uiuo abluero."[78] **<20>**

It is most certain that baptism heretofore was not administered by aspersion as now, but by a total immersion.[79] And as to the baptizing of children, if it were used by any in the first ages, it is condemned by Tertullian and others, and can vouch no precedents or precepts out of scripture.[80] The discontinued usage of baptizing for the dead hath more to show for it since it is mentioned in scripture and not condemned in the Greek Church. Even Nazianzen was not baptized till thirty-three years old, albeit a bishop's son,[81] nor was Valentinian, the Emperor Theodosius, although descended of Christian parents, nor Saint Ambrose, nor Constantine and his son Constantius: so that we may not wonder to read that sundry heretical Christians did reject baptism totally, perhaps it having never been used in their churches. Such were the Seleuciani, Hermiani, Pauliciani, and that ancient and numerous sect of the Manicheans.[82] Even the Jacobites did not use baptism, but with a hot iron imprinted the sign of the cross in the forehead of their partisans.

If I may be allowed to guess at the original of baptism, I would derive it from the pagan custom aforesaid of washing away expiatorily in rivers the most enormous sins;[83] in the doing whereof as the pagans were very tender, so the Christians were more frank, as Zosimus relates of Constantine the Great. And the baptism of children from hence: that because the Romans used the eighth and ninth day to devote their infants unto the *dea mundina* and give them names then,[84] and the Greeks had theirs **<21>** to the same purpose on the tenth day after their birth, therefore the Christians out of compliance with that superstition of the vulgar did hereby incline them to initiate them unto Christ. Such condescension in other cases as in the observation of Christmas, New Year's Day, May-day, Shrovetide and the pre-vigils and wakes of saints,[85] and the form of churches, the praying to the east, processions about parish bounds, the denomination of the clergy by the titles of *antistites, pontifices, sacerdotes,* and the churches by the name of *templa* and *aedes,* the shaving of the clergy, the surplice, the antiphons, and a thousand other things observable in the ancient Gentile Christianity had no other original. Even the sacrament of the Lord's Supper and all its rites seem to be deduced hence: the festivals of the pagan gods were usually suppers. This was so at the first: there was great feasting at them; so in this case at first, they were performed in the temples; so was this at the first, and so continues to be still. All the names of the pagan mysteries are fixed on this sacrament and its rites, et cetera: the procedure from the *catechumeni* to *competentes* and then to *fideles,*[86] the preparation before it, and all austerities so resembling that, they easily show whence they were derived.[87]

But withal I must add that whereas those mysteries were not everywhere the same (for in the mysteries of Mithra they gave to the initiated a cup of water and some bread with some accessional forms of words), so neither were the rites of this Christian sacrament everywhere the same. Where the reverence of the mysteries was greatest and most solemn and accompanied with greater mortifications, there the Christians were more strict. Where it seemed rather substituted to the pagan **<22>** festival suppers, there they were more jocund and the κυριακόν δεῖπνον was no other amongst the Christians than these suppers paganical δεῖπνα, or *pontificum canæ* of the Gentiles.[88] In some places, their ἑταιρεῖαι or assemblies of men at festivals—these were allowed everywhere in Greece and Alexandria and usual amongst the Gentiles. They are termed συσσίτια, θιάσοι, ἔρανοι, and those which assembled there εἰλαπίναι, et cetera.[89] They were either held upon a religious accommodation as the συμβολή —or merely for pleasure and conversation as the rest. Each person contributed his part or share to the defraying the expenses, and that contribution was called συμβολή—*symbola* or *symbolum*. The associates had a kind of admission amongst themselves and the manner of assembling gained it the name of ἑταιρία and κοινωνία,[90] and at those meetings there was usually laid up either the overplus of the money collected or perhaps some further collection made for any distressed member of the society or against such contingencies. These were publicly allowed by authority and held monthly. They were oftentimes held in the temples and also in other appointed places.

He that will compare this with that account which we have of the Christians' Love Feast or *agape* and considers that though the magistrates did not usually allow of private combinations or meetings, and yet approved these if they extended not to the danger of the public, will think that the κυριακὸν δεῖπνον and the κοινωνία were but appellations of some such *sodalitium* or fraternity.[91] And this seems apparent from the communion of the Corinthians where every man brought in his contribution of food and wine and eat and drank thereof. **<23>** The fault which the apostle doth blame in them is that the communists did not import what they brought into the rest of the fraternity, but each fed upon his own *symbola* so that the poorer did rise hungry and the richer did riot it. He tells the Corinthians that if they will eat apart, they may do it at home, not in the church.[92] This procedure was contrary to the rules of such . . . ,[93] and such as were poorer were put to shame and slighted by reason of the meanness of their contributions. He speaks there of the sacrament, and if we compare that and with the *agape* we must conclude the *agape* and communion all one. It is no wonder then if we read of several ways of celebrating this supper amongst the ancients. Even in the apostles' time some communicated with the pagans at their festivals and to the honor of Christ did drink the cup of devils,[94] and did partake of the table of devils (1 Corinthians 10:20–21): from whence we may observe that the rites were the same though they differed in the objects of their devotion.

This being the duality of their rites and ceremonies, let us take a view of the doctrines which the Gentiles were converted unto. These seem to be principally contained in the grand tenet that Jesus was the Messiah of the Jews who was to unite Jew and Gentile under one temporal monarchy. To qualify the Gentiles as befitting subjects for that celestial prince, they were to repent of their sins, renounce idolatry, and entirely to obey the seven commandments under which the Jews did believe all the Gentiles were to be concluded if they would have any person in the life to come or kingdom of heaven. This seems most evident from the apostolical decree made by the synod at **<24>** Jerusalem wherein there was a contest about what obligation the believing were to be brought under, whether they ought to be circumcised and instructed in the whole law of Moses to keep it, or whether they should be subjected to the seven commandments of Noah only. The synod concludes upon the latter. It is manifest from that synod that of these which entertained the doctrine of the Messiah and so became Christians, some were Pharisees and retained the opinions and traditions of their sect, together with the doctrine of Christ. They were not heretics if Ebion and Cerinthus were the persons that occasioned.[95]

It is most certain they which held the opinion were then in good esteem with the church and are said to be the same of the sect of the Pharisees which believed (Acts 15:5), and they were a part in that apostolical synod (though overruled). How else could there have been such συζήτησις—so great a dispute there, as the text avers (Acts 15:7).[96] So there were of the Sadducees that professed Christianity and believed Jesus to be the Messiah yet denied the resurrection. Of such does Justin Martyr speak in his dialogue with Tryphon the Jew, when he reckons up as a third part of Christendom those which were called Christians yet denied the resurrection and tenet of the Chiliasts.[97] It is true he esteems them as wicked and heretical persons, but reckons them Christians. Seeing then that though the converts did retain their former opinions generally, and that Christianity itself was but a reformation of Judaism (as Mr. Selden more than once inculcates): to understand the decision we **<25>** must consult the doctrine of the Jews as to this point.[98]

Now it is a most received tenet amongst them that a Gentile continuing a Gentile was obliged to nothing but the law of nature contained in those seven precepts, and not to the Mosaical Law at all, and that it is needless if we consider the subsequent passage only as an instance of things commonly known to be necessary. Had the synod meant any other way, what a confusion would there have risen upon so great an innovation in the Jewish tenets. How can we imagine that they which were so zealous for the same would have acquiesced therein? How should they suffer this additional clause out of the Mosaical Law to be extended to the uncircumcised: that is to abstain from things strangled, which was permitted to the Gentiles (Deuteronomy 14:21). But that clause is held to be spurious in the text by St. Ambrose and others, and really it is incredible that it should ever have been in that decree. Nor can it be reputed a necessary point in the decree to abstain from things offered unto idols except we understand thereby to abstain from idolatry.[99] For Paul decides that point otherwise to the Corinthians: that it was simply lawful for them to eat things offered to idols and that it is an indifferent matter, except in case of scandal, as Heideggerus doth demonstrate out of the place.[100]

I do therefore take it for granted that this was the fundamental doctrine of the Gentile Christians. But I must further add that as the Jews retained their tenets and usages under Christianity, so did the Gentiles many of theirs. Thus Pantaenus and Clement Alexandrinus mixed Stoicism with Christianity; Origen and others, Platonism and Peripateticism, and I have read of Cynical and Epicurean Christians. It is also to be noted **<26>** that as the Judaizing Christians were offended with Peter for going to Cornelius a Gentile (Acts 11:2), so neither did they come to the same assemblies or communicate with them except it were upon extraordinary occasion and by a paramount apostolical procedure.[101] Thus Peter having at first associated with the Gentile Christians at Antioch and eaten with them: when some came unto him from James, he withdrew and separated himself, fearing them which were of the circumcision. And the other Jews dissembled likewise with him, insomuch that

Barnabas was carried away with their dissimulation (Galatians 2:12–13), which distance continued afterwards in the Judaizing churches. For albeit that the Jews held that the pious amongst the Gentiles might be saved, yet did they esteem them as unclean and such as they might not freely converse or eat with (Acts 10:28).[102]

It may be questioned whether the Gentile Christians did not believe the deity of Christ. They were so accustomed to the deifying and conferring divine honors and worship upon men that it is not to be doubted but many did believe him to be a god in the pagan sense, as other heroes were reputed. And thus Pliny in his inquisition after Christianity found that they did sing certain hymns to Christ *quasi deo*, as if he were a god. And Tertullian relating the same thing says: they did sing hymns *Christo et Deo.*[103] Nor can there be any doubt thereof or that there were many pieces of poetry composed by the brethren which ascribed a divinity to Christ. But if there be any ground for that assertion of Artemon, Apolonides, Hermophilus, and Theodotus, the most learned, subtle, and philosophical disputants (though styled heretics) of the ancient Christians, that all the first Christians, and even the apostles themselves, were taught and did teach that Christ was a mere man (which was their tenet) and that the truth of this doctrine **<27>** was continued in the church until the days of Pope Victor who was the thirteenth bishop of Rome after Peter, and that Zephyrinus his successor did alter and corrupt that truth—if it be true which the Arians said that none but idiots and simple persons believed any such thing, and that till the decision at Nicaea the more knowing Christians did not hold him to be really God.[104]

If we may conceive that they were firmly taught that there was but one God, and that they were too dull to comprehend or invent those subtle distinctions of essence and person, consubstantiation, eternal generation, and if it be certain that the Fathers after the Nicene Council were not agreed concerning the meaning of those uncouth words, and that the world was long after dissatisfied with the use of them, and that such as Gregory Nazianzen and Basil were shy how they taught the deity of the Holy Ghost or of Christ or touched upon the Trinity, *homousianism*;[105] and if we reflect upon the Creed intituled to the apostles and certainly very ancient that there is no intimation hereof in it;[106] if we take notice how differently the Fathers explicate themselves upon that point, and how much the other works of Athanasius do differ from the Creed which goes under his name, we may very well doubt concerning their judgment if not conclude the contrary.[107]

As to their rites and church government, the apostle of the uncircumcision who became all things to all men that he might gain them to Christ did comply with their weakness and prejudice. Many pagan usages and superstitions were retained; their church government was much modeled according to the pagan usages in their temples and sodalities. It is not impossible that they might have had in some places as well priests as temples dedicated and altars; the distinction of their churches into the *ordo* and *plebs* savors of the Gentile customs in the civil government of their cities.[108] It is not to be believed that the Jewish apostles did appoint or ordain officers for them: <28> the Jews did not use to ordain Jews for judges to the stranger proselytes. Neither would they certainly appoint them rulers in their churches. Besides, it is notorious that the first bishops were elected by the suffrage of the people and might be deposed by them, that they might upon a dissension break into a subdivision of episcopacies and erect two or three or more in one city. And of bishops there was no subordination but a parity.

It is easy to imagine that during the numerousness, grandeur, and power of the Jews in Palestine, Egypt, and Babylon, and throughout all Greece, and whilst all the Gentiles expected a Messiah of the Jews to whom they were to be subjected, they did pay a great respect unto the Jews and were much swayed by their dictates. But about fifty-two years after the destruction and government of the Jews under Titus, there arose another Messiah amongst the Jews who accommodated to himself the prophecy of Balaam and styled himself *Bencochab*, or the son of the star.[109] The famed Rabbi Akibba joined with him and saluted him as the King Messiah.[110] Great was his power and a bloody war did he wage with the Romans and the Emperor Adrian. After three years, he and four hundred thousand Jews were miserably slain by the emperor and those that escaped were so angry with their present Messiah that they termed him *Barcozabh* or *Cuzzibha*, the Son of a Lie.[111] Adrian marched with his victorious army to Alexandria (where the Jews in favor of *Bencochab* had destroyed the Romans) and put to death an infinite of the Jews there. The multitude which the Jews say was slain in that war is scarcely to be believed. He put down their synagogues everywhere, so that it is not to be credited that the Jews did anywhere after this appear embodied in the Roman Empire.

And now we may conceive naturally that the Christians must **<29>** totally disclaim the Jews and pretend only to a spiritual Messiah. They could not have preserved themselves but by such an action, and undoubtedly, not long after that, we find mention of priests, temples, and the rites of the church do evidently comply with paganism. What befell the Judaizing churches I know not, but they became in little esteem and sank at last under the name of Ebionites and other heretics. This revolution had a mighty influence upon Christianity, and Adrian in his letter to Servianus, wherein he gives him an account of Egypt, doth avow that all the Christians, besides their devotion to Christ, did worship Serapis.[112] "Illi, qui Serapim colunt, christiani sunt et devoti sunt Serapi, qui se Christi episcopos dicunt. Nemo illic archi-synagogus Judaeorum, nemo Samarites, nemo christianorum presbyter; non mathematicus, non aruspex, non aliptes. Ipse ille patriarcha, cum Egyptum venerit, ab aliis Serapidem adorare, ab aliis cogitur Christum."[113]

Some would have this letter to be false or full of untruths since it seems incredible that the Christians should do so. Besides, since the great patriarch of the Jews did not come into Egypt at all, and it is certain the Christians had then no patriarch at Alexandria or elsewhere, how can this passage be verified? I am of a contrary judgment and do believe that the bishop of Alexandria by reason of the greatness of his power and splendor was called analogically or by way of flattery a patriarch.[114] This appears from Eutychius in his *Origines Alexandrini* and from other oriental writers who speak of St. George as son to the patriarch of Alexandria, though really in his time (under Diocletian) there were none.[115] As to the mixing of pagan worship with Christianity, not to say what the *thurificatores* (one whereof was a pope) did **<30>** upon compulsion,[116] if ever there were such a legion as that formed, fulminating in the army of the Emperor Adrian or the *Legio Thebea* (both famed in ecclesiastical story) or any legionary soldiers that professed Christianity, I am confident they never had any dispensation from worshipping the Roman eagles: "Sequerentur Romanas acquilas propria legionum numina."[117]And I am the more confirmed in this sentiment since under the Christian emperors the imperial banner called *labarum* was worshiped in like manner.[118]

I am sure that the Egyptian Christians were not so scrupulous afterwards but that they procured to themselves and executed the office of *archierosyna* whose power was to superintend over and manage the pagan temples, festivals, rites, and whole religion of Egypt.[119] And this they continued to do until Theodosius the Great did prohibit them to do so, AD 389.[120] It is no less strange a thing that the Christian emperors should for a long time be and wear the habit of the *pontifices maximi*; that the senators, which were Christians at Rome, should as they went to the senate be present at the sacrifices of the Altar of Victory, about the removal whereof Symmachus and the majority of the senate, being pagans, did proffer a complaint.[121] I shall illustrate this point with a strange relation out of Eutychius who was one of the patriarchs of Alexandria. It is thus: When Alexander, the predecessor of Athanasius, was first made patriarch of that place, he found there a temple and a great brazen idol dedicated to one Michael and much frequented by the pagans, and the inhabitants of Alexandria and Egypt did keep a great festival in honor of this idol on the twelfth day of the month **<31>** Haturi and offered up many sacrifices thereto. The patriarch had a great mind to abolish this idolatry, but met with much opposition about it. At last he prevailed by subtlety: he told them that his idol was an insignificant statue, but if they would perform the same devotion and offer up the like sacrifices to Michael the Archangel, he would intercede with God for them and procure them greater benefits than that idol could. Whereupon he broke the idol in pieces and shaped it into a cross, and called the temple St. Michael's Church—which church was afterwards called Cæsarea, and was burnt when the western army took Alexandria. And the festivals and sacrifices were continued in honor of St. Michael, and, even still, the *Cophite* Christians in *Misrar,* or Grand Cairo, and in Alexandria do celebrate the festival of St. Michael on that day and offer many sacrifices unto him.[122]

The relator is a historian of good credit, but I do not remember to have read the like sacrificing to have been performed by Christians elsewhere, though any man conversant in antiquity knows that a multitude of pagan usages crept in among the Christians. And though they did not sacrifice, yet they brought to their priests at the altar the first fruits, as was formerly practiced to the rural gods. And rather the objects of the devotion were changed than the things abolished: the same festivals were retained in a manner to the honor of Christ, the Virgin Mary, or the saints, which were performed before to Mercury, Venus *genetrix*, Bacchus, and the rural deities. As the aforesaid calamities of the Jews did make a great alteration in Christianity, so did the frequent persecutions by the Roman emperors against them who looked upon them as no good subjects since they expected a temporal Messiah and oftentimes disclaimed all subjection to the pagan magistrates, sometimes rebelling, as in the reign of Diocletian did the Christians of Alexandria and the adjacent countries under St. George and in France under Amandus and Ælianus.[123] They looked upon them generally as enemies to the received and established religion or idolatry of the empire and feared the consequences of a change therein. Besides that, the **<32>** people hated them. Upon that account, everywhere, many bickerings and tumults happened thereupon. They did also look upon the mortification and monasticness of the Christians as inconsistent with the government, enfeebling men's minds and alienating them from military employments, the sinews of empire, and spoiling trade, by decrying luxury and all excess as well as in diminishing the sale of cattle and other commodities used in the pagan solemnities.

There, amongst many others (which Papinianus as I remember is said to have digested into seven books concerning the justice of punishing the Christians), were the motives upon which these persecutors went.[124] And though Christianity were not extirpated, yet it changed much its complexion. The opinion of a temporal Messiah was laid aside, subjection to the pagan magistrate preached, many dissolute and enormous assemblies disowned and declared heretical. The Christians fought for the gentile emperors and watched at the temples to defend them, declared them to be no martyrs who disturbed or demolished them. Much of their rigor and strictness was abolished or preserved only in a few monasteries. As the Christians suffered this alteration, they were infected by the conversation and superstitions of the pagans. So those on the other side became much altered by mixing with the Christians: they were inclined to a contempt of their gods and an indifferency in their religion; they were exasperated at the threats of their priests and the expensiveness of their rites and devotions. The discipline of the Roman legions being extinct and the armies composed most of foreign men of mercenary spirits and no friends to the established religion, the soldiery beheld opulent priests and vestals together with their colleges with an envious eye and cared not if a new religion were introduced, so that they might share the spoils of the old.

In this juncture I find Constantine to have made himself emperor. Right he had none, being a bastard and not elected nor admitted by the senate. His sword was his title; success warranted it. His soldiers were not more assured of his courage and conduct than animated by the hopes of honor and riches, which the conquest of Italy and change of religion and government would instate them in. He subverted the power of the senate, removed the seat of the empire, altered much of the religion, and gained most of the sacerdotal lands and revenues by the change.[125] He was no Christian in profession **<33>** till a few days before he died. He never was at prayer among the *catecheumeni* till then, nor so much as baptized, and without that initiating sacrament. It is not to be imagined that he could be instructed in, or admitted to, those doctrines and acts of nearer communion. All that is written contrary hereunto are palpable untruths or deeds of flattery.

It is true his mother seemed zealous for Christianity and built many churches, and he, out of his spoils, allotted some to pious uses thereby to amend the condition of the Christian clergy and oblige them to him. He endeavored the reducing of Christianity into one uniform doctrine: he assembled the Council at Nicaea and there framed a confession of faith and by new honor gave great luster to the church and ensured a secular power everywhere by advancing the ecclesiastical and that of the Christian bishops. These were spies and checks to his governors, and since Rome and Alexandria were the two places that had most influence upon his empire, he and his successors advanced those prelates to a kind of princely dignity that they might gain the greater veneration among the people and equal the splendor of the pagan priests. Then began temples to be dedicated with as much solemnity by the Christians as ever anywhere by the pagans and entitled to the apostles, martyrs, and angels for magnificence and largeness. They were equal to those of the heathens and, as in the fabrics and dedication of the churches, the resemblance of paganism was introduced. So the ecclesiastical government was made parallel to it.[126] You read now not only of temples and altars, but the bishops, *sacerdotes, antistites, sacræ legis,* et cetera. As the heathenish religion was supported by a priesthood under the *Pontifix Maximus* and his college, consisting of the *provinciarum sacerdotes* (*Asiarchæ, Syriarchæ, et cetera*) which were also called *sacerdotes*, the *flamens* (whose power exceeded not their city or town), the *ministri, prefecti,* and *hierophantæ agrorum* which attended in country villages—just such was the reglement of the Christian Church and the jurisdiction in a manner equal.

Thus was the empire to be balanced, but, withal, the Christian emperors strengthened themselves by favoring the Jews, whose aversion from idolatry was as great or greater than that of the Christians. The interest they had in Persia did preserve them still in great splendor, notwithstanding the desolation which Hadrian had brought upon them. And they are a sort of people that so adhere and support each other that they are not to be destroyed. They began to spread again, and Christian emperors gave them not only freedom of religion but permitted their patriarch to gather his *aurum coronarium* in the East and **<34>** Western empires and to live with very great pomp and command. The rulers of the synagogues, lesser patriarchs, presbyters, and others concerned in the government of that nation, were exempted from civil and personal duties and employments by the decrees of Constantine, Constantius, Valentinian, Valens, Theodosius, and Arcadius.[127] They were not only freed from affronts and contumelies, their synagogues protected, but the same respect paid to their rulers was shown to the Christian bishops and hierarchy (thus Arcadius, *Codex Theodosianus,* 16. 8. 13):

> Judaei fuerint obstricti ceremoniis suis: nos interea in conservandis eorum privilegiis veteres imitemur, quorum sanctionibus definitum est, ut privilegia his, qui inlustrium patriarcharum ditioni subjecti sunt (archisynagogis patriarchisque ac presbyteris ceterisque, qui in eius religionis sacramento versantur, nutu nostri numinis preseverent ea, quæ venerandae Christianæ legis primis clericis Sanctimonia deferuntur. Id enim & divi principes Constantinus, Constantius, Valentinianus & Valens, divino arbitrio decreverunt—(AD 397).[128]

Afterwards Theodosius the Younger confirmed their privileges, AD 412. But by reason of several enormities and misdemeanors which fell out by reason of their grandeur, and for reasons of state, the patriarchship was abrogated, AD 414. Yet the particular patriarchs and rulers of the synagogues gather for their own use the said pension of *aurum coronarium* till it was annexed to the imperial exchequer by Theodosius the Younger, AD 429. In this flourishing condition did the Jews spread themselves in great numbers under a regular government over the Eastern and Western empire. Both Palestines and Egypt, Arabia, Babylon, and Persia were replenished with them, their rabbis flourished, their Talmuds and Targums were compiled about this time, and Judaism reduced to that system in which we at present find it in the Empire.

Now we see those grand religions all in a flourishing and powerful condition. The pagans whose interest was continually undermined by the emperors and imperial governors in several provinces and by the Jews and Christians: whatsoever laws were made in favor of them and for their liberty were either directly <35> violated or pretenses daily sought to give color to that injustice. And whether they, being driven to despair, might entertain foreign correspondency is to me unknown but not improbable. It is most certain that they fomented discord among the Christians and on all occasions (as Athanasius particularly relates of the contests at Alexandria) they did abet the Arians and adhere unto them openly; their philosophers did dispute for the Arians in the Council of Nicaea. And as Alexandria had been the seat of the ethnic learning—philosophy natural, moral, and political, physic and mathematics being there most eminently professed and taught—so from hence they were propagated over the Eastern Empire.[129] And the philosophers there did insensibly engage their Christian scholars into several heterodoxies according as their genius inclined each of them, to Platonism or Peripateticism.

It is most certain that the Arians, and all the subdivisions of that numerous sect were profoundly learned in those sciences, and that Origen derived his knowledge from an education under them and the benefit of their libraries there. The Christians had great encouragements and immunities et cetera to support them, and great privileges were enacted for such as turned to that religion and penalties frequently decreased and oftentimes rigorously inflicted on the pagans. But what contributed much to the prejudice of Christianity was their divisions among themselves. Besides the petty sects occasioned by pure ignorance, folly, or madness (of which kinds the catalogues of heretics do present us with many) which were easily extinguished by the imperial power or fell of themselves. There were three potent sects which did give a great check to the more facile and complacent Christianity of the Empire: the Donatists possessed in a manner all Africa and had some hold in Italy; the Arians possessed in great part the Eastern Empire; and the Novatians were with great repute for purity and piety diffused everywhere.

These were all settled under their episcopal reglements with distinct churches. The Donatists began in Africa upon this occasion: after that persecution ceased against the Christians, those whom either zeal or passion had made obstinate sufferers for Christianity detested and refused communion with such as either had delivered up their Bibles and holy writers up to the pagan emperors in obedience to their decrees (these were called *traditores*), or had exempted themselves from danger by paying a sum of money (which were called *libellatici*), or had offered incense and complied for the season with prevailing and persecuting paganism (which were **<36>** called *thurificatores*). And a bishop who either had or was said to have delivered up his Bible, being surreptitiously chosen and ordained at Carthage for that city, the other bishops partly in vindication of their rights which the ecclesiastical constitutions had vested them in, partly out of zeal against such a betrayer of Christianity, declined his communion, excommunicated all that adhered unto him, and ordained another bishop of the place. The people generally adhered to the Donatists. Great was the schism, and two hundred and thirty bishops owned that party,[130] whilst the bishop of Rome and the Italian clergy (who had been universally involved in the like compliance) did adhere to the other, as also did the imperialists at finding that party more pliable and suitable to their political ends and inclined to such a lax discipline that the Gentiles might upon easy terms be admitted to their churches.

The Donatists, exasperated hereby and finding no favor (or rather as they said no justice) from Constantine the Great, sought and found protection in Julian the Apostate by reason of their submissive and invidious address. After Julian the succeeding emperor did oppose and oppress them rigorously, fining them, confiscating their goods, estreating their churches, banishing many, and in a manner outlawing them. But as the resolution with which they suffered did ingratiate them with the populace (who are prone to think they are unjustly oppressed who bear their punishments bravely and with pretense to martyrdom for religion), so the arguments with which they defended their cause being very conformable to the strict Christianity professed in those parts and, rebaptizing those of that side which were converted to them, did imprint in the people every way an opinion or suspicion that the imperialists were scarcely to be reckoned among the number of Christians. The Donatists continued till after the days of Honorius, and, being reduced to great distress by their persecution, it is not to be wondered if many outrages were committed by those who saw themselves, their families and relations, utterly undone by such as, contrary to the general tenets of the Christians, employed force against them. And as it is usual with men in despair, and as Africans disposed to revenge to join with any third party, it is no wonder the conquest of Africa proved easy to the Goths, who were afterwards ejected after a long and fierce war by Justinian, and the Arians no less oppressed than the Donatists before.

And so I leave Africa in a fair way to comply with the designs of Mahomet,[131] the constant wars having made them valiant and bold, their humor malicious, their sufferings angry, and their religion indifferent to any novelty. For during those contraventions, for want of instruction by their own clergy or the <37> imperialists who minded little but ease and ambition (and were extremely ignorant), it is easy to be imagined that they retained only a sense of some generals in Christianity and had nothing of ecclesiastical government or order amongst them: no sacraments, no not of baptism, except they conformed, but this notion so whispered and insinuated into them that the conformists were not truly Christians that it seems to have been the great article of their creed.

The Novatians had their origin from the like occasion. All the Italian clergy, except Novatus and two more (as I remember) had consented to idolatry in the time of Diocletian and Maximinus and, upon the change of condition afterwards, returned with their followers to Christianity.[132] This act of the Italian clergy (the bishop of Rome being involved in it) gave a beginning to the complacent and indulgent Christians of those ages, whereby the discipline of the church was ruined and men admitted and readmitted upon easy terms.[133] Novatus and his adherents who had not apostatized would not communicate with such nor readmit them upon any penance: not that they thought it impossible for such to be saved, but that it was not in the power of the church upon any terms of repentance to associate with them, according to that of the Apostle (Hebrews 6:4–6). These were the Puritans, as I may call them, of those ages: they were men of a strict life and withal of a peaceable disposition.[134] They were orthodox in their judgment about the Trinity which made those that adhered to the Nicene Council to show them great respect, to own their bishops and protect them, who seem of all sects alone not to have intermeddled with the public affairs and revolutions and acquiesced. So in a toleration as never that I know to have endeavored aright to the prejudice of other sects, or sinisterly to advance their own party, they continued till the ruin of the Eastern Empire. And their successions are recorded in our church history, and their oppression under the bishop of Rome is condemned by Socrates.[135] Although this sect did raise no faction in the Empire, yet it is easy to conjecture that their continuance in open schism, the grounds whereof were known and asserted publicly in the Eastern and Western Empire everywhere, and their exemplary lives (in which whatever there was of innocence and true zeal in primitive Christianity seemed then to be lodged and preserved) must needs have added to the contempt of the imperial religion, as if it were corrupted in its discipline and purity, and so far have strengthened the dissenting parties.

The Arians were so powerful a sect in the Empire that the followers of **<38>** the Nicene Council were not equal to them either in number, splendor, interest, or riches, if you will believe the learned Petavius and others.[136] They did offer to be tried by the Fathers that preceded the Nicene Council. At the Nicene Council they were rather condemned by a party there by the general consent of the Christian Church. For Constantine, out of above 2,000 bishops assembled, excluded all but 318, nor were there perhaps (for accounts vary) all bishops that made the council. They were all of a judgment at first and so parties rather than judges.[137] The Arians had not the freedom to dispute their case, and the emperor Constantine was so little satisfied with their prescription that he recalled Arius soon and, a little before his death, was baptized by an Arian bishop. Constantine and Valens were professed Arians, not to mention the Goths. Valentinian, Theodosius, and other emperors protected and honored them with military and civil commands.[138] Their doctrine was not only confirmed by 8 councils, which were at divers times assembled at Tyre, at Sardis, at Syrinium, where 660 bishops were of their opinion—but three of name which held the contrary,[139] but that they also punished others, their adversaries, who were of a contrary opinion to them with confiscations, banishments, and other grievous punishments. Whether the power of their chieftains, the riches of their churches, the magnificence of their worship (they first brought music into the church), the fame of their learning and pretensions to reason, which is always an invidious plea, did raise jealousy in the emperors and hatred against them in the Trinitarians, or what most contributed to their first depression and persecution I know not. Since to persecute for religion was by the Trinitarians—Athanasius, Hilary, and others—then accounted an Arian and unchristian tenet, it is not to be doubted, but after the days of Theodosius the reason of state did prevail most toward their subversion, lest they should join with the Goths who possessed themselves of Italy, Spain, Africa, and other provinces. And terrible to the Byzantine Empire, whatsoever it was, it is easy to comprehend that the depression of them did facilitate the conquest of the Goths. And if you will credit Salvian, the Goths were very pious in their way, mild to the conquered, just in their dealings, so that the wickedness of the Christian rulers of provinces, their depredations upon the people, and the insolence of the foreign soldiers by which they ruled, made even the Trinitarians willingly submit to the dominion of the Goths and prefer it before that of the Eastern Empire.[140]

I come now to the Trinitarians **<39>** who I cannot but represent as enemies to all human learning.[141] They had canons forbidding them to read any ethnic book, and a pique which disposed them to destroy all they met with of that kind. Thus we may suppose them universally ignorant, except some few who appear to be somewhat knowing; and as were the pastors so were the people. Their religion consisted rather in an outside service than inward piety or knowledge; their faith was in a manner implicit, the mysteries of religion (such I call the doctrine of the Trinity and its dependencies) were scarce ever mentioned to them in sermons, much less explicated. Hence the vulgar became prone to embrace superstition, to credit miracles how ridiculous or fabulous so ever. Visions, allegories, allusions to texts were convincing arguments and no demonstration like a feigned story and legend or what might be interpreted a judgment upon a heretic. As to the imperial courts, I know not well what religion to install them into. They did long wear the habit of Roman *pontifices maximi* and, after Gratian and his successor had laid that aside, they exercised their power.[142] You will find a hundred times in the Theodosian and Justinian codes that they assumed the titles of *nostrum numen, aeternitas, perennitas* and that they made their predecessors deceasing to be reputed *divi.* They continued the Circensian games, the obscenities of the theater and scenical women, with a multitude of other idolatrous and even brutal practices for which one would be astounded to read laws made in the Theodosian Code.[143]

As to matters of religion, the emperors enacted what they pleased about it and imposed it on the generality. For synodical decrees did not bind; others then were willing or present and consenting in those days. And you may meet with accounts of the Christian faith in imperial edicts enjoined to be believed by Theodosius as well as Justinian so that I may reckon amongst the Trinitarians a sort of people who were of the court religion and believed as their prince ordained, living unconfined by the dictates of the then declining church. The Trinitarians, though they had resolved upon and subscribed unto the Nicene Council and embraced those forms of speech which are now in use, yet they could not tell what was meant by them: the Latin Church allowed not of three persons but of three hypostases, the Greek Church approved of three hypostases not of three persons, and difficult it was for them to explicate *ousia* or essence. These hard words produced a subdivision amongst them, consisting of Nestorians and Eutychians: the Nestorians believing the divinity **<40>** of Christ held that he was made up of two different persons and so perfect God and perfect man; the Eutychians averred that Christ had but one nature and that upon the hypostatic union the deity and humanity were so blended together by confusion of properties and substances that one person endowed with one will did emerge thence.

Those two sects were of great power in the Eastern Church, and though they were both condemned in the third and fourth general councils, yet did they spread far and near throughout Palestine, Egypt, the Kingdom of Abyssinia, and all Persia. Each of them had their patriarchs, bishops, churches, contradistinct from the Melkites. And now we see the face of Christianity thus represented: those that adhered to the Council of Chalcedon and subscribed to it, as did all the imperial clergy, were called Melkites (that is to say men of the king's religion) by the Nestorians and the Eutychians. The authors of these two sects were learned men and potent bishops: Eutychius was patriarch of Constantinople, and with him joined Dioscorus, patriarch of Alexandria, and Severus, patriarch of Antioch, and Jacobus Baradeus from whom the Jacobites are denominated at this day. Nestorius was also patriarch of Constantinople, and his sect very much diffused.[144]

The truth is: such was the ignorance of the people, and such the debauchery of the ages then, that if a man did but live a pious, strict life, with great mortifications and outward devotion, and were but an eloquent preacher, he might in any place of the Eastern Empire make a potent sect instantly. And to show how ignorant the clergy were in the general Council of Chalcedon in the time of Marcianus the emperor, take notice that at that time the Greek tongue was so well understood at Rome, and the Latin in Greece, that the bishops of both countries, which were 630, were glad to speak by interpreters. Yea, in the very same Council of Chalcedon, the emperor made one speech in Greek for the one part, and another in Latin for the other,[145] the matter of both being the same. The Council of Jerusalem made certain creeds both in Greek and

Latin. The pope's legates at the Council of Ephesus had their interpreter to expound the words, and Celestine's letters were there read. The Acts tell us how the bishops desired they should be translated into Greek and read over again, insomuch that the Romish legates had almost made a controversy of it, fearing lest they should prejudice the papal dignity by such an act and alleging therefore how it was the ancient custom to propose the bulls **<41>** of the See Apostolic in Latin only and that might now suffice—whereupon those poor Greek bishops were in danger not to have understood the pope's Latin.[146]

But the legates were at length content with reason. It was evidenced to them that the major part could not understand a word of Latin. But the prettiest of all is Pope Celestine's excuse to Nestorius for his so long delaying answering his letters, the ground being this: that he could not by any means get his Greek construed any sooner. Pope Gregory the First ingeniously confesses to the bishop of Thessaly that he understood not a jot of his Greek. It is very probable that the proverb of honest Accursius was even then in use: "Græcum est; non legitur."[147]

This was the condition of Christianity in which Justinian the emperor found it about the year 540. He, by conquest in Africa, subdued the Arian Goths and Vandals there as also in Italy, established and enforced the Trinitarian religion by severe laws, suppressed all the different sects and religions in the empire, abusing the Jews, suppressing the Arians and all other heretics (except it be true that he favored the Eutychians). He reigned thirty-nine years. After him succeeded Valentinus, Justinius II, Tiberius, Mauritius, Phocas, and Heraclius, in whose days arose Mahomet.[148] It is observable that all these times were so corrupt and Christianity so depraved that the Church of England and generally the Protestants reject the authority of them and admit no general councils after that of Chalcedon under the Emperor Martianus.[149] Their reigns suggest nothing considerable to the subsequent discourse.

But that Christianity was then degenerated into such a kind of paganism as wanted nothing but the ancient sacrifices and professed polytheism, and, even as to the latter, there wanted not some who did make three gods of the Trinity. Others made a goddess of the Virgin Mary. The reverence to the saints differed little from that of the pagans to their heroes and lesser gods, and images were brought into churches then, though not by public authority. And it is no less remarkable that obscure persons had several times been promoted by fraud or indifferent means to the Empire. Also the Emperor Mauritius, having reigned long and gained much upon the esteem of his own subjects and on the Persians, to whose King Chosroes he had married his daughter, and he had thereupon turned Christian, was barbarously murdered by a conspiracy of Phocas and the bishop of Rome, the last being incensed **<42>** against Mauritius because he had permitted John, bishop of Constantinople, to assume the title of oeucumenical bishop, which title the pope declared to be antichristian. But Phocas, being made emperor, returned this acknowledgment to the bishop of Rome (who had solemnly owned him and given him repute) that he should be head of the church and universal bishop, AD 612. Chosroes, exasperated at the death of his father-in-law, who together with his wife and children were cruelly butchered, and abominating the Christians whose great prelate should countenance such an act, he renounced Christianity, destroyed all the Christians in his country who would not renounce the Melkites and turn Nestorians, which gave an occasion to Nestorianism to spread itself far and near in Persia and those oriental countries.[150] Their patriarch resided in Mesopotamia at *Musall,* or *Mawsell,* which is supposed to be built nigh the old city of Nineveh. He invaded Syria and Palestine, sacked Antioch and Jerusalem, carried away multitudes captive into Persia, and excited the Jews to a rebellion in Palestine. Phocas, having reigned eight years, was slain by Heraclius who made himself to be chosen emperor by the soldiers. Chosroes, having disobliged his subjects in turning Christians and being afterwards unfortunate in his wars, was deposed by his son Syroes and murdered by him. He lived but a year and was succeeded by Hormisdas.[151]

Whilst the Grecian Empire was thus unsettled by the frequent change of emperors, and the detestable means by which Phocas had gained the throne, having much alienated many from the love of Christianity, and the Eastern Church was divided into factions by the means of the bishop of Rome promoting his new authority there, and the Nestorians and Jacobites or Eutychians multiplying under their several patriarchs to the great disturbance of the church, anathematizing and being anathematized; and whilst that Persia was broken by intestine divisions and wars, and the people indifferent as to their princes, who should rule them, and divided by the mixture of Jews and Christians spread among them in great numbers everywhere, Mahomet arose and began the empire of the Saracens and a new religion.

It may perhaps seem strange that the general description of the primitive Christians which is here represented should differ so much from the usual accounts thereof which are given by the divines and vulgar historians. But in answer hereunto, I desire the reader to consider first the grounds and <43> proofs which I go upon, and if the authors be good, the citations true and indisputable, if the progress of Christianity be such as is conformable to the constant course of human affairs and great revolutions, that then he would not oppose me, by discourses of miraculous accidents, unimaginable effusions of the Holy Ghost, and such like harangues as no reason can comprehend nor example parallel.[152] Secondly: let him consider that since we are destitute of any solid chronicles or Christian annals before the days of Constantine the Great (for so Eusebius saith), and that he could find nothing substantial to establish an ecclesiastical history upon except the Acts of the Apostles, and that whatsoever is alleged against me must be out of suspected or spurious writers, partial in their own case and ignorant either for the want of learning or want of books and opportunities to be informed aright, or a prejudiced opinion blinding their judgments, I conceive the credit of what I write ought to seem most valid, because it is consonant to the Acts of the Apostles and the real existence of things.

It ought to seem a complete refutation of them all: that if what I say be true as undoubtedly it is, the contrary must be false. If it be further urged that the apologies of the ancient Christians are inconsistent with the relations I make, and that so great a deformity in the tenets and practices of the first Christians can never be reconciled to what they say, I answer that the apologies ought to be looked upon no otherwise than as rhetorical pleas and the defenses of advocates for their clients, wherein all things are managed as much to the advantage of the defendant as it is possible, and that it is most evident that this course was taken by those Christian Fathers. Neither indeed do I want testimonies of their imprudence whereby to satisfy any man that they would not scruple at palpable untruths if they might derive any benefit from thence. Justin Martyr in his apology to Antoninus Pius the emperor (not to mention that Irenæus, Eusebius, and Tertullian do relate the same) doth aver that Simon Magus did miracles at Rome and that he had a statue erected to him in the reign of Claudius Caesar with this inscription, "Simoni Deo Sancto,"[153] of which relation there is not a word true. And was not this most impudently done to obtrude a narration upon the Roman emperor which all

Rome must know to be false? And even Justin who lived at Rome must have understood it **<44>** to be so.[154]

So Apollinaris, bishop of Hierapolis, and Tertullian, in their apologies, say that the emperor Marcus Antoninus, being reduced to great straits for want of water in Germany, and in danger to be taken thereupon by his enemies, the Christian legion called Legio Fulminea, did obtain such a return from God to their prayers, that at the same time a plentiful shower supplied the Roman army, whilst thunder and lightning destroyed the hostile Germans; whereupon the said emperor should write to the senate to decree that the Christians should not be molested, that any man might turn Christian, and that no governor of any province should divert any man or turn him from being a Christian. All which story is a mere forgery, as Vossius hath demonstrated at large and most imprudently urged to those who were certain of the contrary.[155] I shall instance but in one more case and that is of the Sybils, whom Justin Martyr allegeth in favor of Christianity, as also doth Constantine in this oration in behalf of it. Yet are those Sibylline prophesies supposititious and feigned by the Christians as Casaubon, Blondel, Valesius, and others do acknowledge.[156] A thousand such pious frauds might be instanced in, but that many learned men within this last century have saved me the trouble of prosecuting any such discourse.

I must add that the church history of the primitive times seems mainly deduced from the Latin and Greek writers who give no account either of the Syriac or Judaizing churches so that we hear no news of the latter till St. Jerome and Epiphanius came to represent them as heretics for adhering to the same doctrine and discipline which St. Peter and St. James and all the apostles (except Paul) had instructed them in, and wherein they had not been controlled during the lives of those who first founded the church. What . . . authority had power to do it, or how doth it appear that they had either corrupted their tenets or depraved their gospel, the Jews being so tenacious of tradition, and those being men that pursued no designs or worldly interests besides, were they ever heard by an indifferent judge or general council of all Christendom?[157] No affairs were in so unlikely a posture as to that matter amongst the Greek and Latin Christians that, if they had been convened legally and fairly, not one of their adversaries could have understood what they said or judged of their allegations otherwise than according to their own prejudiced opinions.

But to speak more closely: it is evident that the first Christian Fathers when they would magnify the number of their converts or adherents would not only bring into their catalogue such pagans as opposed idolatry, though they no way pretended unto **<45>** Christ and Christianity, but even all such as did profess it in any way and under how great variety so ever of rites or tenets—just as the Jews did reckon the Sadducees, Pharisees, and Essenes and other lesser sects in the number of Jews and as the modern Christians do compute in the Eastern Church, the Grecians, Melkites or Syrians, Georgians or Muscovites, Nestorians, Indians or Christians of St. Thomas, Jacobites, Cophites, Armenians, Abyssinians, and Maronites, and in the west Papists, Calvinists, Lutherans, Anabaptists, Socinians, and such like even to the inhabitants of Liefland where they would make an estimate of Christianity and its extent.[158] Nor doth there want reason for this procedure, for as we denominate men and estimate those to be of human race who have the general resemblance, propagation, speech, and laughter, how different so ever their morality and rationality be: so in Christianity the external profession in general doth entitle them unto the appellation. And if all persons grossly ignorant—demi-Jews, demi-pagans, demi-philosophers, and such like as posterity has concluded under heresy—may not come under this notion, I do not know where to find the primitive church or Fathers. Since most if not all the Fathers of the three first centuries come under this number and the martyrs were no others, it is a caution suggested to us by the learned Casaubon and subscribed unto by all men of understanding that the Fathers do most frequently mistake in point of history as well those of the Greek as Latin Church (either through ignorance and inadvertency or because they inconsiderately need use of any story that seemed to make for their advantage in their sermons or writings).[159] And that they deserve as little credit in reference to matters of faith is apparent by writings of Mr. Dale, Hottinger, et cetera,[160] the sole consideration whereof made the judicious Protestants reject their authority and pay them but a precarious veneration. As to the subsequent condition of Christianity, that which we seem descended from is no other than a mixture of the religion of the Essenes, the Jewish heretics, and of the Egyptian *therapeutæ* which likewise were Jews, but not Essenes, together with the superadded tenet of Jesus being the Messiah and of other doctrines derived from the Gentile philosophy, and of certain paganical rites and ceremonies.[161]

It is apparent that Eusebius and Epiphanius reckon upon these Essenes and *therapeutæ* as Christians, disciples of St. Mark, and the great ornament of the profession.[162] Monkery deduces its original from them, and their lives were the patterns and precedents of those Christians who are renowned for the austere practice of piety, which the first apologies represent. It is apparent that the first Christians **<46>** from whom we are derived were Alexandrian proselytes which, retaining the name of Jews, did adhere unto the Septuagint. And hereupon these Christians whether of the Latin or Greek Church had no other Bible than that, or a version of it, and from hence they read those books which after ages called apocryphal. Neither had our gospel any other original than from Alexandrians or other Hellenists. It is confessed that Luke was of Alexandria; that Mark also was such is most probable. And, as to the others, it is evident that either they are but versions or not to be entitled to any other beginning than that some Hellenists published them in the name of Matthew and John. For Matthew may certainly be said to have written in the common Syriac which was then the Hebrew tongue.[163] The Gospel of Mark is thought to have been dictated by Peter and only translated by him into Greek as most of the ancients inform us. And the apostles did not understand Greek at all: the gift of tongues lasted but for that time, and all the sacred books except what bears the name of Paul (who did understand Greek) are but translations or counterfeits performed by unknown persons whose fidelity or integrity those questioned who rejected them or who embraced them.

But it is manifest that they are written by most illiterate persons. As to the Greek tongue,

> Pro vero sane tenendum est, omnes fere discipulos Christi & Apostolos, ut erant idiotæ & plebaei, piscatores nimirum, nautæ & portitores, non aliam novisse linguam praeter vernaculam, hoc est Galilaeum, & Syriacum idioma quod in illa regione obtinebat. Etsi enim multi in Syria & Iudæa Græcè sciebant, hoc ad infimæ plebis homines nihil attinebat qui vernaculam tantum noverant, Græcè prorsus ignari. . . . Scribebant igitur Apostoli idiomate suo, & lingua sibi familiari & vernacula, quæ protinus à Syris ἑλληνίζουσι vel Graecis ipsis ad fidem conversis, quos cecum habebant Euangelii praerdicandi adjutores & administros, in Græcum transferebantur. De quibusdam hoc certò' compertum est, de aliis ignoratum, quia non proditum: de omnibus

tamen verisimile est, quia de quibusdam verum est. Non enim disparatio eorum, qui gente ac genere & vocatione ac munere pares. . . . Quod ad Novi Testamenti libros attinet, ea causa quoque asseri potest cur multum diverso ab elegantiore & puriori Hellenisimi loquendi genere conscripti sunt. Ab idiotis quippe partim compositos dicere licet, partim à metaphrastis, & ipsis non ad modum Græci sermonis peritis.[164]

I have transcribed this passage out of Salmasius (whose entire discourse upon the Sixth Question there deserves to be read). Not that I believe that either the **<47>** Gospel of Mark or John were penned originally in Syriac (for then the Judaizing Christians would have had them as well as those of Matthew), or that the Epistles of Peter, James, and John (or that the Hebrews which is but a translation said to be made by Clement or some other) were ever penned in that language, which the supposed authors only knew, but to evidence how little certainty we have of their original and authenticness. And if they were not derived from those Hellenistical Jews, I know as little whence to fetch them as when they were written. It is true that Paul did understand Greek, but his epistles were as little regarded as his person amongst the Judaizing Christians. And they had as bad an opinion of him as the Jews themselves. It appears by Paul's carriage (Acts 23:6) that he did act by somewhat like to juggling in his proceedings.[165] How else could he cry Christianity assuring each of them singly that he was in the truth and that afterwards, when Paul was dead, each of them pretended his religion to be the true religion derived from Paul, whence arose great feuds amongst them.

To pass from this discourse to that other concerning the ignorance of the first Christians and their enmity to all ethnic learning: It appears that in the days of Christ none but the vulgar sort (the Galileans were the worst among the Jews) did believe in him. The wise, the rulers, were such as the truth of the gospel was hidden from. And in the days of Paul, not many wise men after the flesh, not many mighty, not many noble were called, but the foolish things of the world were chosen, 1 Corinthians 1:26. And truly afterwards, till near the time of Constantine, very few of any better rank or intellectuals did embrace Christianity, which made the heathens upbraid the Christians as men that gained only on children, women, and the poorer and more ignorant sort of persons. Nor did they pretend to learning as appears out of Lactantius, Annobius,

Minucius Felix. Nay, they were enemies to all human learning, as appears by the old constitution of Clement whereby all the books of the Gentiles are prohibited (Clement Romanus l: 1 Constit. caput 6). And the Council of Carthage did prohibit the clergy to read any such books, et cetera.[166]

What I have said is notoriously true as to this point and needs no further proof except that I illustrate the condition of Christianity by that passage of **<48>** Avicenna who, being to relate the nature of medicinal simples according to the Greek Alphabet, says that he follows *Alphabeta Barbarorum.*[167]

I proceed now to the particular narration of the birth and actions of Mahomet whose rise, that we may the better understand, it is necessary that we consider the situation of Arabia and search into the original of the Saracens, a nation not mentioned by the ancient Greeks or Romans, and of whom there is no account given by the Christians contemporary to Mahomet.

CHAPTER 3

A BREIF ACCOUNT OF ARABIA AND THE SARACENS

The History of the Saracens and of Mahomet

HE BETTER TO UNDERSTAND this particular history of the Saracens and Hagarenes, it is necessary we make a relation of the Arabians in general.[1] For the general situation, constitution, and religion thereof had an influence upon the Mahometan revolution, and the whole religion of Arabia was interposed in the production of it. The Arabians received their denomination not from Arabus, a son of Apollo, as the Latins imagine, but from Araba, one of the provinces of what is vulgarly called Arabia, situated near Medina where it is thought Ismael did first seat himself.[2] But this Araba or Arabum or Arabia usually includes all that peninsula which was inhabited by the Arabians. These divide their country into several kingdoms whose names being unknown to the European geographers I shall forbear to use as much as I can and shall acquiesce in the vulgar distinction of it into Arabia Fælix, Petra, and Deserta.

It is of great compass and extent, having on the west the Red Sea for its bounds, on the south the ocean, on the east the Persian Gulf, and on the north Syria and the River Euphrates. It is as large or larger than Spain, France, Germany, and Italy. Pliny reckons a great part of Mesopotamia within the precincts of Arabia and the Arabians to be styled Syrians. And, as to this last, there is this ground for it that Arabian *Salihenses,* called *Al Dajannuini,* did conquer Syria.[3] And a second time that province was reduced under the obedience and possession of the Ghassanian Arabs which came out of Yemen, or Arabia Fælix, and were of the tribe of Azdenses.[4] And Aretas (whose lieutenant at Damascus sought to apprehend Paul, 2 Corinthians 11:32) must probably have been the first or one of their kings, if Christian and Saracen chronologers agree.

Arabia Petra (so called from Petra the chief city) is bounded on the west **<49>** by the inmost nook of the Red Sea and Egypt, on the north by Palestine and Cælo-Syria, on the east by Arabia Deserta, on the south by a track of mountains which disjoins it from Arabia Fælix. This country Pliny, Strabo, and Ptolemy call Nabatea the Desert. Arabia Deserta is bounded on the west by Petra Cælo-Syria, on the north by Euphrates, on the east by sundry mountains which divide it from the country of Babylon, on the south also it is severed from Arabia Fælix by a ridge of mountains. As for Arabia Fælix, it runs out like a peninsula between the Arabian Gulf (or Red Sea) and the Gulf of Persia. It is the largest of the three divisions and said to contain in compass 3,504 miles. It is called by Solinus and others Ayman, by the Arabians, Yemen.[5]

What share Arabia had in the Chaldean monarchy I know not, nor whether it were ever all reduced under the obedience of one sovereign. Most certain it is that the Arabians were divided into tribes and were as exact in preserving their genealogies and marrying in their own tribes as ever were the Jews.[6] And as to their ancient religion and learning: though the accounts thereof be but slender, they not having had the use of writing and letters till or little before the birth of Mahomet, yet it may be conjectured that the astronomy, astrology, and other knowledge of the Persian Magi and Chaldeans was derived originally from them. There want not some who essay to prove this, but to insist thereon would not be to our purpose. Their language at first seems to have been little different from the Hebrew or at least Syriac, until one Yaarab introduced the Arabic.[7]

Of the Arabians there are said to be two sects; the pure Arabians who are said to be descended from one Joktan or Kahtan (the son of Saleh, the son of Shem, the son of Noah) and the *Mosta-Arabs* or denizened Arabians.[8] For Ismael being ejected by Abraham came into Arabia, seated at Yathrib (since called Medina), and married into the tribe of Jorham, of the pure Arabians who lived in Yemen or Arabia Fælix, and from him descended the Coreischites and other *Mostaarabick* tribes, who, notwithstanding, are not able to deduce their pedigrees with any certainty from Ismael, but from Adnanus who was of his race.[9] Ismael marrying into the tribe of Jorham conformed himself to the language, manners, and way of living practiced by his new relations, and so he and his posterity became incorporated into the Arabians. And the tribes of the *Mostaarabes* and Jorham did diffuse themselves into several provinces without retaining any national distinction but what arose from their genealogies or governments and language.[10] For, as to this last, it is said that the progeny of Joktan or Jorhamide, did differ in dialect from the **<50>** Ismaelites, the former using the Arabic dialect of Hamyar, which Ismael corrected and reformed into another called pure Arabism or the dialect of the Coreischites.[11]

The progeny of Joktan had at first the preeminence and a kind of rule which they might well challenge not only upon the account that they received Ismael as a stranger, and his progeny were but *Mostaarabs*, as because of their strength, number, and riches which arose from the fertility and opulence of their country, viz. Yemen, whereas the Ismaelites were possessed of Yathrib and the desert Arabia. The inhabitants of Yemen were called Sabei or Sabii from Saba the son of Yashab, the son of Yaarab, the son of Joktan, concerning whose religion it is necessary that I speak somewhat.[12]

They avowed that their religion was exceeding ancient, that it was descended from Enoch (whom they call Edris) and Seth, and they pretended to have the books of Seth preserved from all antiquity down to them.[13] This undoubtedly was the religion which Abraham professed when he was in Harran in Mesopotamia before God is said to have reclaimed him. This was the religion of the Nabathei, or inhabitants of Arabia Petra and of the Chaldeans, and the inhabitants of Harran or Carr in Mesopotamia.[14] Nay, it was diffused over the face of the whole earth as Maimonides said, and as Abulfeda.[15] It was the most ancient of all religions. They did believe there was but one great God, whom they called the Lord of Lords, and in their disputations they alleged most strong arguments for the unity of the Godhead. The chief God they called *Olla* or *Alla taall*,[16] the highest or greatest God. Besides this chief God, they had other lesser gods to whom they attributed no intrinsic, essential, underived power, but only an efficacy communicated by the supreme deity, whereby men were intermediately influenced and ruled, whereupon they did adore them with a secondary, divine worship as mediators and intercessors for them. And this was their way of address to the great God: "I give myself to thy service; thou hast no companion but such as are in thy subjection, and thine is all that is devoted and offered to them."[17]

It was their opinion that there could be no communication between the divine essence and man but by some intermediate beings,[18] and that the pure invisible spiritual substances were employed to this end, and that in a subordination to their influences it was necessary that there should be other intermediate visible bodies. For those, some of the Sabii did feign *sacella* or mansions: such are the gross bodies of the celestial planets (for those they principally addressed themselves to, though many had equal reverence for the fixed stars), which they imagined to be animated by those intelligences, as our bodies are by their **<51>** souls. Upon this account, they observed diligently their houses and stations, rising, setting, conjunctions, oppositions, benevolent or malevolent aspects; they assigned to them days, nights, and hours; they ascribed unto these figures and shapes, subjected regions and particular persons to them. And agreeably hereto, they made prayers, incantations, and seals. As for example if, upon Saturn's day (which was their last day of the week denominating each day from the planets as we do), a man came to pray to him at the first hour having his seal on, made according to art and suitable to that planet, and he clothed in a fitting garb and made use of a convenient form of prayer: whatever he shall ask that is in the disposal of Saturn, it shall be granted to him; so for the rest of the planets whom they called lords and gods. And by this ascent from the creatures to the creator, from visible to invisible things, they did intermediately proceed to the intelligences and supreme deity.

And from hence arose the fabric of talismans of which there was such use among the Arabians and Egyptians, and whereto they attribute such power, and by which Apollonius Tyaneus is said (by the Christians) to have affected his miracles.[19] Upon the same sentiments did others of the Sabii proceed, who yet went higher to erect statues and images to those lesser deities to intercede for them, they supposing it necessary for man (who is liable to so many contingent necessities) to have his mediator always ready that he might have recourse to him.[20] And that these planetary bodies (the chapels of the glorious intelligences) were itinerant and moveable, sometimes rising, sometimes setting, sometimes continuing under/over hemisphere; whereupon they proposed to detain their influence and preserve their benevolent power by lodging it in some statue or image made of a metal and figure convenient to this or that planet; the days, hours, degrees, minutes, and all other circumstances being astrologically observed in order thereto, and such sigillations, prayers incantations, suffumigations, attire, et cetera, being used as are appropriate. Hereby they did apprehend they should always have their mediators ready to assist them; and these images they called vicegerents in reference to the celestial mediators by whose interposition a man was to propitiate their superior planets.

This is the sum of their religion and the foundation of all that idolatry which diffused itself thence into Chaldea, Egypt, and all parts of the world: the Chaldean discipline being the same with this, and the Persian magi having no other origin.[21] Not to multiply my discourse into two many particulars, I shall in what is to come <52> observe only what may conduce to my principal design:

The Sabii rejected the Jewish canon or sacred books and relied on those which they deduced from Edris, Seth, and other their patriarchs and prophets.

They say that Noah preached against their images and worship of mediators, and therefore they generally speak against him.

They say Abraham opposed their image worship and talismans, and therefore he was banished by them.

That many people in the Levitical Law were purposely enacted by Moses in opposition to the Sabii that the Israelites might not be ensnared in their ways.

They shave their heads close, abstain from the blood of animals, esteeming it the food of demons (though some want food thereon that they might contract an affinity and correspondence with them).

Though the principal place for their devotions was near the city of Harran or Carr, which Abulfeda calls the city of the Sabii, yet did they preserve a great esteem and reverence for the Caaba at Mecca.[22] They kept sundry fasts, whereof one consisted of thirty days.

They continued in repute not only to the days of Gregory Nazianzen the inhabitants of whose diocese were generally Sabii, but even to the rise of Mahomet who often mentions them.[23]

As to the inhabitants of Arabia Petra, I have already showed that they were of the religion of the Sabii. I shall only add that they were esteemed the meanest and most despicable tribes, insomuch that *Alnabat* or *Nabateus* in vulgar signified a mean and despicable person.[24]

I come now to speak of the inhabitants of Arabia the desert which, as it had been the seat of Ismael, so the inhabitants pretended to a nobility even above those of Yemen. Of all the tribes of the Ismaelites, the

Coreischites were the most illustrious, their military condition made them proud, and their poverty and inaccessibleness had hindered them from being conquered, so that their speech was more refined, and their glory less stained than that of the other provinces. But there were other grounds for their preeminence: for a Coreischite signified proverbially a gentleman of quality, as did *Alnabat* an inferior person. And it is the general tenet of the Arabians that the Coreischites are the most noble of all the Arabian tribes, as Erpenius and Hottinger assure me,[25] and notwithstanding the distinction of the pure Arabian and *Mostaarabs* (which Abulfeda saith was the most received tenet of the Saracens of his time). Yet there want not good authors who believe the ancient tribes of the pure Arabians to have been extinct, and that all the Arabian tribes **<53>** tribes recorded as in being, since the Saracen records are strangers to the country, some being called *Mota Arabs*, the progeny of Joktan, others *Mostaarabs* as coming from a remote place.[26] Nay, they say that Joktan was of the race of Ismael and certain it is (they own) that none of them can deduce their genealogy beyond Adnanus, a descendant of Ismael.[27]

If so, the Coreischites must have been the noblest tribe of all. However, it is certain that at the time of Mahomet they were the most illustrious tribe, for they were possessed of Mecca the metropolis of Arabia Deserta, and which the Arabians call the Mother of their Cities, and inhabited in the center of Arabia,[28] and, which is more, had the keeping and were a kind of priests (*aedili*) of the *AlCaaba, Caaba, Kabe* or *Cabea*, a temple reverenced universally by the Arabians and the chief place of their devotions. It is said that the tribe of Chozaah had the keeping of it once (they were of the number of the tribes of Yemen and forced by an inundation to alter their dwelling) and were esteemed thereupon the chief of the tribes, but that one Abu Gabshan sold it to one Kosa, a Coreischite, for a rundlet of wine.[29] He repented heartily of his foolish bargain, which gave occasion to the Arabian proverb: "More vexed than Abu Gabshan."[30]

The Caaba was so called either from its eminence and height or because it was a square building.[31] It is also called *Albait Alharam*, or the prohibited house of refuge.[32] They report that Adam, being cast out of paradise, desired of God that he might build such a house as he had seen in heaven towards which he might pray, and which he might compass about in his devotions, as the angels and blessed spirits do about that celestial mansion that, thereupon, God sent down a glorious light embodied and shaped in the form and model which Adam desired, towards which he might pray and compass it about.[33] After the decease of Adam, his son Seth did erect a fabric of clay and stone in that place, according to that model which, being destroyed by the deluge, Abraham and Ismael built a temple by the command of God in the same place, an angel showing them the ground and model. This temple was kept up by the succeeding Arabians, but while it was in the possession of the tribe of Coza, idols were first brought into it (also Hobalus, Asaphus, and Nayela) by King Amrus, who being of Yemen and a Sabian.[34] That they were talismanic is no doubt. Afterwards Abu Corb Assad, a king of Yemen, did beautify it with stately curtains about seven hundred years before the birth of Mahomet.[35] So great, so general was their veneration for this temple that when the tribe of Gatsan built another temple to themselves in imitation of the Caaba, the other tribes made war upon them for that and destroyed that schismatical edifice. [36]**<54>**

In the temple there were a multitude of idols undoubtedly accommodated to the superstition of every tribe. Within was Abraham's statue, attended with a multitude of angels and prophets, and on the outside were ranked 360 idols, whereof Hobal (which perhaps imports *Ha-ball,* the great Baal or Bel), Asaf, and Nayela.[37] Hobal was the chief, being a red statue shaped like a man holding seven unfeathered arrows in his hand; Asaf was also like a man; and Nayela like a woman. These two are said to have been turned into stones for having committed fornication together in the Caaba. Hither did all the tribes make pilgrimages and, in order to it, did solemnly devote themselves. Sometimes they went round the temple in a kind of procession and came betwixt Safa and Meriah (which are the same with Asaf and Nayela).[38] This Safa was a blue stone at the foot of the mountain of Abikobais, and Meriah a great stone near the mountain of Koaikaban.[39] They were distant from each other (about 780 cubits). They professed their reverence to the great god and some also to his associates as each particular person fancied—saying: "Thou hast no companion or associate besides—who is at thy disposal together with all that is devoted to him."

Thus they went through each station and offered their gifts and cast stones in certain places. And all the Arabians did agree to set certain months apart for this religious performance in which it was unlawful for any tribe to make war on the other or for any man to molest another. This they all did—except the tribes Tai and Cathaam and some of the race of Alhareth Eb. Caab.[40] For those people made no pilgrimages nor reverenced the Caaba nor observed religiously any months or place as sacred.

This was the condition of Arabia, if we abstract from particular conquests and the mixtures of religion arising from the Jews who dwell among them, ever since the dispersion of Babylon, and the Christians whom either Peter converted to Christian Judaism or which fled thither upon several persecutions by the Roman emperors in Egypt and Syria. Of the Christians, it is notorious that the Nestorians and Jacobites or Eutychians were dispersed through those provinces, and the Arians were propagated that way since the generality of those provinces were infected from the Academy at Alexandria and the neighboring bishops. Nothing was more tenacious of their old rites than the Arabians and, withal, none more prone to admit of novel opinion under the specious color of religion. It is natural for men by cohabitation to infect each other with a mixture of devotion, as diseases are propagated **<55>** by contagion, and we may believe that the Arabians, being possessed with an opinion of their being descended from Abraham and Ismael, did pay a great respect to the Jews who were spread through their country—yet not so as to relinquish their worship and pilgrimages to the Caaba. It was always a part of their religion to circumcise (as did the Cholchi and Egyptians) but not till thirteen years as Ismael was circumcised. About seven hundred years before Mahomet , those of Yemen did turn Jews, and about seventy years before Mahomet their King Du Nowas did compel all to Judaism and burnt the dissenters, many whereof were such mongrel Christians as that age usually produced.[41]

Whereupon, to vindicate the Christians, the king of the Abyssinians invaded Yemen, conquered the country, and reigned there seventy-two years. The second of the Abyssinian princes or governments there, Abrahah Alashram, viceroy to the Negush, built a Christian church there to divert the people from their pilgrimages to the Caaba. But the generality of the inhabitants retained obstinately their ancient reverence for Mecca, and one of them, easing himself in this new church and otherwise defiling it, Abrahah swore he would destroy the Caaba. He marched with his army for that purpose directly for Mecca, but, when he approached Mecca, they say the elephant he rode on, called Mahud,[42] kneeled down and refused to go forward, though he went cheerfully any other way: and withal a flock of birds carrying stones as big as peas in one their beak and two in their claws so weighty that they killed therewith his followers striking through helmets, men, and elephants so that the survivors relinquished their journey. And the Arabians, who usually computed their years from some remarkable accident, began a new account, from the year of the elephant.[43]

After Mahomet was born, and not long before he begun to declare himself, the inhabitants of Yemen addressed themselves to the Greek emperor Heraclius for aid against the Abyssinians, but he refused it as being unsettled in his empire. Anusherwan, King of Persia, did relieve them and gained so much power in Yemen that he appointed them their kings out of the natives. It is to be noted that the Christian writers call him Cosroes whom the Arabians and Persians call Anusherwan, for Cosra or Cosroes was a common name to all the kings of Arabia Petra and Deserta.[44]

I find they embraced Christianity in the time of Alnooman, the son of Almondar,[45] and according to our ecclesiastical history under a queen called Mawia in the reign of Valentinian and Valens.[46] And although they were Trinitarians, and in behalf of them made war upon the Arians, afterwards **<56>** they turned Jacobites, and during the reign of Justinian they made war upon the Christians in their behalf.[47] Upon the murder of the Emperor Mauritius, Cosroes, king of Persia, compelled all the Christians in his dominions (and Arabia was in a manner subject to him) to turn Nestorians upon pain of death,[48] and erected them a patriarch at Mausell,[49] so that we may believe the Arabian Christians or such as were fled thither at several times to have turned to that opinion. But, notwithstanding these revolutions, the reverence for the Caaba did in great part continue, it being incident to human nature oftentimes to turn their religion in obedience to their princes. But inveterate superstitions are not so soon exterminated as is the outward profession of religion, it being evident that most of the Coreischites retained their idolatry. Nor was the Caaba destroyed with its idols all this while.

CHAPTER 4

THE TRANSACTIONS FROM THE BIRTH OF MAHOMET TO HIS FLIGHT FROM MECCA

URING THOSE TRANSACTIONS, Mahomet was born about the year of Christ 580. Some place it in 570, others in 600, others in 620; but I follow the most probable account since it is generally agreed that he was forty years old in 620, at which time he began his prophesy.[1] He was of the most noble tribe of the Coreischites. His father's name was Abdalla, his mother Amena or Emena, both of that tribe.[2] He was born at Mecca; his father was curious to have his nativity calculated, and it was predicted that he should be exceedingly advanced by the propagation of a new law and monarchy. Not long after his birth, his father died, as did his mother when he was about six years old, whereupon his grandfather Abdolmutleb took care of him and he dying about two years after, his uncle Abutaleb undertook his education.

The Mahometans report several miracles which happened at his birth, but would be tedious to relate here. During his infancy he gave pregnant signs of a singular nature, great wit, and good behavior. His uncle gave him all the instruction the country could yield, which being then divided into sundry religions of the Christians, Trinitarians, Jacobites, Nestorians, Arians, Idolaters, and Jews, and those each as it were refracting other (as contrary elements do upon mixture), he was not ignorant of what each of those religions held. Abutaleb his uncle, having occasion to go to Jerusalem and not only to Damascus, carried him with him where he was more perfectly instructed in the principles and various sects of Christianity.[3] As he went to **<57>** Damascus, about Bosra,[4] as soon as he saw him was astonished and seizing upon his hand said it was a prodigious youth, that, as he came along, he saw a cloud overshadow him and that the renown of that stripling should fill both eastern and western world.[5]

Being returned from thence, as well educated as was possible for his uncle to breed him, and being educated to all the martial exercises of the Arabians, at twenty years old he gave great proofs of his valor and conduct in a fight between the Coreischites and the tribe Kais Ailan, which happened in the month Moharra, at what time it was unlawful for the Arabians to fight, it being the time of pilgrimage to the Caaba, whence the Arabians called it *dies sceleris*, or the wicked day.[6]

After this, his military genius not permitting him to live idle at home while many of his countrymen served in the Christian armies, he went into the field under his uncle Abubacr who commanded a brigade under the Christians.[7] For albeit the Arabians were not tributaries or subjects to the Christians or Persians, yet their country lying between both empires, some of their princes confederated with one and some with the other, according as their situation made them obnoxious, and served either prince upon certain conditions.[8] Here he accomplished himself in civil and military prudence and withal discovered the divisions and weaknesses of the Christians. During his being abroad in Syria, a noble lady being a widow (and who, for riches and birth, was courted by sundry Arabians, princes) falling in love with him (or directed by a vision as was pretended),[9] invites him to relinquish the war and live with her, promising him a noble maintenance and to accommodate him in order to further travels with a large cargo that he might improve his intellectuals and estate together.[10] He who thought (according to the opinion of his country) that merchandise might very well consist with nobility accepted of the overture.[11] Nor is this more to his disparagement than it is to the nobles of Venice or Genoa; such were Vespasian, Pertinax, Tarquinius, Priscus among the Romans and even of late Spinola.[12]

Being thus accommodated, he made several advantageous expeditions to Alexandria and other parts of Egypt. And curiosity or ambition prompting his great spirit, he undertook a voyage into Africa from whence he passed into Spain (AD 605), where he found the kingdom unsettled in religion. For the Goths, having been from the beginning of their Christianity zealous Arians, were forced to turn Trinitarians (AD 589) by their King Ricaredus. And it not being so easy to extirpate inveterate opinions as to alter the profession of them, the **<58>** populace (and many others) retained their former sentiments. And after the death of

Ricaredus, endeavors had been made (AD 603) to resettle Arianism. He finding it in this condition is said to have endeavored to instill into that nation some of his principles and had embroiled them. But the return of St. Isidore from Rome (whose esteem and power in that country was very great) enforced him to return the same way he came.[13]

This voyage gave him an opportunity of seeing the weakness, the secret animosities, factions of the Christians, not only in Spain but Africa (where were the remains of the Donatists and Arian Vandals) and in Egypt. In his voyage I suppose he discovered the plantation and use of rice wherewith he acquainted his countrymen, recommending it to them as an excellent nourishing durable food: for which he was honored that it is still a tradition among them that Mahomet, being in paradise (before his assuming to be a prophet) and compassing the throne of God, fell into a sweat and one drop falling from him to the earth produced rice.[14] Another became a rose.

After his return, Chadija married him.[15] And it being the custom of the Arabians that the husband should endow the wife upon marriage, since his fortunes were not proportionable to the quality and riches of Chadija, I find that Abutaleb did make her a dowry of twenty camels and twelve ounces of gold, adding this speech:

> Glory be to God who hath caused us to descend from Abraham and to be of the race of Ismael, and hath given us the holy land to possess, and the Caaba to keep where to pilgrims from all places resort; who hath also made us judges and rulers in our country. Mahomet, the son of Abdalla, my nephew, with whom none of the Coreischites can compare for virtue, bravery, glory, understanding, and wit, although his riches do not equal his birth and accomplishments (in truth riches are transitory as a shadow, and are lent to us by heaven so as to be recalled when Allah pleaseth) is passionately in love with Chadija, the daughter of Chowailed, and she likewise with him: whatsoever is demanded by way of dowry I will see it settled.[16]

I think I follow the most probable story by placing Chadija in Syria, though she were a Coreischite. But it makes nothing to the prejudice of my narration, if Chadija be supposed to live in Mecca and there (upon a dream) fall in love with him and invite him, upon a large salary, to live with her and oversee her estate and conduct her merchandise into Syria and Egypt.[17] The Arabians acknowledge the poverty of their prophet, and, for his being retained in her service, they plead that it hath often been the fortune of such as God hath designed **<59>** for His prophets and the greatest dignities that they should arise from servitude to empire and by a long practiced obedience learn to command; that Joseph was a servant in Egypt, and Moses in Midian; that nobility is not extinguished by poverty; that Noah was a carpenter; that Isa (so they call Jesus Christ and so I shall name him in the subsequent story) followed the same trade.[18] That since the nobility of his extraction is not questionable, it is malice and envy to upbraid him with this employment, as if it had been servile and mean; that this objection did not become the followers of Isa; that Mahomet had rendered eminent testimonies of his valor in the wars and might have been rich if he would have been less generous or more rapacious and extorting.

That whereas they said Mahomet was but a camel driver: there is nothing of contumely in that if we consider that wealth of the Arabians consisted much in camels; that the most illustrious and rich nobles of that country did usually attend their own business and drive or feed them themselves; that it is not imaginable he was the most inferior servant of Chadija, his warlike spirit would not have submitted to it, especially his uncle being of such quality and riches, or that Chadija would put him to any such inferior duties whom from the beginning she designed for her husband, dissembling only her passion for a time.

Mahomet, having added to the splendor of his family the riches and power of Chadija, entertained no mean thoughts of himself. She had an uncle called Warekeh or Varkah who understood Hebrew or Syriac well and could write the character.[19] Him she did employ to teach Mahomet to write (for amongst the Coreischites scarce any could write at all). The invention of Arabic letters was then but new, one Moramer had found them out, one Ebn Mooklah three hundred years after Mahomet, and after him Ali Ebn Bozea perfected them as they are now.[20] Of the Arabian tribe thence they were propagated to the Cendian tribe, and by one Bashar introduced at Mecca a little before the original of Mahomet's usurpation.[21] Mahomet immediately acquainted himself with this new character, and it added much to his repute that he seemed ignorant of nothing. At Jerusalem he had been perfectly instructed in Christianity and had in sundry places conversed with the Nestorians, Jacobites, and Arians: by them he had been informed of the vanity of idols and talismans, **<60>** of the unity of the Godhead, providence, virtue, and vice, the tenets of the Jews and Jewish Christians.

Thus he became very well versed in the scripture, the doctrine of the Old and New Testament, the traditions of the several sorts of Christians, especially of those Judaizing Churches which Peter had planted all along from Jerusalem to Babylon and all Mesopotamia. Nor is this all which I find written of him: for Rodericus Toletanus assures me that he was well acquainted with natural philosophy.[22] In fine, the Arabians had such a repute for his universal knowledge that they believe he understood all things. Though the Arabians did much affect the glory of being eloquent and excellent poets, yet in those qualities did Mahomet surpass them all, not only in sublimity of thoughts, quaintness of speech, wittiness of his parables or apologies, but in choice of words and phrases.[23] To all which as his great learning and education had much contributed, so it was an artifice of his to conceal those arts by which he had attained those excellencies. Being asked how he attained to so refined a language, rather than discover the means he had used, he told them that he had learned it from the Angel Gabriel who had taught him the dialect of Ismael himself.

Thus Mahomet gained upon the admiration and esteem of all men, and, by way of gratitude to his uncle Abutaleb, he contracted a particular friendship with young Ali his son and instructed him in writing and all manner of knowledge.[24]

Ali was of a brown complexion, a little man with a belly somewhat large. He had a contempt for the world, its glory and pomp. He feared God much, gave many alms, was just in all his actions, humble and affable, of an exceeding quick wit, of an ingenuity that was uncommon.[25] He was exceeding learned, not only in those sciences which terminate in speculation, but those which tend to practice and are the useful arts of life and supports of civil society. He had a great dexterity in managing the great house and a courage so extraordinary that it seemed to approach to rashness. In his company did Mahomet pass much of his time, and Ali was so surprised at the extraordinary abilities of his cousin that he did believe him to be no less than a prophet. It was no unusual thing for prophets to arise and to be owned in Arabia: the common traditions of the nation and the Sabian **<61>** principles did incline them to believe it possible that, under certain configurations of the stars, a prophet might be born and that he might do great miracles.

It is most certain that those people were much addicted to judiciary astrology, and this is one tradition of it. The nativity of Mahomet had been calculated, and it had been predicted by a Jewish Genethlia that he should be a great prophet and prince.[26] Abu Maasor said of him in defense of those (as Elmain) who write that he was born in the latter end of the night: "Necessariò Muhammedem fuisse natum in fine noctis, quando libra medium cœli teneret, media nocte verò meridiem transiisset signum tauri aliâs enim Prophetiam & principatum ei competere non potuisse."[27] Nor was it held unusual among them for a prophet to bring his Coran, or sacred writ, derived from God.[28] So they held that Edris, and Seth did so, Zaradast or Zoroaster, Moses, also his laws, and Isa and his apostles their gospels, so did Mani who gave a beginning to the Manichees, a sect diffused through Persia and Arabia even at that time, which they avowed to be the incorrupt word of God. Nor were the Manichees singular herein: the Gnostics, Nicolatians, Valentinians, Montanists had their sacred writs, which they reverenced, and contemned as spurious the testament or canon of the Trinitarians; and that the Nazarenes and churches planted by Peter had their peculiar gospel I have already showed.

Whilst the esteem of Mahomet thus began to grow, and that the people beheld him as an extraordinary person, the death of Mauritius with its odious circumstances, having taken off from the value of Christianity, and Chosroes having destroyed all the Christians in Persia or made them revolt to Nestorianism, and having wanted and made desolate Palestine, Jerusalem, Syria, and Egypt, and those Arabians who usually adhered to the Christians and served for pay, being discontented that Mauritius first, and then Phocas, denied them their salaries, and that they were involved in the troubles and calamities which Chosroes brought upon the Christians, Mahomet saw a fit opportunity to erect a new empire among the Coreischites. It did not a little contribute thereto that the other Arabians of Yemen had joined with Chosroes and shared in the rich booties of Egypt, which seems to have raised envy in those of Arabia the Desert. And afterwards, Heraclius having murdered Phocas and gained the empire, he marched against Chosroes, won three general battles, carried on the war into Persia, having in his army Abubacr and a brigade of the Scenites or desert Arabians.[29] These misfortunes did create such troubles in Persia that Chosroes resigned his kingdom to Medorses, one of his sons, but Sirces, his other son, being disgusted at that, puts his father to death, assumes the crown, makes an ignominious peace.[30]

Now were the Arabians of Yemen miserable, divided and **<62>** broken into factions, and disquieted with the troublesome consequence of so disastrous a war.[31] Those Scenites who had served valiantly under Heraclius, finding no acknowledgments proportionate to their merits, were sufficiently discontented. Mahomet gains to his friendship Abubacr surnamed the just, and Omar, and Othman, all persons of great power and esteem among the Coreischites, and men of mortified lives, so unconcerned in ambitious aims and private ends that they were able to give any party a luster and to any cause the face of justice and piety.[32] Now began all Arabia the Desert to ring with the fame of Mahomet and Othman and Ali being his secretaries; his divine poems were divulged, nor was anything ever read with greater applause. The Arabians were great admirers of poetry (songs were their pandects, their laws and chronicles were contained in them),[33] and when any poet had gained renown above others, all his tribe kept a public festival: the drums were beaten, processions made to him by men, women, and children to congratulate him.[34] This, as it added to the glory and interest of Mahomet, so it was much to his advantage that in token of his humility and to show how great an enemy he was to luxury, he always wore woolen garments (a garb said to be used by the ancient prophets, and then much used by the ascetics or such Christians as pretended to austerity of life), and that he lodged commonly upon mattresses, whence he had that double appellation of the man clothed with woolen and the man that lodgeth on the mattress.[35]

The Christians say he lodged thus because he was troubled with epileptic fits. But what is that to his garb or lodging? These fits seize the patient in any place, and most seldom when they are laid down. In the Arabian writers, though Christian, I find no such account of him nor can I believe it, because he was much addicted to venery and so able therein to gratify forty women in one night,[36] whereas nothing is more inconsistent with, or pernicious in, that disease than immoderate venery. Besides, it is a disease not to be dissembled and in which no dissimulation can be used. I grant he might either naturally or by some other unknown means frequently fall into ecstasies, and lie entranced, but as this differs much from the falling sickness, so it was no incredible accident among the Arabians who might have learned from the Jews and Christians concerning the ecstasies of the old prophets and of Paul.[37] But it was a common tenet with the Arabians that some men might fall into such raptures, and might converse with angels: I find of late that Cardan and his father could fall into them when they pleased.[38] And I am apt to believe that the illustrious Cardinal Ximenes did the like sometimes.[39]

Let us then imagine that in all those cases, nothing befell, nothing was done by Mahomet but what served to imprint in the people an opinion **<63>** that he was a prophet, which he the more fomented in them by framing his poems to the great God and magnifying him and frequently, in public, crying "*Allah Allah Howa Cabah Allah, God, God, the great God.*"[40] Having given these testimonies of his piety, and in his discourses enlarging in defense of the unity of the deity, he began to inveigh against the mediator gods or idols erected in and about the Caaba and write a *surat* or chapter of the Alcoran called "Anaan," in which he introduceth God, complaining that the Arabians did pay really more honor to the associate gods than to Him,[41] and that they robbed Him of that veneration which was due to Him.[42] He told them that the Caaba was the temple of the great God, that Abraham and Ismael had dedicated it to His worship alone, that the introduction of idols was a novel practice, that the prophets and patriarchs, especially Abraham, Isaac, and their father Ismael, did worship God without associating any with Him; that all associating of others with the great God, either in worship or in essence or both, was idolatry and therefore the Coreischites and other Arabians that did worship these idols were idolaters. So were those Christians who either held a trinity of persons or trinity of gods or did hold the deity of the Virgin Mary. So also were the Jews who did associate Ozair or Ezra to the great God, saying that he was the son of God.[43]

Among those, for whom the Arabians had a traditional reverence, who though he were not a prophet, yet was he for his witty apothegms and fables of as great credit as any of the prophets in a manner, there was one named Lockman or Lusman (most of the learned imagine him to be Æsop, the author of the vulgar fables).[44] But Mahomet either feigned or met with other stories of him and fixed him in the time of King David. Him he bringeth in giving this character to his son. "Oh son, do not thou join with God any companion."

Those latter discourses occasioned Mahomet a great deal of trouble, for the chief of the Coreischites, the rulers of Mecca, and others that were devoted to idolatry and Sabiism began to resent these proceedings, and some out of religion opposed him and his followers, others out of interest, fearing that this doctrine might destroy the glory of the Caaba and prevent the usual resort to it and so extinguish the repute of the Coreischites, whose honor and profit seemed now at stake. Mahomet strengthened his interest by a marriage with the daughter of Abubacr and used all manner of insinuation and address to increase his party. But the number of those that firmly adhered to him was but small, and he placed so little consideration in the respects of the vulgar not cemented to him by a religious tie that he would not adventure his design upon their affection, it being too mutable to build any dangerous lasting design upon. He made some small sallies into the countries and endeavored **<64>** to draw them into his party. But though he could not so effect his designs as to engage them into his religion or defense, yet by his demeanor and eloquent and sage apothegms he contrived them all in the opinion that he was a prophet.

He daily spread abroad relations of his discourses with God and his conferences with the angel Gabriel and used such a sagacity in discovering all plots and counsels held against him that his followers believed God almighty did reveal all to him. And Abutaleb did vigorously protect him, forbidding any to approach the presence of the prophet having a sword or any offensive weapon about him. The number of his adherents were now increased to forty when Abutaleb died at the age of eighty years.[45] The reputation of that prudent and ancient person, and who died in the religion of his country, was a great support to Mahomet. Yet did not his decease abate the courage of Mahomet. He considered well the juncture of affairs that whilst the Christians and Persians were so embroiled, and the Arabians so divided into several factions and more religions, it became him to protract his designs. For great attempts like great trees must have a deep root or every contrast overthrows them.

Not long after, there came to him seventy-three resolute men from Awas and Chezra and two women.[46] They came with great devotion and took oath unto the prophet that they would live and die in the profession of the faith of Ismael their common parent and patriarch and first propagator (under Abraham) of the Mahometan faith, who now denominates his followers Moslemin, that is, such as believe in God alone.[47] He knew well enough the importance of giving his party a specious appellation: his adversaries he calls associates, very invidiously if we consider what influence those appellations would have upon such as could look no further than the names and appearances of things.[48] Out of these last assistants, he chose twelve as principals or doctors, who, departing, did inveigle the inhabitants of Medina that they resolutely declared for him to assist him.[49]

Medina, then called Yathrib, was the second city of Arabia Deserta, distant from Mecca 10 days' journey or 270 miles and the ways difficult to pass.[50] It was seated conveniently so that he might upon any occasion retire into Yemen or Arabia Fælix (which it borders upon) or otherwise draw any converts or aid thence or even out of Persia. And it is observable that the more remote the people are from the court, church, or chief cities, the less devotion they retain for them. And the frontiers, by reason of the mixture of passengers and conflux of several strangers, are more civil and gentle to all comers than the more inland countries. Mahomet, understanding now the multitudes that would be faithful to him **<65>** in Medina, demeans himself with more haughtiness than before at Mecca. He declares that he was the apostle of God sent to revive the glory of Ismael and the religion anciently professed amongst them.[51] He commands all people to relinquish idolatry, to destroy their idols and worship only one God. He declares his faith to be the true faith, yet so that all which believed Moses or Isa might be saved, and should be protected, paying a moderate tribute. He enjoins all to believe the truth of the apostles and prophets, and to receive the sacred books, not declaring which were they particularly in favor of the Christians.[52] He approved their laws and declared Christ to be the spirit of God and the word of God.[53]

The Christians, finding such a declaration, entertained a favorable opinion of him, resorted unto him and recommended themselves to his most benign protection, and took a cartel of security from him. He commended them for opposing idolatry, as he did also the Jews, never mentioning any of the patriarchs, or Moses, Isa, or the apostles but with this honorable addition: "God's peace be upon them."

These tidings engaged the Coreischites against him, seeing all Arabia to divide. Hereupon Mahomet commands his followers to depart for Medina and promiseth to follow them. He retained with him Abubacr and Ali, sending the rest before. All of them arrived safe at Medina, Mahomet lodged at the house of Chalid Abiol till he had built a temple and a house for himself.[54]

CHAPTER 5

MAHOMET'S CONDUCT AT MEDINA, THE EMBASSY OF ALI TO THE HAGARENES AND SARACENS

ND NOW WE SEE HIM seated at Medina. There he erects a prophetical monarchy, and entitling God and the angel Gabriel to his dictates, he imprinted a greater awe thereof in his followers and was more absolutely obeyed than force or terror could otherwise make him. He declares that after Moses, the Jewish state being corrupt and apostatized from the law given by Moses and grown wicked in their lives, that Isa was sent to reform them and all the world, by a spirit of meekness; that the Jews persecuted and would have crucified him, but that the divine providence substituted a phantasm in his stead, and so he was only put to death in effigy, being really translated into paradise that he should save all at the last day who believe in him and mortify themselves to the world, should observe his precepts. That God, finding that the mildness and gentleness of Isa had not proved effectual, had now sent him who was the comforter promised by him to protect his followers from further persecution, to propagate the doctrine of the prophets and of Isa: all which taught that there was only one God ruling the world by His providence, a rewarder of the just and punisher of evil doers, that God having patiently expected the issue of Isa's preaching and of his apostles, and finding it fruitless, even the Christians being much **<66>** apostatized, and some lapsed into open image worship and idolatry, he was now sent to enforce all men to the truth (Islamism) and to make war upon them till they confessed one great God.[1]

The Christians, who had been so persecuted by Chosroes, and finding their condition very uncertain among the Arabians according to the humors or interests of the governors, were very glad of his rise and magnified his undertaking. No less pleased were the Jews who were reduced to a mean condition by reason that the wars of Persia, and the animosities and jealousies of the Greek emperors, had abolished all grandeur and extinguished universities, patriarchs, and governments. They hoped, by fomenting Mahomet so, to embroil Arabia that they might draw advantage from thence to aggrandize themselves and either at last destroy Mahomet or see him reduced to such straits as that he should turn to them and become Jew. But Mahomet was too politic to be deceived by the Jews. However he cajoled them, he trusted them least of all.

He considered with himself that to pursue his designs an army was necessary and consequently money to raise and maintain them: to preserve an army in command and to render it serviceable discipline was requisite. And, that he might multiply his soldiers, he penned a *surat* or chapter exciting and obliging them all to promote Islamism with fire and sword and made it meritorious to die in such quarrels.

The security which he gave to the Jews and Christians that they might live under him without molestation brought a great deal of riches into the public treasury, and these securities were observed with so inviolate a faith that it was a great invitation to the next neighbors to come under his government and for those afar off to wish him prosperity and increase of empire. It was the excellency of the Arabians always to be the best and most active horsemen in the world. Though their horses were lean, they were bold and well managed; they were fed with small sustenance and could endure the want of water in extraordinary manner.[2] Their exercises were on horseback to shoot an arrow and spurring their horses to catch it before it came to the ground; to see an arrow shot at them and to avoid it by stooping or hanging on either side of the horse as occasion required and immediately put themselves again in a posture of defense. They would ride a full career and yet gather up javelins or arrows, which lay on the ground; they would hit the least visible mark with sling, bow, or javelin.[3]

Water was their constant drink, their food coarse bread milk (new or sour), cheese, the flesh of goats or camels, pulse, and especially rice which he recommended to them as the most nourishing and venereal food in the world, saying that he himself did in one night **<67>** gratify forty women after a supper of rice.[4] Their diet was without luxury, and the same at home and abroad, in field and in garrison, by which his forces were preserved more healthful and were sustained less burthensome and expensive wherever they marched or quartered. Whereas the forces of an enemy not so disciplined would exasperate the country to a revolt by oppressing them to support their riot and mutiny, or disband upon any straits such as his men would not be sensible of, he frequently preached to the people in the temple of Medina leaning upon a column made of the body of a palm tree. But afterwards he had a desk made of tamarisk wood with two steps to ascend into it.

In Medina he wrote at sundry times the greatest part of his Alcoran.[5] Upon every occasion that his dictates might be more authentic, he published a *surat* or chapter of it, some whereof were at first very brief, not exceeding one period.[6] He constituted for his emirs or generals four friends: Abubacr, Omar, Othman, and Ali. And here, he gave Ali his daughter Phatemia in marriage.[7] Many resorted to him and became Muslemin, for I do not read that he armed and disciplined any others, not thinking it safe to put arms into the hands of new and unsettled friends.[8] Besides that, the populace thought a happiness to be freed from so laborious a militia and other molestations upon paying a moderate tribute, having liberty to attend their employments and enjoy their own religion with security, provided it were not idolatrous. Many of the Christians even of the monks, perceiving with what reverence he spoke of Isa, now acknowledged him to be the word and spirit of God, though otherwise a mere man born miraculously of a virgin, and how much he preached up acts of mercy, justice, and did embrace Islamism. And so did sundry of the Jewish priests.

It had been always from the time of Ismael (if not before) the custom of the Arabians to circumcise their children, as Ismael was, at thirteen years old. Mahomet not only continued this custom among the Ismaelites, but extends it to all that would turn Muslemin. This was not done out of complacence to the Jews who circumcise on the eighth day, but to continue an inveterate use of the Arabians, the neglect whereof would have begot a great distaste in that people, and the imposing whereof upon foreigners, becoming Musulmen, was justified by the Mosaic precedent of circumcising proselytes.[9] Mahomet's thoughts being wholly bent upon the introduction of a new religion and empire, he had Mecca frequently in his memory. He considered that place as the center of Arabia and metropolis of Arabia the Desert. He knew of what importance it was for a prince to be master of the chief city in his dominions, and that the sovereignty of Arabia **<68>** were half gained, if could possess himself of that place. He had gained the esteem of the populace, who reverenced him as a prophet and were satisfied of the truth of the miracles related of him. They admired his poetry, perpetually sang them and thought it a great honor to their tribe and city to have so eminent a person reside among them. They were witnesses of this valor and piety and saw his deportment and the doctrine he spread to be such as they needed, not fear oppression from his cruelty, extortion from his avarice, nor tyranny from his government. Tyranny consists not in the unlimitedness of power, but in the extravagant use of it.

The military men or Scenites and nomads saw in his design all that might oblige them to him since his religion would involve them in a perpetual war which would furnish them with opportunities to gain honor and riches. And the other inhabitants, which were artisans and tradesmen, saw that under him they should find all encouragement and protection since they should neither be compelled to war nor exhausted with burdens. They saw the resort to the Caaba lessened and, if these divisions continued, the advantages they derived thence and the glory they retained thereupon would all vanish, and they saw the troubles and hazard of a nation broken into factions and each party wherein was weak and, which is worse, dissolute and insolent. They saw that though the rulers and prevailing party in Mecca were against Mahomet, yet the most upright, just, and popular were for him, that the prophet retired from Mecca out of tenderness to the people lest they should be embroiled in civil dissentions and the holy Caaba defiled with blood, that Abubacr, Omar, Othman, and Ali had relinquished all to adhere to him. And, at Mecca, they saw continual objects of their commiseration: their friends imprisoned and tortured for befriending and retaining a veneration for the prophet. Balal, Zohaib, Cabbab, Ammar, Abes, Abu Handen, and Sohail with many others were cast into prison and used outrageously.[10]

The resolution with which they underwent those torments wrought effectually upon the commonality who pitied those that suffered so gallantly and could not hear with astonishment these words echoed out by the martyrs: "God God, the great God, and Mahomet his Apostle."

They saw that the Coreischites, which opposed Mahomet, were in profession absolute idolaters and, to support their grandeur and render their religion more mysterious and awful, find that God being all sufficient needed not any outward testimonies of their devotion, besides that they might be secure of His benignity by freely propitiating these associates.

But they saw that in <69> reality those Coreischites were men of no religion, perfect Sadducees (and it is in vain to attempt to excite others to a cordial defense of a religion which they themselves appear not to believe heartily). Moreover, there had fallen out an accident since the birth of Mahomet which was fresh in their memories and I suppose contributed to his reception. One Gawius Abu Abdoluzza, a priest or sacristan to one of their principal idols, having one day by negligence not shut up the door, two foxes came in and pissed upon the statue. He coming in, and perceiving what had happened, thought that idol was unable to help others, who could not avenge himself of the paltry foxes, and broke out into this expression: "Is he the lord upon whose head the fox pissed? Surely, he is despicable upon whom foxes do piss. Oh ye tribe of Salem (those were they that worshiped that idol), assuredly this statue doth you neither good nor hurt. He neither procures nor hinders your happiness." And, having said so, he broke the idol to pieces. Mahomet honored this man with a memorial in his Alcoran and changed his name, which signifies an erroneous person or son of a worshipper of Uzza (an Arabian deity) into Rashed Ebn Aba Rabehi—that is an orthodox person, the son of one that worshipped his Lord.[11]

Whilst affairs were in this posture at Mecca, and the Coreischites exceedingly distracted, Mahomet seemed to have a happy prospect of his designs, his only difficulty was to adjust the interest of Mecca and of the Caaba with his new religion. In order hereto, he declares that his journey to Medina was not a flight from, or desertion of, Mecca, but a religious pilgrimage to that place where Ismael first settled himself and whence the Coreischites were issued originally, and calls it the Hegira or journey taken out of devotion. And his four companions (together with the others that accompanied them) were entitled *Almo Hajerin* or the devout pilgrims.[12] In this appellation he cunningly made use of a paranomasia in which he alludes to the nation of the Hagarenes, the Arab *Elhagiar,* a warlike and potent people living thereabouts, called by Strabo and Ptolemy Ἀγραῖοι, *Agrei,* and their chief city Agra.[13] Of these there is mention made in the Chronicles that the Hagarenes were overcome by the Raabenites, 1 Chronicles 5:10.[14] Such an artifice and anagrammatical allusion he made use of in styling his sect *Aleslam* which by transposing the letters becomes *Ismael.*[15]

These Hagarenes are mentioned in the Roman history for their valor.[16] Trajan, having carried his conquests over all Persia as far as the Indies, was repulsed here with great damage, and neither he nor Severus could subdue them.[17] Of this nation of the Arabians did Mahomet make particular account <70> and invite them to Muslemisme, for it was his mode only to send to princes to invite them thereto, and they commonly submitted. But I am apt to think arguments and motives were made use of by his emissaries, and in an affair of this importance which required so much address as was requisite in the nonage of the empire. That it might not be dissolved before it was settled, I imagine Ali to have been employed in the negotiation, who was most dexterous in such affairs, who best understood the sense of the prophet and knew when to explain and when to intrigue his speeches. Besides, his youthful courage and address in horsemanship made him most fit to excite this warlike nation to so great an enterprise as the advancing the glory of Ismael and his descendants under the conduct of Mahomet.

Let us then fancy the gallant Ali mounted upon as good a horse as that he used afterwards called Duldall (which carried the miller from Medina to Katchan in Persia in one night which is above two hundred leagues),[18] with a small but brave troop of Moslemin, martial in their aspect, grave in their speech and carriage, exact in their discipline and obedience, armed not for show but service.[19] And though they valued their tulipants as diadems, yet they more esteemed the goodness of their swords, by which they seemed to design for each man a royalty.[20] Such was their reverence to their commander that one would have thought they had been all slaves and could not retain a bold spirit under so imperious a general. But the dexterity of the prophet showed that tyranny that the prudent may be absolute without tyranny and without regret or enfeebling the spirits of the most valiant; that the arts of government consist not in the show but use of authority, and the true use of it is to insinuate itself into, not impose upon, men's reason.

His Coran acquainted those Hagarenes with the heavenly wisdom of their prophet and the spectacle convinced them of his sovereign prudence and conduct. The Hagarenes were astonished when they saw the motto of this incomparable leader to be "Dominion belongs to God alone"[21] and observed their deportment when dismounted; and discerned that they equaled the most pious monks in their devotions and the most liberal princes in their alms; and that their affability, humility, with a detestation of all riot, luxury, and vainglory was such that the world was to receive examples from them since no age had produced any for the

Muslemin to act by, and they were their precedents. But that which most endeared this people to them was that, at their first approach, they saluted the people of Agra with that exclamation so well known to the Arabians: *"Allah Allah Howa Cobar Allah God, God the* **<71>** *great God,"* and in their standard they observed the lunulet or half moon, the ancient arms of the Ismaelites which they had seen placed on the head of Astarte or Ashtareth, the great goddess of Arabia and Syria, to which these countries had been immemorially devoted;[22] with which lunulets the Ismaelitish kings as Zebah and Zalmunna (Judges 8: 21. 24) did usually deck themselves and their camels. And thus the Jews expound the Shahoronim in that place.[23]

They were received with all the expressions of joy and welcome imaginable. But the Muslemin declared a greater satisfaction in the sense that they were welcome than in any empty or luxurious expressions of it. They exercised themselves upon this deportment that it was not any scorn of their entertainment, or that they did not think themselves happy to have given so good a beginning to their negotiations, but that the wisdom and felicity of man chiefly consisted in serving the great God; that joy of this world was but imposture; that a man was to consider there was a time when he was not in being, and there would be a time when he should die; that the interval between both was so short and so uncertain the only difference between men was their good actions in this life, and their rewards in the future; that he mistakes his course who places his confidence in any but God, and misplaces his delights who takes pleasure in anything but what is agreeable to his will.[24]

After these and suchlike discourses, the sun beginning to decline, they desired the opportunity of a retirement and water to wash themselves, wherein it was particularly observed with what care they washed their eyes, ears, nose, mouth, and hands for which they gave this reason: that though our knowledge was bred in us by our senses which were as the windows to let in the light, and as those senses, if duly employed, were the instruments of the soul to discover the wonderful works of God, yet human nature was so inclined to misapply them and to be led by them into an excess of sensuality that men ought to have a diligent watch over them. And to remind the Muslemin hereof, the prophet had appointed them such washings always before their prayers, and undoubtedly such memorials are not only efficacious to restrain men from vice but very acceptable to God, being silent testimonies of an aversion from sin and of a resolution to be cautelous for the future. After this, they went to their *sallah* or prayers. They began with the solemn introduction of "*Allah Allah Howa Cobar Allah*," then they proceeded thus in the words of the first chapter of the Alcoran: "Glory be to the Lord of all creatures, the king of the last judgment. We honor thee, we invoke thee: assist us in our necessities, lead us in thy ways, bring us into the path of those to whom thou hast done good, and not into the way of those upon whom thou hast poured out thy wrath, nor into that **<72>** of such as thou sufferest to go astray. Amen."[25]

Those and other prayers made up of sentences out of the Alcoran, repeated with show of great zeal and inward sincerity, added much to the good opinion the people had of them and their prophet. The multitude either employed their eyes in observing each action of theirs or their tongues in inquiring after the discourses and deportments of these illustrious persons. At their prayers, they turned their faces toward Mecca and the Caaba as if they paid as much reverence to the temple of Mecca built by Abraham and Ismael as every Jew did to that of Jerusalem. This was interpreted by the Arabians as a novelty and liable to exception till they were assured by Ali that the *Reblah* was changed from Jerusalem to the Caaba and that it was the pleasure of heaven that all Muslemin should pray towards the temple of Ismael.[26] This reason was satisfactory because it made for the glory of their progenitor, and every man readily believes pleasing news. The prayers the Muslemin went to again before bed time, and those which they renewed in the morning at break of day, administered fresh cause of admiration and discourse.

And the more for that: it was observed that the Muslemin did express some signs of reverence to Venus or the Morning Star, which had been an ancient deity of the Arabians,[27] and that they did also in the subsequent week observe as a kind of Sabbath the *Guimia* or Friday which had been always a day of weekly adoration to the goddess Urania (portrayed as corniculate or with a crescent on her head) in Arabia. It is most certain that in the whole Alcoran there is not any precept for the observation of this *Guimia*, but that Mahomet, understanding the wonted superstition of the Arabians, continued the solemnity of the day but altered the object of their worship to that of the one great God.[28] So he retained the lunulets upon the mosques and in their ensigns, suggesting new reasons for a custom grown sacred, inveterate, and not to be abolished without hazard to his main design. "Non institutum sed relatum a Mahummde ut festud

Guimia quod Oraniæ corniculatæ sacrum; a corniculata ejus & vetustissima effigie lunularum apud eos honere manasse videtur."[29]

It is agreed by the most knowing in the oriental transactions that Mahomet resolved to make no greater change in Arabia than was necessary to his purpose and did ingeniously accommodate to his ends those superstitious usages which were imprinted in the breasts of the Ismaelites.[30] It was a saying of that great personage: "He that knows not how to get up the ladder shall never get to the top of the house; that many things might be wished for which a wise man cannot hope for or pursue; that great designs are often frustrated when the authors discover **<73>** their greatness. Let others cry this is good, this is gallant: the prudent consider what is possible, what is requisite, and how to turn to advantage the successes of each day."

These circumstances having sufficiently prepared the minds of the Hagarenes, the principals among them resort to Ali and his companions to be informed concerning the desires and commands of the prophet. Ali first gives them an account of his original, the prodigies at his birth, the miracles done by him, his conversation with the angel Gabriel, the austerity of his life, the incredible prudence of his deportment, the quality, virtue, and numbers of those that adhered to him, and whatever else might endear the prophet to them, omitting nothing that might gain upon their reason or credulity. He added that the Coran which Mahomet brought was in general no other doctrine than all the prophets had taught, the sum of whose documents was that God alone was to be worshipped and idols exterminated; that this was the religion of Noah which he preached and for contempt whereof the world was drowned, seventy-two persons (so the Arabians say) only escaping in the ark; that this was the doctrine which Salehus came to preach long ago to the Arabians betwixt Hijaz and Syria in the country of Heir (one of the tribes held to be totally extinguished).[31]

The prophet Salehus came from God to the tribe of Thamud or Thomud, commanding them to desist from the worship of idols and associate gods and to worship only the true great God.[32] Few believed the message; the rest demanded as a miracle that he would produce a camel out of such a rock, which Salehus did and that camel foaled another. Yet they persisted in their infidelity and hamstringed the camel, whereupon the almighty caused a thunder to arise and destroyed them all, the houses wherein they dwelt yet remaining, which the Hagarenes were not strangers to. That this was the doctrine Abraham taught when he was banished their country, and which Ismael afterwards settled there when he planted himself in Arabia, Ali doubted not but they had a traditional knowledge preserved in their songs of the time when idols were first brought into the Caaba; that it was an innovation in the true religion planted by Ismael who, together with Abraham, built that temple;[33] that besides the introduction of a multitude of idols and associate gods they had by the mixture of lies and fables depraved, and in a manner, abolished the religion of Ismael; and that God had now at length been pleased to extend his mercy to the Arabians; that the Jews having lost their Coran which Moses gave them and made Ozair or Ezra an associate with God, receiving a Coran (this is the canon of the scripture and the Cabbala which the Jews derive from Ezra) of this as it were from the great God, and destroying the prophets, persecuting Isa when he was **<74>** sent to reform them.

Also, the followers of Isa had lost the Coran sent to them, and associated Isa and Mary his mother with God, and in most places introduced idols into their churches and houses—that now God had raised a prophet out of the lineage of Ismael to publish the truth and restore the doctrine of Ismael to its purity. The Caaba we reverence more than any Coreischite at Mecca, and since it hath pleased God by His prophet to remove the *Reblah* thither, towards that we direct our faces when we pray. The pool of Zamzam we hold no less sacred than they though not upon an idolatrous account, because we now know that when our mother Hagar was delivered of Ismael, he, dancing with his little feet, made way for a spring to break forth.[34] But the water of the spring coming forth in such abundance as also with such violence that Hagar could make no use of it to quench her thirst, which was then very great, Abraham coming to the place commanded the spring to glide more gently and to suffer the water might be drawn out if it to drink. And having thereupon staid its course with a little bank of sand, he took of it to make Hagar and the child drink. The same spring is to this day called Zamzam from Abraham's making use of that word to stay it. We honor those stones which they so idolatrously worship: they are neither Mars, Bacchus, nor Venus, though upon the one they can observe the portrait of Venus, the last within the cloisters or court of the Caaba. On the ground, enclosed in an iron grate called *Makam Ibrahim*, or the place of Abraham: upon that he stood when the Caaba was built. And there are the impressions of his feet in it, the print of the right foot being deeper than that of the left.[35]

That other, called the Black Stone, which is riveted to the wall in a corner of the Caaba on Basra side is no idol either, but one of the precious stones in paradise brought thence by Adam, carried up to heaven again at the deluge and brought to Mecca again by the angel Gabriel when Abraham built the Caaba. It was as white as milk at first, but the sins of men have caused its color to degenerate into black.[36] We are so far from detesting the Caaba and from dehorting them from going on pilgrimage thither that it is a fundamental article of our religion to undertake it, **<75>** and none can be a Musulman who thinks himself not absolutely obliged to go thither to perform the usual rites and do his devotion at those stones, as now it is done but out of piety to the Great God only and reverence to our holy progenitors.[37] The stones are blessed memorials of Abraham, Hagar, Ismael, not objects of our devotion, and we must worship not them. But there we doubt not but there is a benediction attends such as piously kiss the Black Stone and stepping do pass under it. There is a heap of stones near the way betwixt Medina and Mecca where the idolaters do now cast each three stones in their peregrination in honor of Merkolis or Mercury.[38]

"Behold," said Ali, "to what a height of idolatry the true Muslemitical religion of our father Ismael is corrupted.[39] After that the Caaba was built, and Ismael grown a stripling, the angel Gabriel appeared to Abraham and told him that God intended to make the highest trial of his affection and gratitude, and that he would have in acknowledgment of so many favors to sacrifice his son to him. Abraham immediately consented and being returned home bid Hagar call up her son and put on his best clothes that he might be better looked on at a wedding to which he intended to carry him. They departed the next day in the morning betimes and took their way towards mount Arafat, Abraham carrying along with him a good, sharp knife and some cords. But as soon as they were gone, *Sceithan*, that is to say, the devil represented himself to Hagar in the shape of a man, reproached her with the easiness wherewith she had consented that her son Ismael should go from her, and told her that what Abraham had related unto her concerning the wedding was to which he was to bring him was pure forgery, and that he was carrying him to the shambles. Hagar asked him why Abraham would use her so since he had always expressed a great tenderness to her son. The devil made answer that God had commanded it should be so, whereto Hagar replied since it was God's good pleasure that it should be so to make that disposal of him, it was but fit he should comply therewith. Whereupon the devil, pressing harder upon her and treating her as an unnatural mother, endeavoring by those aggravations to bring into rebellion against God, she pelted him away with stones.[40] **<76>**

The devil's endeavor, proving unsuccessful that way, and too weak to overcome the obstinacy of a woman, he applied himself to Abraham, revived in him the tenderness and affection of a father, represented to him the horribleness of the murder he was going to commit and remonstrated unto him the little likelihood there was that God should be the author of so abominable an action. But Abraham, who was acquainted with the subtlety and artifices of that wicked spirit, sent him away and, to be the sooner rid of him, cast also a stone at him. The last attempt the devil had to make was to represent to Ismael the horror of death and the unnatural procedure of his father, but he found the same treatment from him as he had from the other two and had a good stone flung at his head. The father and son, being come up to the top of the mountain, Abraham said to his son: 'Ismael, my son, I cannot imagine thou knowest the occasion of our journey and the reason why I have brought to this place. It is only this that God hath commanded me to sacrifice thee.' Where to Ismael made answer that since it was God's pleasure it should be so his will be done. 'Only let me entreat thee father to grant me three things: the first is that thou have a care to bind me so fast that the pains of death may not engage me to attempt anything against thee. The second is that thou whet the knife well and after thou hast thrust into my throat that thou hold it very fast and shut thy eyes out of fear lest the cruelty of the action should dishearten thee from going through with it, and so leave me to languish a long time. And the third that when thou returnest home, thou remember my duty to my mother.'

Abraham, having promised to observe all those things, and whetted his knife, binds his son, directs his knife to his throat, and shutting his eyes holds it as fast as he could. But finding when he opened his eyes again that the knife had made no entrance, he is extremely troubled and tries the edge of it against a stone, which he cuts in two. He was so astonished thereat that he addressed himself to the knife, **<77>** and asking it why having so good an edge as to cut a stone it could not as well cut his son's throat, the knife made answer that God would have it so. Whereupon the angel Gabriel took Abraham by the hand and said to him: 'Hold a little. God would only make trial of thy faith. Unbind thy son and sacrifice this he-goat.' And immediately, there came into the place a he-goat which Abraham offered to God for a burnt offering. The three stones which Hagar, Abraham, and Ismael threw at the devil are yet to be seen near the highway betwixt Arafat and Mecca, and these two great heaps of stones there have been made partly by our Muslemitical ancestors, partly by the deluded of the first. Of each of them brought three stones to be cast at the devil at the same place where these heaps are, to the end he may not distract them at their devotions at the Caaba or mount Arafat."

"I know," added Ali, "that the Jews and the pretended followers of Isa do say that it was not Ismael but Isaac that was to be sacrificed. But this is one of the corruptions of their Coran, for the intendments of God were greater towards Ismael than Isaac. Therefore, Sarah was made to be barren till our father was born. This Sarah foresaw and therefore hated him. This Abraham understood and therefore took such care (as also did the Angel Gabriel) of him. In Ismael was circumcision first celebrated.[41] It was concerning Ismael that the promise was made to Hagar: 'I will multiply thy seed exceedingly; it shall not be numbered for multitudes.'[42] The generation of Hagar was greater than the generation of Sarah: it shall reign unto the east and to the west, and God shall let them to rule over all the nations of the earth.[43] Behold renowned Hagarenes your illustrious ancestors; view the country that you are possessed of: the three Arabia and the rich appanage in Mesopotamia and Syria, and compare them with the narrow and barren land of promise designed for the promise of Sarah. Inquire how often they have been totally conquered and carried away captive into foreign countries and their temple destroyed whilst you retain the ancient habitations. Nor can any monarch boast of an entire conquest by the most valiant **<78>** Hagarenes. Your Caaba hath been profaned with idols but never destroyed, nor totally alienated from the worship of the great God."

These discourses raised in the Hagarenes not only a great attention but in one instant seemed to have gained them to the party of the prophet. They heard with a great deal of pleasure the glories of their extraction, the share that their progenitors had in the love of the great God that so high promises were made to their tribes and that was so mindful of the deserts of Arabia as to design it to be the seat of the most potent and renowned empire in the world. These fellows that understood no other delicacies than sour milk and parched peas or beans, no better array than what the hair of their goats or camels, and that coarsely spun and coarse woven did yield them no other beds or pallets than the ground, no other riches almost than a few camels, a lean horse or two, a bow and arrows, no other deity than a few mistaken stones which at a pilgrimage to the Caaba they or their ignorant ancestors had brought home and devoutly worshipped; or if any had been more illuminated, their religion mounted no further than to make some ill-favored cringes to the moon and mumble an orison to the Morning Star, crying: "*Allah, Allah, Howa Cabar.*"[44] For this was their old form of prayer or doxology, which Mahomet most subtly turned into *Cobar.*

These fellows, I say, now began to imagine themselves the darlings of heaven, the heirs of paradise, and monarchs of the universe. And since they now comprehended the true original of the present religion and what it was whence they had degenerated, they resolved to be as good Muslemin as their father Ismael, and to own that worship (especially it being more facile and easy than their idolatry and present superstition) which all the prophets had preached and adhered unto. It is one of the most difficult parts of a prince to adjust employments unto **<79>** their ministers and to make choice of suitable instruments for carrying on each affair.

The youth, the spirit, the fire of Ali did not a little contribute to the happy success of his negotiation. His success was the less suspected because he was not arrived at the years of dissimulation. His good mien, his prudence, and other virtues made the greater impression upon them because they were set off by an age in which they were extraordinary. His courtesy was able to compel his enemies to quell their passion and rendered his friends his slaves; his eloquence and his reason, which he could form according to the persons he dealt with, and he was of opinion that true eloquence and solid reason were but relative names and did not depend upon select words, numerous periods, apt cadence or arguments concluding in modes and figures, but in being operative and efficacious upon the persons he was to deal with; that there were times when the greatest artifices was to abandon all art, the greatest prudence to neglect its severe rules and where a wise . . . might have drawn the greatest advantages from untruths and fables without endamaging his reputation.[45]

Such, I say, was his eloquence and reason that he seemed to have charmed their senses and possessed himself of all the affections of their souls. He prepared their courages as he pleased, infused boldness into the most fearful ambition, into spirits incapable of it, and which even then did not apprehend what they were instigated by, and persuaded the most impetuous and undisciplined to such a moderation and regularity of military discipline as might be subservient to their great ends. The example of his small and well-trained retinue did conduce not a little to this last point, and if the prophet had only commanded it from God and not introduced the practice of it in his domestics, the Coran would have been ineffectual and the design become abortive.

The Hagarenes were all eyes and all ears and their souls distracted between what they saw and what they heard. But the approach of noon gave Ali and his companions **<80>** occasion to withdraw from their presence to prayer and so they had the greater liberty to recollect themselves. Dinner being brought in, which was served with more plenty and neatness than is usual amongst the Arabians, the illustrious pilgrim and his associates declined to taste of anything that appeared to be more delicate than ordinary, and the viands which were there added nothing to the entertainment of the Muslemin but as they testified their welcome and the kindness of their friends. They said that it was the command of their prophet that the Muslemin should not indulge themselves in such sensual pleasures in this life, that God had reserved them for the divertisements of paradise and the future world, that here our bodies are frail, our senses easily glutted so that such momentary delights were not worth our serious thoughts and regards, that they did but effeminate and intenerate the body and beset the soul, that courage and luxury were inconsistent, that since the great God did by the prophet call forth the Muslemin to extirpate idolatry and propagate Ismaelisme or Islamism by arms, they ought to prepare themselves for that holy but laborious militia, and that nothing did more conduce thereto than that a man should live at home as he did abroad, in the town as in the field, in the court as in the camp, that this was most healthy and withal would preserve their minds (which sympathized with their bodies) in an equality of temper and uniformity of disposition, and would render them more firm in their religion, fixed in their friendships, equal in their humors and tractable in their passions; that luxury was the seminary of all mischief, that even the first approaches thereto were dangerous, that if a man once indulged himself therein, the evil would become remediless, that our desires are apt to grow boundless when they transcend the limits of what is absolutely necessary, that inordinate desires were a perpetual torment never satisfied but always spurring **<81>** men onto new projects, that content was the greatest felicity which was only attained by extinguishing our desires, and a Musulman was happy enough if he did not want.[46]

The Hagarenes astonished at their parsimony and abstinence, inviting them to drink some Persian wine, adding that persons who fed so would stand in need of some refreshment by a draught thereof, which would recruit their strength and renew their vigor impaired by a laborious discipline and slender diet. But Ali declined their offer saying that their prophet had severely interdicted the Muslemin to taste any wine, that there was more pleasure in obeying the commandments of God than in the flavor of that generous liquor; that he who made man best understood his fabric and would not prohibit him anything without which he could not subsist; that Adam, Seth, Edris, lived to the greatest age without it; that it was but in imagination of our weakness which put us upon the pursuit of such cordials the sense whereof is only in opinion. It was true that the God of wine, Bacchus, was worshipped in Arabia and that foreigners held he was fostered there, but this was a corruption of the true Ismaelism:[47] that both the idol and the liquor entitled to him were now to be banished and the Arabians to know that *Baccha* signified no more than great and renowned, and however depraved now, was only a religious exclamation in praise of the great God; that whatever pleasure there was in wine, those sensual pleasures are inconsiderate in this life and therefore God had reserved the entire satisfaction of our senses till we come to paradise where all such delights will have their perfect relish and gusto, our immortal bodies being qualified with senses never to be dulled with satiety.

Hereupon he related the dialogue in the Alcoran between Mahomet and Abdias, a Jew. Abdias demanded of him what use there would be of wine in paradise.[48] The prophet answered: "Your question is so subtle, that I must return a double answer to one interrogatory. I shall therefore satisfy why it may be drunk there and why not here. There were two angels, Azot and Marot, sent down from heaven by God into this world to instruct and govern mankind with this caution: that they should never judge unrighteously or **<82>** drink wine. This being known, many repaired to them for justice, which they impartially administered amongst others. Appeared before them a very beautiful woman to complain against her husband. To incline them to favor her case, she invited them to dinner and treated them magnificently, charging her servants to ply them with wine to the drinking whereof she also frequently urged them. In short, they were made exceeding drunk and their feeling those impressions from her beauty which before they were not satisfied of, they importuned her to that compliance which the most amorous sigh after. She promised to consent provided that one of them should acquaint her with the way whereby they came down from heaven and the other with the passage up thither. They did so and she having disengaged herself, mounted straightways to heaven which when God perceived and inferring Himself of the manner of her arrival, He turned her into the Morning Star that she might there shine with as great luster as ever she did on earth. The two angels, being called to an account, were commanded to choose whether they would suffer torments in this world or in the world to come. They elected the first and remain hung to this day in iron chains with their heads downwards in the abyss of *Babilli*. What say you now, Abdias? Is it not reasonable that wine should be prohibited here on earth and yet allowed hereafter?"[49]

The Hagarenes hereupon fell into admiration of the Coran and did not doubt but he who published such divine things must be the apostle of God and an intimate of heaven. They were convinced that it was not fitting for men on earth to drink wine since it had so evil effects upon those pure and angelical bodies. They then perceived the reason why their first progenitors paid a reverence to the Morning Star: that they did not worship the star as the idolaters did since but uttered an "*Allah Allah howa Cabar*" to the honor of God who had placed that bright star in the firmament to put them in mind of the inconveniencies of drinking wine on earth where our life is an errand to serve and glorify God (not pamper our selves). And, to acquaint them of the future pleasures of the celestial paradise, all the topics that rhetoric itself yields should not have persuaded them so powerfully as this single apologue.[50]

But the abstinence from wine being of such importance to the preserving of civil and military discipline, mutual friendship, obedience, dispatch, secrecy without which the Arabian **<83>** monarchy could not be achieved, Ali thought fit to enforce that point by a second relation: that their prophet, being invited by a friend to an entertainment at his house, chanced in his way thither to be detained at a nuptial where he admired to see the innocent cheerfulness and mirth of each guest, how friendly they embraced and kissed each other and rendered mutual testimonies of unfeigned love.[51] And, inquiring of the master of the house what it was that created in them so debonair and complacent a humor, he was told that this was the usual effect of wine and that they had drunk some, whereupon he pronounced a blessing upon that liquor which did produce so amicable a disposition in the breasts of mortals.[52] The prophet departed thereupon, and as he returned the next day called there again, but he found things in another condition than he left them. Here lay a scattered leg, and there lay an arm cut off in one place: he saw a cripple lie in the other, some bereaved of one or both eyes. Hereupon he demanded whence that passion and mutual animosity betwixt friends, what occasioned the fray. The landlord told him that this was the usual consequence of drinking wine: that after they had drunk hard, they became mad and, from misunderstanding one another, proceeded to blows and so had killed some and maimed others. Upon this, Mahomet changed his benediction into a curse and prohibited his followers that they should never drink wine here.

Ali put a period to those kinds of discourses. And dinner being concluded, now that he found the Hagarenes sufficiently at the devotion of Mahomet, he determined to accomplish the utmost ends of his negotiation by an additional harangue to their purpose.

"Valiant Sons of Hagar and Ismael: If I thought I needed to speak any more to you, either to convince you of the truth of the religion our prophet teacheth, of the divine authority of the Coran each line whereof is a durable miracle and will always appear to be so as long as the language of Ismael doth continue upon earth, since no human wit or learning can produce anything equal to the least *surat* or chapter thereof. If this were necessary, I would insist upon further arguments and add new motives to persuade you to Islamism, the sum whereof is avowed to be this by **<84>** the testimony of the angel Gabriel himself: that a man confess there is no god besides the great God, and that Mahomet is the apostle of God, that a man observe strictly the five times of prayer daily, that he give alms, that he fast during the month of Ramadan, and that, if he can possibly, he make a religious pilgrimage unto Mecca and the Caaba.[53]

I proceed to another point which makes as much for all your interest as it doth for the glory of God: that life, which heaven hath given you and which God may at any moment deprive you of, he is pleased to give an occasion particularly now to serve Him. And if you lose that upon this occasion, which a fever, a fall, the least casualty might otherwise bereave you of, the supreme joys of paradise are ascertained unto you. It is the divine pleasure that idolatry should be destroyed out of the earth and the progeny of Ismael are these whom God designs this high favor for, to compel all men to the true worship. But such is the divine goodness that besides the future rewards allotted for Muslemin, he hath annexed to this difficult and laborious employment empire and glory on earth! It is hereby that the promise concerning Ismael must take place, and it is by this means that the valiant Hagarenes must give laws to the utmost ends of the earth and extend the dominions as far as there is any habitable region.

The work is happily begun. The great God hath sent you a prophet to conduct you such as the sun never beheld. Edris, Noah, Abraham, Ismael, Moses, Isa had these characters imprinted on them that we reverence their memories and esteem each of them truly great. But none ever equaled Mahomet the last and chiefest apostle of God, nor was there enjoined to the world this double testimony viz. that God is the great God, and Mahomet the apostle of God.[54] No Coran ever equaled his for subject or eloquence, and, to make way for him, you see that the Coran of Musay or Moses and the Coran of Isa are perished or so corrupted by the wickedness or negligence of their followers that there is no affiance to be placed therein. It is by a belief herein that Muslemin shall obtain the highest glory in heaven and on earth. No monarchy was ever parallel to what God by His prophet doth summon you.

If you behold the condition of the Greek monarchy and Christendom, all things **<85>** will appear facile unto you. The subjects are so exasperated by oppression, so debauched in their manners, so indifferent in their religion, and after so many quick revelations by the death of the Emperors Mauritius and Phocas and the usurpation of Heraclius, so unconcerned for their prince who governs them, that you need no more than attempt their conquest to effect. There is no unity in their councils, no duty, no obedience in the soldiery so defrauded of their pay during the reigns of Mauritius and Phocas. There is no conduct or prudence in their generals or commanders, no union in their church. You shall no sooner advance your standard but the Arians will become your friends. Nay Muslemin, the numerous Jacobites (and the historians will enlarge their divisions) and rather live peaceably under your protection than anathematized, scorned, hated, persecuted, and depressed under the Melkites.[55]

It is natural for mankind to endure more patiently and willingly the rule of a foreigner and of one differing in profession from them than to be tyrannized over and trampled upon by one of their fellows of the same religion and of no better extraction than themselves. And those potent sects will bear with some content a yoke under which the domineering Melkites shall groan.

They are not unacquainted with the Arabian force. Your armies have lately carried terror over all Syria, Palestine, and Egypt: this a parcel of you heretofore did under Queen Maria in the reign of Queen Mavia, in the reign of Gratian and Valence.[56] You vanquished their armies and enforced them to sue for peace by their solemn embassy to you in the time of the Emperor Justinus who preceded Justinian.[57] King Almonder made the like conquest and enforced the emperor to send an embassy to him for peace.[58] And, lately, did not a party of the Saracens under Chosroes, in the time of Phocas and Heraclius, overrun Egypt and added to the victories of the Persian King? I must tell you, renowned Hagarenes, though others know your puissance, you never understood it yourselves. You have always been the stipendaries and appendage to the Roman and Persian Empires; you have fought to make them great, not yourselves; you have, as it were, been subjects to the one sometimes, to the other sometimes. [59] We find that Arabia has been divided betwixt both, and Aretas hath fought in favor of **<86>** Justinian while Almondar hath fought against him, and Chosroes hath appointed princes to be one party and the Greek emperor to the other.[60]

And what have you acquired by all the victories you have gained and the services you have rendered? Lo the Greeks: have they continued unto any of you the usual pay? Are they not indebted unto you by long arrearages, and what answer have they made to your just demands? And is it not that they have no money to spare for Hagarene dogs? Certainly you deserved a more civil and obliging a return, and you need not that heaven should excite you by a prophet to revenge this indignity, make them to feel your power once more, convince them how necessary your friendship is to them by letting them see you can be their masters? Bostra or Vostra gave birth and original to Marcus Julius Philippus, and an Arabian swayed over the Roman Empire but deprived him of the empire.[61] To effect this, let us not live divided under more petty princes than we have tribes; let us all unite into one monarchy as we are all of one language and one parentage. We are all Hagarenes, all Ismaelites. The same Hegira will suit with all, the same crescents is our common standard. It is a pitiful thing to see into what necessity the petty princes are reduced to maintain themselves and to how many real evils they are exposed to, to conserve that vain image of liberty and that sweet delusion of sovereign authority that doth bewitch them. In expenses they consume themselves for their defense and almost give all that may be taken from them. That nothing may be taken from them, they are obliged to observe all the fancies and notions of the enemies and friends, and if they subsist it is not by their strength, for they have none but by their weakness. And because their countries are of so little concernment that they beget not a desire in ambitious persons, or their justice should be violated in the conquest of them, or they are under shelter from the enterprises of the one by the jealousy of the other, and conserve their liberty by this only reason. Let the ambitious hinder one another to seize upon them and to become their **<87>** masters.

Consider with yourselves how often your divisions and subdivisions have made you a prey to the invading Persian or Roman. Have you not seen the Roman armies and been almost reduced to desolation under Trojan, Severus, and others? Has there ever been a war betwixt these two potent empires under which Arabia has not been harassed and the blood of Ishmaelites shed on one or both sides? Think of the calamities you have endured and examine from whence they have sprung; inquire what renown Arabia was arrived unto under Odenatus and Zenobia, but that some of you were inveigled and brought of to combat the others.[62] They confess it: they confess they owe more unto your petty princes that could be mercenary than to their forces which you singly baffled. Independency is an empty name if poverty, weakness, and contempt are the consequences of it, and a commodious subjection is to be preferred before a shadow of sovereignty and a precarious insignificant power. The liberty is greater, the repute greater, the riches greater, and all are more secure if a small principality become the accessional of a puissant monarchy than if it subsist of itself.

I speak not this that our prophet demands or that God enjoins that you should lay down your power at the feet and submit it to the disposal of Mahomet. No, he is designed our prophet, not our emperor, and brings us no laws but what are to guide us to heaven or which God enjoins to be observed here when a nearer view shall have convinced your eyes. As fame no doubt hath filled your ears that he is altogether averse to the concerns of this world, that he is so far from depriving any Ishmaelite of his liberty, that he would set even a bird free if he saw him encaged and so remote from ambition and avarice that the greatest pleasure he takes in having anything is that he may give it away to some more indigent Muslemin. You will then lay aside all suspicions should the Coreischites of Mecca instill any into you now.

No, no, it is unity amongst the Ishmaelites; it is Islamism amongst all that our prophet is sent to promote. Learn but from him to worship one God, to reverence and pray towards one Caaba, to advance one pure religion and leading your forces. And whilst you yourselves dispose for the happy success of affairs, we pilgrims beg the honor of a precedency **<88>** in the most laborious, perilous, and troublesome."

This speech being ended, Ali found the Hagarenes wholly bent to adhere to Mahomet and resolute to adventure their lives for the propagation and defense of the religion of Islamism. Nothing was to be heard but the *Allah Ekbar* or exclamation of God the God and Mahomet His apostle.

He left two of his companions to instruct them in the *sallah* or prayers and otherwise to form them into a convenient discipline that they might be ready upon any urgency, it being the determination of the prophet not to draw any greater forces together as yet, partly because the country about Medina was so very barren that even the Scenites or most wild and hardy Arabians could not be accommodated thereabouts. So excessive were the heats, so scorching the sands, so sterile the soil, and so great the scarcity of fresh and wholesome water, partly also because that his were Muslemin being as yet novices in their religion might be drawn into faction and mutiny or otherwise relinquish him. And it was prudential for him not to embody others than such as were firm to him than to be deserted by any that had been his follower. He knew the nature of the Arabians: how prone they were to listen to novelties, and how obstinate to maintain even with their lives whatsoever they were prepossessed with. Nor did he doubt by his emissaries to inveigle as many as should most resolutely support him against any that should come to attack him there. And it was not his intention to take Mecca by force, but by surrender, since he could not choose but profane or violate the respect which he had for the sacred Caaba by assaulting and storming the city.

Ali now prepares to depart from Agra and on the morrow hastens to Saraka which was the chief city of the Saracens. I find St. Jerome and

Sozomen and many of the ancients to have believed that the Saracens were denominated from Sarah the wife of Abraham and that they took that name to conceal their descent from the handmaid Hagar.[63] But this is so ridiculous a conceit that Scaliger, Fuller, Hottinger, Pococke, and all the intelligent moderns laugh at it.[64] Nor did the Saracens ever claim kindred with Sarah or renounce Ismael and Hagar, but vowed that the majesty and greatness of Hagar was to transcend that of Sarah. **<89>** I could willingly assent to Fuller (that since Saracens, usually in writers, is taken for all the Scenites and inhabitants of Arabia the Desert) that they were so called from *sarak,* which in the Syriac tongue signifies empty and barren, their country being such. But since Hottinger thinks it strange that the Arabians should give themselves a Syriac name and not Arabic, I shall decline that.[65]

But withal, I can as little think they would admit of a name from the Arabic *sarak*, to *shark*, to steal privately, which yet is the opinion of Scaliger, Hottinger, and Valesius, though Dr. Pococke dislike it (since they were public robbers, not private). He thinks therefore they were called Saracens from *sharkion* which signifies the East because they lived eastward of Judæa, which reason had been better if the name had been of Jewish extraction. But in that or the Syriac language it signifies no such thing, nor could the Saracens call themselves so, there being others more easterly than they; nor could they do it in reference to the western Arabians—they being thus termed in history before any Arabians were settled in the western world contradistinct from them. I believe they were one province only of Arabia which was called Saraka and lies beyond the Nabatheans or Arabia Petræ, the inhabitants of which are called Saracens. Ptolemy calls the country Σαρακηνοί. I am persuaded of the truth hereof because the geographers, in distinguishing the Arabians, denominate them from their particular region as the *Cedrei, Agareni, Saraceni,* et cetera.

And therefore I suppose Ali to have gone to the city (I have authors who style it so) of Saraka, and that in his journey and reception there happened nothing that need relation after what I have said of the Hagarenes, the Saracens being no less prepossessed by emissaries with the fame of Mahomet and his apostleship than those of Agra, and their customs and manners being the same. The most remarkable accident in the journey, and which contributed much to the veneration of Ali, was that toward the dawning of the day when the morning *sallah* or prayer was to be said by the Muslemin, and they had begun their devotions, an unexpected fire consumed the cabin wherein two of the followers of Ali were lodged. The one of them chose rather to be burnt than to preserve his life by discontinuing his prayers, upon which he was so intent that neither the sight of the fire nor the noise and concourse of people, nor the importunities of such as called to and plucked him could any way divert his thoughts or make him express any sign **<90>** that he heard or regarded them. The other escaped by a timely flight.

The news hereof coming to Ali, he immediately pronounced with extraordinary zeal the *Allah Ekber* or Mahometan exclamation: "God, God, the great God."[66] And, calling for the Musulman who had escaped, he told him that the man was happy who trusted in God; that the world was not constant or perpetual to anyone, but that our wisdom and felicity here consisted in resigning ourselves to the will of God and devoting our hearts entirely to him; that to serve God was our duty as his creatures and subjects to whom it was enjoined, our glory as Musulman and the way to eternal happiness. He declared the deceased to be a martyr and prayed that God's peace might be upon him, and his memory glorious who had expressed so great a devotion to God and so great a contempt of life that he would not interrupt his prayer to save himself: that prayer was the pillar of religion and key of paradise; that nothing ought to detain or divert a Musulman from his devotion;[67] that he who could at such times think upon or mind anything else did not entirely resign his thoughts to the worship of God and did not merit the name of Musulman or true believer; that the value of life and of this world was inconsistent with a true faith concerning the felicity of the future; that this world was no other than a dead carcass or carrion; and they were dogs which pursued it.[68]

This said, he commanded that he who had escaped should be severely bastinadoed, which chastisement he endured with a great deal of fortitude and cheerfulness, kissing afterwards the hands of him that chastised him and making him a present thereupon. The Saracens were astonished at this affair and to understand the patience with which the Muslemin underwent their punishments, though they received one hundred stripes and these so cruel that several pounds of flesh were to be cut afterwards from the bruised parts to effect their recovery;[69] that they hold the first batons (such as were used to these purposes) to have been sent from heaven and that all of them were sacred, and those which were bruised or touched with that instrument of justice were exempt from torments after death; and that the party punished ought to kiss the hands of the lector **<91>** and give him thanks and a present for every blow given.[70]

The impressions which this spectacle made in the Saracens are not easily conjectured. Ali, who understood to derive advantages from any emergency without seeming to do so, omitted nothing that might engage that valiant nation to the service of the prophet. He instructed them in Islamism, made use of all those arguments which had prevailed on the Hagarenes: whatever might work upon their passion or reason, he urged unto them and drew motives as well from honor and interest as from piety. He desired they would do more for the great God than they had done in the behalf of the associate gods and show themselves as valiant under the apostle of God as under Odenatus and Zenobia, Almondar or Alhareth, Justinian, Heraclius, or Chosroes; that the Arabians were the same they always were, but that Persia and Christendom were so degenerated that they needed not to apprehend any difficulties in the conquest of either.

CHAPTER 6

THE RETURN OF ALI AND THE WARS OF MAHOMET

E SET ALL THINGS in such order here as he had done at Agra and retired back to Medina with a numerous retinue of volunteers who came of their own accord to attend and guard the prophet. They disciplined themselves there every day, and what time could be spared from their *sallah* and their military exercises was employed in working upon some trade, the prophet teaching them that that food was most pleasant, nourishing, and blessed which every man gained by his particular industry and labor and that God delighted in those alms to be given which a man had gained himself. Mahomet received Ali with as much honor as became the gravity of the Apostle of God, and Ali prostrated himself before him with such reverence that he seemed really to believe what he usually professed—that the shadow of the prophet was as the shadow of God.

At the same time, there arrived news from the kingdom of the Abyssines, how Giafar, the son of Abutaleb and brother of Ali, had converted the Aluajash or Negush, called Aitshama, emperor of that kingdom, together with his subjects to Islamism. This Giafar, with other adherents of Mahomet at Mecca being **<92>** persecuted by the Coreischites, desires Mahomet's permission to retire, which obtained, he withdrew into Ethiopia for protection. This Hegira or flight was some time before the pilgrimage of Mahomet to Medina.[1] Now Giafar, residing in the court of Aitshama, did instruct him in the rise and doctrine of Mahomet. The Abyssines had always used circumcision not upon any religious but civil account and are said to have been converted to Christianity by Queen Candace's eunuch,[2] and that Matthew and some others of the apostles preached there.[3] Undoubtedly they were at first of the number of the Judaizing Christians and afterwards, as did the Arabians, they turned Jacobites.[4] This affinity in religion, in circumcision, and in rejecting the

Melkites (not to mention that the Abyssines had not long before reigned in Yemen for seventy years or more),[5] and the general ignorance of the Christians whereby they did not understand the notions they had of the Trinity, did facilitate the conversion of the Negush who was soon convinced that it was impossible there should be three persons in the deity and that God should have a son. And hearing that Mahomet did not only style Isa prophet, but superlatively honored him as the word and spirit of God, he embraced Islamism.

Upon this intelligence, Mahomet commands Ibn Omar to prepare for an embassy to Ethiopia in the sixth year of the Hegira. The retinue had much of splendor and Ibn Omar carried a letter from the prophet which began thus: "In the Name of God, merciful and gracious, from Mahomet the Apostle of God to Negush Aitshama, King of the Abyssines, et cetera."[6] His reception there was no less solemn than magnificent. Aitshama descends from his throne to receive the letter. He laid it presently on his eyes, and sitting on the ground, read the contents and returned a submissive answer which began with the *bismillah* or form with which the strict Mahometans usually begin their discourses and letters and is the proem of every chapter in the Alcoran, viz: "In the Name of God, merciful and gracious. To the Apostle of God of glorious memory, from Aluajash Aitshama Ben Ahahar. **<93>** Health, O Apostle of God, who are sent of God, et cetera."

This letter was carried by Giafar Aritha, the son of the Negush, and sixty of the princes of Abyssinia, who accompanied Giafar Ibn Omar and Aritha. The arrival of the Abyssines at Medina was attended with all the solemnity and splendor which became the prophet. There were in Medina several Christians. Mahomet commanded them, their presbyters and monks, to be present at the reception, and, after the first ceremonies were past, the prophet, having caused the people to be ranked with their faces towards Mecca and the Caaba, he commanded Giafar to read to them somewhat out of the Alcoran. He fixed upon the *surat* of Mary (or Isa), and when they heard it they wept and publicly declared themselves Muslemin.[7]

It is easy to apprehend what effects this embassy had upon all Arabia. Those of Yemen could not but call to mind their late subjection to the Abyssines and feared again a second conquest; those of Mecca were terribly affrighted and suspected the Islamism of Abyssines as a trick of state and rather feigned than real. They remembered the attempt which

Abrahah Alashram had made upon the Caaba, which before related, which happened in the forty-second year of Chosroes or Anusherwan at which time Mahomet was born, and from which the Arabians made a new epoch, and to which there is a *surat* in the Alcoran relating. The adherents and confederates for Mahomet were very much strengthened hereupon and more assured in the truth and success of his apostleship.

It became the Coreischites now to look to themselves and to prosecute him by a vigorous war. Mahomet, to amuse them the more and the better to discipline his few followers, had not embodied any such numbers nor made such show as might terrify the rest of the Arabians, the petty princes whereof might be thereby induced to hasten into a close league and confederacy to his destruction. In the end of the first year in which he came to Medina, he sent out his uncle Hamza (with white flag hallowed by himself), accompanied with thirty men. But this small troop produced no change anywhere, nor attempted anything memorable by reason of their small force, or that Mahomet would make no show of invading others till he was in a condition to defend himself.[8]

SECOND YEAR OF THE HEGIRA[9]

In **<94>** the second year, his parties being better formed and more numerous, he resolved to distress Mecca and thereby render the people mutinous against their leaders. He sent out of Medina 319 to intercept a rich caravan belonging chiefly to the Coreischites and was going into Syria under the conduct of Abusofian and other principal captains of the Coreischites, guarded with 900 or 1,000 soldiers.[10] Abusofian, the son of Hareth, finding himself in danger to be attacked, and knowing the discipline and valor of the Muslemin and the difficulty of protecting a large caravan and at the same time fight the enemy, designed to retreat. But in Beder, or Bader, the Mahometans reduced him to a necessity of fighting.[11] Neither the number, valor, nor policy of the Coreischites could resist the fortune and prowess of the Muslemin. Seventy of the stoutest and bravest of the Coreischites fell that day, most of them commanders and as many more were taken prisoners, with the loss only of fourteen Muslemin who were declared martyrs. The fame of the victory and the spoil added much to the renown of the prophet. All of the riches were brought into the public treasury for the general benefit. For Mahomet had so principled his followers that they regarded nothing beyond a mere subsistence and the propagation of Islamism.

Mahomet was resolved to take Mecca and the Caaba by surrender and therefore would no further prosecute his victories. Besides, he did not think it prudence to grasp at more than he could securely manage. He knew that young converts are not so fixed to their profession and party, but easily become factious and mutinous or revolt again, and that a nearer approach to Mecca might render the Coreischites desperate and so alarm their neighbors that they might join in their defense. He knew that in the territories he had already acquired, as also in Yemen and the neighboring provinces of Persia, were a multitude of Jews who were not so obliged by the protection given them but that they would upon any opportunity advance the interest of their own nation and endeavor to resettle themselves in their old monarchy at Jerusalem as they had lately attempted under Chosroes and formerly upon diverse occasions. Nor was he ignorant that the Jews did hate him for magnifying Isa and advancing him (above Moses) to the dignity of a prophet whom they had put to death as a seditious person and esteemed the son of a whore. Whereupon he resolved to secure them before they should make any head and, by subduing them, increase the number of his victories, it being certain that the Coreischites would be glad to see him **<95>** otherwise employed than in distressing them and would wait the issue of these new troubles.

I know not what open cause of jealousy the Jews gave to the prophet. But he dispatched Abubacr to them to demand that they should embrace Islamism, repeat the *sallah* or Mahometan prayers, pay the tenth of their estates, and lend to God a considerable sum of money. No man was so fit for this employment as Abubacr, for, besides his great courage, he was exceeding passionate. No Jew could be a greater bigot in his way than Abubacr was in Islamism. They could not believe so little concerning Mahomet, but on the contrary he believed as much. He believed all that Mahomet said and all that was said of him. When the prophet reported that he had been carried in one night from Mecca to Jerusalem, the Coreischites laughed at it as a bold figment and imposture and asked Abubacr if he believed it. He readily answered that he did not only give credit to that but would believe and justify matters more incredible than these. He came to the Jews and pressed them to receive the commands of the prophet, urging them with the miracles of Mahomet, that being the most prevalent argument with that nation. But they were not moved thereby. How confidently so ever he reported them, they said they expected a Messiah of their own, the son of David, whose dominion should extend far and near, and, as to the lending any sum of money to God, Phinhas the son of Azura demanded if their God were so poor that he needed to take up money at interest.[12]

The insolence of this question did so enrage Abubacr that he gave him a box on the ear protesting with all that he would have slain him but that the prophet had given them a cartel of security. He departed and acquainted Mahomet with their refusal, but mentioned not the words of Phinhas, protesting he durst not repeat their blasphemies. Mahomet was not displeased with the ill success of the negotiation, but presently curses the Jews in a particular *surat*, declares that they are enemies to the Muslemin and aim at a distinct monarchy of their own, that they had always persecuted the prophets of their own nation, and were so arrogant as to imagine that God could not raise a prophet but from among them.

THIRD YEAR[13]

In the third year therefore, he sets out against them, and in fifteen days destroys their castles, plunders them of their riches, and reduceth them to his mercy, killing Caabas the son of Alaszasi who was his most bitter enemy.[14] It was well for him that he distressed the Jews in so short a time. For the Coreischites, thinking to find him so busied against the Jews that he would not be able to defend **<96>** Medina against their powerful forces, sent Abusofian with three thousand foot and two hundred horse and three thousand camels (the milk whereof was their victuals) to attack the town. Mahomet draws forth his army to fight them. A bloody battle ensued thereupon in which the Muslemin were at first victors, but were at last overcome with the loss of Hamza, Mahomet's uncle, and seventy others of their party. Mahomet acted all the parts of a good commander and a valiant soldier and, since he despaired of conquest, determined to make good his retreat to Medina, the neighborhood whereof preserved from any great damage that day. The Coreischites, discovering him rallying his men and bravely fighting in the rear of his flying forces, bent all their power to destroy him, and Ochas, the son of Abumugid, wounded him in the lip with a javelin and shook out some of his fore teeth.[15] Abdalla, the son of Sidhab, hurt him in the forehead. He was also wounded in the jaws. Notwithstanding all which, he escaped safe into Medina, and Abusofian, being distressed for want of water and necessaries, was obliged to withdraw his army to Mecca.[16]

A man of less courage than Mahomet would hardly have subsisted after the ignominy of this discomfiture. But the prophet was undaunted, and casting the blame upon the Jews who had so unhappily diverted the Muslemin to flesh his vanquished troops with their slaughter, he fell upon the sons of Nadir, a tribe of Judaizing Arabians, routs them and pursues them into Syria, showing the country far and near his victorious troops when they thought him in a manner ruined. This happened in the fourth year of his stay at Medina.

All Arabia was alarmed at this last success, and the Jews and several other nations combined with the Coreischites against Mahomet and drew out ten thousand choice men to fight him. The prophet musters what forces he could from Medina, Agra, and Sarak, and determines not to be enclosed in any town, nor engage too near Medina lest the vicinity of a refuge might take of the courage of his soldiers. He marches forward to encounter them, but finding a consternation in his army, he declined the engagement and put in practice a stratagem which was new in Arabia. He caused his men to encamp and drew a strong line of circumvallation betwixt the Coreischites and the Jews, and gaining over one Naimus of the tribe of Gatfan, a potent man in the army of his enemies. By his means, those of Mecca and the Jews so quarreled that they broke up their army and departed without doing anything.[17] Six of the Muslemin were slain in this expedition, and three of the infidels, two of which were **<97>** slain by Ali in duel in the view of both camps, to the great encouragement of the Mahometans and terror of their enemies, one of them being a very valiant captain and as it were the soul of their army.

Great was the renown of Mahomet, who had, without any loss or hazard, caused so powerful an army thus to dislodge and dissolve. He pursued a brigade of them, besieged them five and twenty days, reduces them, cuts off the heads of 670 of the men, and distributes the women and children among the Muslemin for slaves. This happened in the fifth year of his stay at Medina.

SIXTH YEAR[18]

In his sixth year he resolved to carry the war into the country of the Coreischites, gains several considerable victories as he goes, and marches to Hadibia, a place near Mecca.[19] The Muslemin had their courages inflamed by this succession of victories and by the sight of the Caaba. The inhabitants of Mecca were disconsolate to see the danger so near them, and that so many expeditions against Mahomet had proved fruitless, and, being divided and distracted among themselves, knew not what to do. But the generous prophet, continuing in his resolution of taking Mecca rather by surrender than fight, comes to a treaty with the Coreischites which ended in a cessation of hostility for ten years to come. One cause of this truce was that if Mahomet or any of his followers had a pious intention to visit the Caaba, they might come without arms and perform their devotions.[20]

Hereby the prophet gained many advantages. The inhabitants of Mecca were convinced of his strength and of his generosity to them and devotion to the Caaba. He had the opportunity of sending in emissaries under pretence of devotion and the glory of having faced and brought to composition the capital city of Arabia. His army hereupon inaugurates him solemnly of their own accord (without any solicitation of his) to be their *xeriff* or prince.

He retires from Hadibia and marches against several little territories that had been in arms against him who, being excluded the cessation and deserted by the Coreischites, were easily subdued and forced to pay him an annual tribute of half their dates and to hold their lands at the pleasure of the conqueror. His armies now seemed invincible throughout Arabia, and the Jews, as well as others, were subjected upon the same terms. In this expedition Ali signalized himself at the battle of Chaibar where he seized on the gates of the town and managed them on his arm like a target.[21] This was the event of the seventh year.

EIGHTH YEAR[22]

In the eighth the Coreischites, finding the prejudice of this truce and that whilst they stood neuters their allies were destroyed, renounced the cessation and drew upon them the forces of Mahomet. He marcheth thitherward by **<98>** easy journeys, and many of the great men, being no less sensible than the inhabitants of their weakness, turned, some really, and some out of fear, to Islamism. His uncle Abbas and Abusofian were of that number: the first withdrew out of the town to Mahomet, the other remained behind to render the prophet more important service by his stay. Mahomet entered Mecca without any opposition, having first proclaimed that all who retired to the house of Abusofian, all who shut their doors and offered no injury to the Muslemin, and all who fled for refuge to the Caaba should be secure. His entry seemed rather a procession to the Caaba than a triumph. Aljanabus tells us that upon his approach to the temple all the idols (even the great Hobal) did prostrate themselves unto him.[23]

In the Caaba he broke in pieces the wooden pigeon which was there and cast it away, Ali being busied (as were the rest) in demolishing those idols. And, not being able to reach one that stood aloft, the prophet suffered him to stand upon his shoulders till it was done.[24] The inhabitants immediately became Muslemin, but the rulers and chiefs who had been his enemies, and either scorned to believe him or despaired of mercy though they should do it, he put all to death, it being inconsistent with the absoluteness of the monarchy which he designed to permit a hereditary nobility. The people, thinking themselves happy in their own safety, did the less mourn for those which were slaughtered, and, whilst their minds were set upon a peaceable enjoyment of their own, they forgot revenge, nor did they think of remote consequences, and that whilst every one singly courted their prophet and emir, they did introduce an universal servitude.

Now we see Mahomet possessed of the metropolis of Arabia the Desert. Yet doth not all this power and series of prosperous attempts infuse into him new pride or outward grandeur: whatsoever fortune hath put into his hands doth only enable him to do more good, to bestow more alms and more to advance the glory of God. His Muslemin seem to be all animated with the same spirit, nor do the inhabitants of Mecca find themselves governed by an emperor and an army but by a prophet. It is not arbitrary power but the ostentation and abuse of it that makes it odious and tyrannical.

Whether it were the consummate wisdom of Mahomet that continued him in this equable temper, or the source of the mutability of human affairs in a man who had tried such vicissitudes, or whether the custom of dissembling was become natural to him, or that old **<99>**age had secured him from those sallies which indiscreet youth is subject to, I know not. But it was very advantageous for him that this prosperous revolution did make no change for the worse in his demeanor. For there happened an insurrection within a few months after the destruction of the idols in the Caaba, which reduced his new religion and government into jeopardy and would have dethroned any but the prophet. Those who would not stir in behalf of Mecca and the Coreischites: whether it be that vulgar heads will not believe things till they fall out or out jealousy that they should run into a certain inconvenience of being subject to the Coreischites to avoid the uncertain apprehensions of Mahomet.[25]

When they were ascertained that the idols were destroyed and the substance of the Arabian religion changed, some shadows and circumstances only remaining, the Thakifii and Hawazine Arabians take arms under one Melic, the son of Aufus. Their number was not formidable, being but four thousand in all, but they were Arabians and animated with zeal and revenge.[26] Mahomet was determined to act securely and not obscure the last actions of his life by rashness or want of foresight. He drew forth an army of twelve thousand men, whereof ten thousand were veterans and the rest captives of the Hawazines and people of Taiph, and prepared to encounter them in the valley of Horam.[27] Whether it were that fortune is seldom constant to her greatest darlings or that the Muslemin acted too securely presuming upon their numbers, tried valor, and discipline, so it happened that the idolaters totally routed them and pursued them to the gates of Mecca, where the gallant prophet, accompanied only by Abbas and Abusofian, made a stand and, leaning on his javelin, persuaded some of the Muslemin to rally and by the appearance of a new charge to put an end to the furious chase of the idolaters. The prophet must be owned to have showed the highest courage and prudence who could retain his judgment and valor amidst so universal a consternation, disorder, and flight.

The idolaters withdrew their forces, either not having strength enough to besiege the town (which is as big as Amsterdam),[28] or that few know how to improve advantages when they transcend expectation, or that an undisciplined army is not fit to prosecute a tedious siege, or that they were forced to it by the sterility of the country and want of water (whereof there is little good and potable thereabouts), Melic retreated and gave Mahomet respite to infuse fresh resolution into his dismayed troops.[29]

The angel **<100>** Gabriel presently brings him a *surat* that no enemy could be safely despised, nor any human strength presumed upon; that albeit infidelity and idolatry were things odious to God, yet pride and presumption were also abominable to Him; that the Muslemin were puffed up with a conceit of their own strength; and that God had defeated them now to convince them of the necessity of His aid and blessing in all designs; that, if they would abandon the opinion of their own worth and puissance, He would repair their loss by sending an invisible legion of angels who should fight in their behalf.[30]

This oracle gave new life and vigor to the Muslemin and made them more punctual in their obedience to their emir and prophet. He determines to fight Melic before the noise of this rout should run through Arabia, knowing that new conquests are always unsettled and that the minds of men, quickly reduced to obedience, are as soon lost and that since prosperity was the foundation of his apostleship, adversity would overthrow it. His success was such in the second engagement that with the loss only of four Musilmen and the slaughter of ninety infidels, he gained a complete victory and made himself master of all their riches: six thousand head of cattle, twenty-four thousand goats, forty thousand sheep and four thousand ounces of silver, and their wives and children taken prisoners. The infidels yielded themselves tributaries and vassals on condition to have their wives restored, and Melic rendered himself to the prophet and became a Musulman whereupon Mahomet restored to him all his possessions.[31]

NINTH YEAR[32]

In the ninth year of the Hegira he had no great difficulties to contest with: the remaining wars did rather exercise than endanger his forces. His followers became more fixed and endeared to him, and they who had embraced his religion out of fear persisted in it out of affection and conscience. They no longer resented the destruction of their idols, seeing that success attended on the followers of the great God. Many that had been his obstinate enemies became converts, and the princes of Dauma and Eila became his tributaries.[33] He disarmed those which he suspected, leaving his forces in excellent discipline under good and faithful commanders, and placed a confidant of his governor of Mecca. He went to visit his old friends and assistants at Medina.

In the tenth year of Hegira he received no tidings but such as confirmed the daily growth and progress of Islamism. He received continual **<101>** addresses and submissions from the new converts, and all Arabia seemed at his devotion. But that in Yemen there arose one Mosalleina who pretended to be his associate and partner in the apostleship and found many followers.[34] But the sage Mahomet despised this new imposture, either because he thought the same cheat was not to be acted twice with success in so short a time, or that he fancied the renown of his valor and conduct was enough to retain all men in his obedience, or that he despised the luxury and effeminacy of the inhabitants of Yemen and imagined that such who had much to lose would not hazard their estates nor endure the hardships of war for a new religion, or whether he did suppose that petty insurrections contribute to the establishment of an absolute sovereignty. It is certain he despised Mosalleina.

CHAPTER 7

MAHOMET'S LAST PILGRIMAGE, HIS DEATH, AND BURIAL

E DID NOT SUPPRESS this year nor the next, which was the last of his life, but to testify his veneration to the Caaba, to return thanks to God for his success, and to give an example to the Arabians in what manner they should continue their pilgrimages of devotion to Mecca. He, in the company of all those who had followed him to Medina, began the most illustrious procession that ever was in the world. As you might at any time have seen these conquerors of Arabia at work, mending or making their cloths, cultivating rice, picking of oats, or selling parched peas, so now you will see them marching a long pilgrimage with a train of seventy-two thousand persons, with a garb and postures that would better suit with madmen than those who were to give laws to the universe. But there are different ways of getting esteem, and, in a diversity of circumstances, some lose their empires, glory, and riches by the same courses wherewith others acquire them.

Medina was the place whence Mahomet determined to begin his pilgrimage, and the fame thereof soon gathered together seventy-two thousand persons (men and women) to complete the train of the apostle. They say that Noah, when he went into the ark, took along with him seventy-two persons, and, for that reason, it is requisite the pilgrims of Mecca should amount to the number of seventy-two thousand,[1] and that number ought to be so exactly observed that more must not be received as such that year, but that number must be complete. Otherwise (they say) the angels would be obliged to make up what were wanting, and it were want of respect to those spirits to put them to that trouble. When they set forth they are covered only with a shirt, nay, some go naked down**<102>** to the waist. They march continually and after a particular fashion, for they are obliged to go after the rate of a trotting horse or rather of a camel galloping, and that with such earnestness that they hardly take the leisure to eat, drink, or sleep, out of an imagination that the sweat forced out of their bodies by that violent motion carries away with it all their sins and cleans them of all impurity. The women who might not be able to bear the inconveniences of such a march have the privilege to swathe up their breasts with a scarf.

The illustrious pilgrims continued thus their procession from Medina till they arrived at Mount Arafat, which is half a day's journey from Mecca, by the foot whereof lies the ordinary road to that city. Here the prophet related to his followers the sacrifice of Ismael and Hagar, adding that they must divert out of the way, as was usual of old in those pilgrimages, and fulfill a commandment of Abraham's to cast several stones in a certain place at the devil, in imitation of their father, and to drive him away that he might not instill any wickedness into them or divert their thoughts from the pure worship of God during this sacred pilgrimage: that though they seemed only to cast the stones in Akabah (the name of the place),[2] yet indeed each stone did hit the devil and either wounded his face or broke his back; that not only Abraham, Hagar, and Ismael had found this way to avenge themselves on him, but also Adam in the Valley of Mine did pelt the devil with stones and put him to flight.

From hence, Mahomet conducted them up to Mount Arafat to view the place where Ismael was to have been sacrificed, and here they spent that night in a great devotion. At the foot of Mount Arafat, the people of Mecca had prepared a multitude of white rams: every one of the pilgrims bought one and carried up with him which there they slew (every one his own) in imitation and as a memorial of their fathers, Abraham and Ismael.[3] After each hath killed and dressed his oblation, they eat a little thereof and give the rest to the poor (which flock thither in great numbers to receive alms) without reserving so much as the skin, saying that neither did Abraham when he performed his sacrifice. Towards the dawning of the day, they come down and go to the city of Mecca,[4] where the high priest or chief imam of the Caaba makes procession conducting through the chief streets a camel which is appointed for sacrifice. The hair of the camel they account a very precious relic, which so that the pilgrims all throng as near as they can to the beast to snatch some **<103>** of his hair which they fasten to their arms. After the priest hath walked the camel sufficiently, he leads him to the market place where the *Daroga* or judge of the town, attended with other officers, kills him with an ax.[5] As soon as the camel is dead, all the pilgrims endeavor to get a piece of him and throng so confusedly with knives in their hands that these devotions are never concluded but many pilgrims are hurt and killed which are reckoned as martyrs.

After this ceremony, the prophet leads the pilgrims to the Caaba. At their first approaches, they with a great shout proclaim the *Allah Ekber* or "God, God, the great God," and then the double testimony of "*la Illah Mahumed resul Allah*: the God and Mahomet his Apostle." They went seven times round the precincts of the Caaba, but with a variety of postures and some difference of pace. For thrice, they went a good round trot, and four times they walked gravely about it, agitating their bodies and shrugging their shoulders in a strange but Arabian manner, especially as they passed between the two stones of Safa and Meriah, the sight whereof reminded them of the sacredness of the Caaba and the judgments of God against impiety and irreverence. After all this, they all came to the *Hagiar Alasvad,* or Black Stone, which he told them was brought from paradise and changed its color by reason of the sins of men.[6] Here the prophet devoutly said his prayers, kissed the stone, and begged pardon for his sins and prosperity for the future, enjoining all his followers for ever so to do. It is advanced from the stone seven handfuls or a cubit and a half, being fixed in the wall, and under it every pilgrim did most submissively creep, weeping and deploring his sins and praying that he might arrive at paradise. Then they went to the other stone whereon Abraham stood when the Caaba was building. It lies in the midst of the court of the Caaba enclosed within an iron grate and into the prints of his feet they pour some water fetched from the pool Zamzam. And, having said their prayers, they drink it up thence and depart carrying home with them in a vessel some of the sacred water of Zamzam.[7]

Thus Mahomet performed the pilgrimage and left an example for his followers how to continue it. It was the policy of the prophet not to reject all rites that had been abused to idolatry, nor to affright the Arabians into a rebellion or irreligion by making a total change in the substance and ceremonies of their devotion. The casting of stones was an usual rite in the honor of Mercury;[8] to run naked or with no other garment than a loose linen covering was a part of the worship **<104>** of Camosh. The other ceremonies appertained to Baal-Peor which there had been the deities of the Ismaelites.[9] Nay, he continued the pilgrimage upon the same day that it had always been held, upon (viz.) the tenth of the month of

Dulhagiiah.[10] So he retained circumcision which was nationally used there always, as also the fast of Ashura was of ancient observance among the Coreischites.[11] In like manner, their washings and rites of cleanliness were old usages which he confirmed. I am confident that I have read that the fast Ramadan, which lasts a month, was of an original more ancient than Mahomet; at least the Sabii kept one of thirty days. I meet with a particular reason, given by Ebnol Ehir, why Mahomet did undertake this difficult and laborious pilgrimage: and that was to convince the idolaters that his followers were as hardy and able of body as the other Arabians and that neither the scorching heats of Medina nor strict diet and discipline had any way enfeebled them.[12]

For my part, I am apt to believe that he retired to Medina that he might not seem to relinquish and scorn his old assistants, or thinking himself safer there than in his acquests at Mecca where he had put several eminent persons to death, or to keep his men in their former discipline which might be corrupted at Mecca, or to show the Arabians that neither his victories nor his power had altered him, that he designed no monarchy but to conserve the repute of being apostle of God.[13] For he did not abandon his deity dignity, nor the real exercise of it, but the show and appearance thereof. And, although devotion might engage him to the pilgrimage or a design to fix the people in a good opinion of him, by resettling after so many broils the usage and freedom of pilgrimages to the Caaba, yet I do believe that he thought it also a part of wisdom to visit again the dominions and not to invite the envious or ambitious to create new disturbances by his being absent so long.[14] Besides that, the solemnity of this procession did manifest unto the people of Mecca that the demolishing of the idols had neither abated the resort, emoluments, or honor of their city which was now assured to be in a manner the metropolis of all the Mahometans.

Mahomet, having performed the pilgrimage and instructed the Muslemin in all points of their religion and worship, retires again to Medina, either out of pretended modesty or self-denial or to keep those countries **<105>**which bordered upon Yemen in obedience. For not only Mosalleina had formed a considerable party thereabouts, but in the eleventh year of the Hegira one Aswad Absites declared himself a prophet of several provinces and cities in Arabia Fælix and had become very formidable. But a Musulman called Firus of Dailam assassinated him in his own home and put an end to those troubles.[15] These little insurrections could not create any trouble to the prophet who was now possessed of the Caaba and had at his devotion so good an army well commanded and a rich exchequer.

But the end of his life drew on, and he who had begun so late those vast attempts, and had proceeded therein so leisurely, had only the satisfaction to see all Arabia, part of Syria, and Mesopotamia reduced under the obedience and become subjects to the religion and empire. A slow fever seizeth this great spirit and bereaves him of life. It was originally occasioned by poison given to him in a shoulder of mutton hashed at the taking of Chaibar in the seventh year of the Hegira by one Zeinaban, a young maiden, the daughter of Alhareth a Jew, who being asked why she did so horrid an action, briskly replied: because thereby she should either discover him to be a true prophet and apostle of God or free the Jews from the persecution of a fierce tyrant. No sooner had the prophet eaten of the mutton but he said this shoulder of mutton tells me that it is empoisoned and Bashar, a Musulman who did also eat of it, died presently.[16]

Mahomet lived above three years after it and rendered great testimonies of his ability of body as well as prowess. Yet he did frequently say, and particularly in his last sickness, that the morsel which he ate at Chaibar still molested his stomach, and, when the mother of Bashar made him a visit as he was dying, the prophet said to her: "O mother of Bashar, I now feel my heartstrings break by the poison I swallowed with your son at Chaibar."[17] His sickness continued thirteen days only. He died in the climacterical year of his age being sixty-three years old. As writers differ about his age so they disagree about the day of his death, which some say was the same with his birthday. It is confessed it was about that time.

When the prophet lay upon his deathbed, he called for pen, ink, and paper and told them he was very sensible how the Coran was written and that he was afraid lest they might fall into **<106>** sundry errors and mistakes after his decease. And therefore he purposed to write them a treatise to preserve them from the danger of such an inconvenience, and (either I am strangely deceived in my memory or I have read that he told them then that were three thousand errors in the Coran, which it was the will of God at first to have divulged and now it was his will the Muslemin should be undeceived). [18] But Omar and some others being by, and either tender of the repute of the prophet (and their own credit and safety), lest he should reveal anything which might derogate the Alcoran, or being apprehensive that the prophet was become frantic with his fever, they forced any to bring him pen, ink, and paper. And so he died leaving no such *surat*.

No sooner was he dead and the report thereof spread abroad in the city but the multitude flocked to his house and cried: "Do not ye bury the apostle of God. He is not dead. How could he die who is to witness for us to God? No, no, he is but withdrawn aside as Isa was. Forbear to bury him." With these did Omar join saying: "If any one aver that Mahomet is dead, I will kill him presently. He is not dead but assuredly conveyed away as Isa was, or rather as Moses was, when the people missed him forty days."[19] But Abubacr wisely composed the tumult shewing out of the Alcoran that it behoved Mahomet to die as well as the other prophets, adding that if any purposed to worship, the prophet was certainly dead, but the God of Mahomet was the living God.[20]

There arose a further contest where the prophet should be buried. Some said at Jerusalem, where most of the prophets were buried. Others said at Mecca, but the inhabitants of Medina prevailed to have him buried there. So they buried him in his own house, the house of Ayesha, under his bed, he having formerly told them that the prophets were constantly buried in the place where they died.[21] There is a stately temple since built by the Mahometans upon the place and richly adorned within and without. Within this temple there is a chapel with a roof contrived by an extraordinary architect. In it there is a tombstone called *Haijar Monaour*, or the bright stone, said to have appertained to Ayesha, the wife of Mahomet, and within that is lodged the body of the prophet.[22] Nor is the tomb suspended in the air by loadstones or any other contrivance, but is placed in the floor and hung about with rich hangings of silk and **<107>** gold and environed with rails of iron sumptuously gilded. The Mahometans do make pilgrimages to it as to the Caaba, the prophet having promised happiness to such as do this. None can approach the tomb, but they devoutly kiss the bars enclosing it.

He was forty years of age when he first began to pretend to the apostleship at Mecca.[23] Thirteen years he continued there, and ten years of the Hegira were passed when he died. How far he carried his conquests in his lifetime is uncertain: some say he subdued not only three Arabias but Egypt, Antioch, Syria, Armenia, and all Palestine (except Jerusalem), that he vanquished the Emperor Heraclius in a battle slaying fifteen thousand of his men, others that he only secured himself of Arabia and part of Mesopotamia and Gaza together with the passages of Mount Sinai. Some would even subject Africa to him also. But this is certain, that, according as he by his travels had informed himself of the weakest parts of Christendom, he directed his successors to trace their steps with their victorious armies and first to Palestine, then Egypt, then Africa and Spain, and, within about fourscore years after his first appearance, you may read how his Musulmen were possessed of all those countries, and as much more on the side of Persia and Indostan, and which would seem incredible did not all agree to it.[24]

Within twenty years after his first rise, AD 643, you read of nothing but of vast armies of the Greeks being beaten, Damascus, Jerusalem, Antioch, Egypt taken, and seventeen hundred sail of ships of theirs covering the seas, and terrifying Constantinople, Cyprus, and Rhodes. For discipline, the Spartans or old Romans never equaled the Saracens, and their empire did not grow by slow degrees.[25] No sooner was their sun elevated above the horizon but it was in its meridian. And when it will decline no man knows.

CONCERNING THE JUSTICE OF THE MAHOMETAN WARS, AND THAT MAHOMET DID NOT PROPAGATE HIS DOCTRINE BY THE SWORD, WITH A VINDICATION OF MAHOMET'S CARRIAGE TOWARDS THE CHRISTIANS

T IS A VULGAR OPINION that Mahomet did propagate his doctrine by the sword and not only compelled the Arabians at first to receive his doctrine but obliged his successors by a perpetual vow or precept to endeavor the extirpation of Christianity and all other religions. But how generally so ever this be believed, and how great men so ever they be who assist it, this is no other than a plain mistake. It is most true that Mahomet did levy war in Arabia, but it was **<108>** under the pretense of restoring an old religion, not to introduce a new one. He taught his followers to abolish idolatry everywhere and that all the world was obliged to the profession of these truths: that there was one God, that He had no associates, that there was a providence and a retribution hereafter proportionate to the good or evil actions of men. But that all mankind were to be enforced to the profession of his religion or that he compelled any thereto is a falsehood.

It is plain that many Christian doctors have held that Christianity may be enforced and that it is a just cause for one prince to invade and conquer another's territories to propagate the true religion. Thereby, they say that if one king may chastise and reduce under obedience the subjects of another, they may do as much for the Lord paramount of the universe. That kings are the ministers of God to execute wrath upon such as do evil, and that, being the viceroys of the almighty, they ought to assert the glory, cause, and sovereignty of God to be everywhere submitted to, there want not precedents for such actings. Amongst the Jews, Hyrcanus compelled the Idumeans to be circumcised and turn Jews,[1] and all Christian annals furnish us with instances of the like nature. It is likewise true that several Christian doctors teach that a nation guilty of enormous sins may be invaded and that it is a just pretense of war to reclaim them from notorious wickedness, it being lawful to compel them to observe those laws of nature, whereto God hath originally subjected them.[2]

These and sundry other titles of war are treated of and maintained by the divines who write concerning the Spanish rights over the Indians.[3] But though the Christian doctors and some popes have urged them, and thereby prepared apologies for the Mahometans, I do not find that Mahomet proceeded any further in Arabia the Desert than to exterminate idolatry everywhere, but not to force men to the profession of Islamism.[4] He himself did give letters of security and protection to the Jews and Christians in Arabia and never used any violence to them upon the account of religion. At Medina such Jews as peaceably paid tribute continued unmolested, though mortally hated, until the days of Omar, the son of Alchittabi, who expelled them out of Arabia, **<109>** he being told that Mahomet had prohibited that two different religions should be tolerated within that country, the seat of his empire. But though they were thereupon expelled thence, which was rather an act of civil prudence than religion, yet were they never compelled to Mahometanism, nor banished his other territories.[5]

The same Omar did give the Christians his security upon the taking of Jerusalem: "In the name of God, merciful and gracious, from Omar the son of Alchittabi to the inhabitants of the city Elia: Security and protection is granted as to their persons, children, wives, estates, and all their churches, that they be neither destroyed, alienated, nor prohibited the Christians to resort to."[6] And when Amurcus the Saracen general under Abubacr did besiege Gaza, he made this declaration to the Christian governor thereof:

> Our Lord hath commanded us to fight and conquer you except you will embrace our religion and so become our friends and brethren pursuing the same common interest with us, so you will have us your faithful allies. But if you will not accept of these terms, then submit to pay us tribute yearly, yourselves and your posterity forever, to us and our successors, and we will protect you against all opposition whatsoever, and you shall be in league with us. If you agree not hereunto, then the sword must decide our rights, and we will not desist until we have subdued you and put in execution the will of God.[7]

By this declaration, it is manifest that the Mahometans did propagate their empire, but not their religion, by force of arms, and, albeit they did not permit others than Musulmen to enjoy any military or civil commands in their territories or entire conquests, yet the Christians and other religions might peaceably subsist under their protection if they paid the tribute demanded. In Spain the *Mozarabick* Christians always lived quietly and safely under them, and others in their other kingdoms and dominions, an inviolate justice being preserved towards them; and though the rich and potent nobility and rulers were destroyed or reduced to nothing, which was done to prevent future rebellions, yet it is observed by Scaliger—and it is an assured truth—that the vulgar Greeks live in a better condition under the Turk at present than they did under their own emperors when there were perpetual murders practiced on their princes and tyranny on their people. But they are now secure from **<110>** injury if they pay their taxes, and it is more the interest of the princes and nobles than of the people at present which keeps all Europe from submitting to the Turks.

The decree of Mahomet in his Alcoran concerning the Moslemicall wars does run thus: Make war upon those which do not believe in God, nor that there is a day of judgment, nor that those things are forbidden them which God and His prophet have forbidden unto them. Nor do administer due justice unto them who have taken cartels of security and, being subdued, do readily pay the appointed tribute.[8] Hereby, such as have taken cartels of security he understands such Jews and Christians as had yielded themselves to Mahomet and taken protection under him. Thus Mahomet Ben Achmed expounds him. Elmomin, who collected his "History of the Saracens" out of the best Mahometan writers and was himself secretary of state to one of their princes, avowed that

Mahomet did give protection and security to the pagans, Magicians, and Jews, and Christians also which swore fealty to him and paid him yearly tribute.[9]

Moreover, that he sent Omar to the Christians to assure them that they should live securely under his dominion, and that he would esteem their lives as the lives of his Moslemin and of their goods as the goods of those others:[10] to this purpose, there is extant a compact or league betwixt Mahomet and the Christians, published in France by Gabriel Sionita and reprinted by Johannes Fabricius a Dantzicker, which is by him affirmed to be most authentic, and mentioned by Selden, though Grotius takes it to be but a figment of the Christians that they might gain favor with the Moselmin.[11] I shall not transcribe it because I think it to be suppositious. It is published in English by Mr. Rycaut in his "Relation of the Turkish Government" liber 2, caput 2. The sum of it is that the Christians submitting to him and paying their tributes duly shall live and enjoy the liberty of their religion without any molestation, and that there shall be a perpetual amity betwixt the Musulmen and them.[12]

There are also sundry passages in the Alcoran wherein he permits the unbelievers to hold their own religion and declares that every of them—Jew, Christian, or other—might be saved if he hold that there was one God creator, a day of judgment, and lived justly and uprightly. In fine, it is **<111>** manifest that Mahomet and his followers do make war not to enforce others to their religion but to enlarge their empire and reduce all under their subjection. This is the direct injunction of the Alcoran in the place already mentioned, and is avowed by Selden and Salmasius, and albeit they do call the territories of the Christians *Dar Elharb*, or the enemy's country, and think they have a perpetual right to make war upon such, yet it is only upon the grounds aforesaid. So that the controversy betwixt them and the Christians is not whether religion may be propagated by arms, but whether it be lawful to make war on others nearly for the enlargement of empire. And herein Mahomet, as in other cases, hath the Jews for his defenders whose opinion for the affirmative is generally the same with his as to this matter. And it was heretofore the sense of most emperors. And if the Christians do not own the same sentiments, few princes do believe other, though they cloak their own ambition with different and more specious pretences. Maimonides and the Jews call such wars "praelia majestatis contra gentes alias, ut dilatet terminos regni & augeat magnitudinem ejus una cum famâ."[13]

As Mahomet seems to have deduced his laws for an offensive war from the Jewish doctors, so did he derive his laws for conquest out of them.[14] If he did everywhere destroy idolatry and not only within Arabia and the Caaba, this is agreeable to the Jewish rulers who did oblige the conquered nations to become stranger proselytes and submit to the seven commandments of Noah, one whereof was against idolatry.[15] But if he did only condemn and not extirpate idolatry, if he only conquered the Gentiles and left them tributaries with permission to continue idolaters (which is probable), since the Turks and Moguls do so, and they would not do it were there any passage in the Alcoran or any *Assoniah* or tradition to the contrary,[16] then likewise, had he the Mosaical Laws for his precedent. For by the Mosaical direct law against idolatry, Deuteronomy 12:2, Exodus 34:13, such false worship was only to be extirpated out of the land of promise, and not in other acquests. It was by force only of an intervenient and prudential law of the Jewish Sanhedrin that idolatry was well to be exterminated out of the conquered territories lest thereby the Jews should be perverted from the worship of **<112>** the true God thereunto.[17]

So that Mahomet, in that he commanded all other religions to be excluded Arabia the Desert (for they are not prohibited elsewhere), did imitate the divine institution for the holy land, and in permitting variety in other places had the same great example for his precedent. But this is not all. The demeanor of the Saracens upon a victory is entirely consonant to the Jewish laws of war, as a Jew taken in war did not become a slave to a Jew, but all other captives did become slaves and were at the disposal of the conqueror, to be sold or employed in what service he pleased. So neither can a Mahometan be enslaved by a Mahometan, but all other captives are at the disposal of the conqueror and he may employ or make sale of them as he pleases.[18] As to those that were not taken captive in war, but yielded themselves by surrender on articles, it was a perpetual law among the Jews that all places subdued by them should be reduced under bondage and the inhabitants be retained in servitude, though not absolute slavery. They were to live in an abject manner, paying a great submission and an arbitrary tribute to the victor, and never to bear any command in Israel, and were also liable to sundry personal services, occasionally in the building of public edifices, fortifications, the temple, et cetera. So the nations that, upon invasion, did render themselves were to be brought into servitude and made tributaries (Deuteronomy

20:10–11). Thus upon the children of the Ammonites and who had yielded to the victorious Israelites upon terms did Solomon levy a tribute of bond service, and they wrought personally at his public buildings (1 Kings 9:21, 2 Chronicles 8:7). So did David (1 Chronicles 22:2).

As the Mahometans do herein conform to the Mosaical Law so that they do nothing herein that is repugnant to the most exact rules of war, I find Grotius to justify.[19] And if there be no injury offered thereby to them that are made captives, or subdued, I do not comprehend any reason that the Christians should complain of their hard usage under the Mahometans.

But to proceed. How equitable that Mahometan tenet is that wars are just for the enlargement of empire I will not determine.[20] **<113>** It is an opinion not so barbarous or uncouth but that old Greece and Rome, as well as Jewry, will avow it. But most certain it is that Mahomet did render a great testimony of his wisdom by introducing it among his followers, for it conduced much to the vastness of that empire which he designed, since the Mahometans could never want a pretense for war against others. It conduced much to the public tranquility of that empire which, being erected upon a military prudence, would run into civil broil and confusion were not there that Mahometan precept enjoined them to be continually solicitous to enlarge their territories. It brings also this additional benefit that since great kingdoms ought to know no period of their growth (it being therein as in natural bodies which when once arrived to a determinate pitch immediately decline and go to ruin), their opinion contributes to the subsistence and perpetuity of their monarchy.[21] And how repugnant so ever the continuance of slavery be unto Christian charity, it is not absolutely unlawful or any more repugnant thereto than is war itself.

Nay, it is a moderation in the effects and rights of war, and I am sure Christian statesmen such as Busbecq have condemned the European policy for relinquishing so wise and so beneficial a practice.[22] For the advantage to particular soldiers doth add to their courage, as also doth the continual sight of those they by servitude lead in a continual triumph. It makes the same enemies always despicable to them, whose ancestors and kindred they see every day to be their slaves. It makes them more desperate in fight,[23] the indignities of a lasting slavery seeming worse than death to a valiant person, besides the profit that accrues to the public thereby, it being in vain to expect that such extraordinary pieces of architecture and fortification should ever be performed by the moderns as the ancients effected by their slaves.[24]

To conclude: though the principles of the Christians seem to condemn slavery, yet in Portugal and other places it is frequently practiced, and perhaps the Christian laws and customs against such usage had no higher rise than ecclesiastical and civil policy, which the successors have indiscreetly (and not out of conscience duly informed) retained still.[25] **<114>**

CONCERNING THE CHRISTIAN ADDITIONS

HAVE ALREADY SHOWN that Arabia was the common receptacle for the persecuted Jews and Christians of all sorts and sects to retire unto. I must add thereto this limitation: that persecution works this effect upon all religions that such as then do continue firm and constant are more pious and devout than at other times, the indifferent and the vicious usually adhering to that religion which prevails and prospers. And the martial spirit seldom persists in that profession which excludeth him from employment. Upon this account, the Nestorians, Jacobites, the Arians, Arabians, and Judaizing Christians were of more exemplary piety in those days than the Trinitarians, either out of policy to ingratiate their partisans by such speciousness, and to inodiate those who oppressed so innocent and religious persons, or out of a real conscientiousness. The Judaizing Christians had the fairest pretences and were most tenacious of their customs and traditions, and by a series of persecutions from their first conversion until the days of Mahomet, and by the principles of their Christianity which was conformable to the self-denying doctrine of Isa and the discipline of the Essenes, they were a harmless religion such as might win much up the melancholy temper and suspicious humor of the Arabians. They were diffused from Pella in Judea to Cochab in the confines of Arabia toward Syria and so on to Yemen or Arabia the Happy and Chaibar or Mesopotamia.[1]

The kings of the Arabians and their tribes, several of them, had been Christians, as I related: first Trinitarians, then Jacobites, and amongst several of their tribes as that of Gassan in Syria and its confines and of Rabia and Codan, and many other tribes had their churches and converts as the Jews had also in others towards Arabia the Happy and elsewhere. As Mahomet seems himself to have been a Judaizing Christian and a great honorer of Isa, so he always expressed a great reverence for them. And it is concerning them that he says that Isa their prophet should save them in the last day. But as to the Trinitarians (that is those Christians who advanced Christ and the Holy Ghost or the Virgin Mary into the deity whom Mahomet calls *Almushrikuna* or Associators), these he universally judges to hellfire in his Alcoran as well for their tenets as wicked lives.[2] That the Arabian Christians were men of just and strict deportment appears hence: that Mahomet **<115>** saith of them that one might safely entrust them with any sum of money and they would restore it again.[3] But the Jews were such villains that no man could trust them with a penny.

It is known how severe enemies the Christians were against all images and pictures. The Mahometans were so likewise, insomuch that upon their coins they stamp some pious sentence and not any effigies. And so bigoted were[4] they as to this point as that not only the former Saracens but the Turks, till of late, would not receive as current any Christian money with an effigy stamped thereon.[5] And they universally demolish all pictures and images where they conquer. Mahomet, though he did not force the Christians to his religion, yet he told them that such as believed in Isa ought to live according to his precepts with great humility, piety, and unconcernedness for the pomp and vanities of this world, that they ought neither to seek nor retain honor nor riches or go to war, or intermeddle with state affairs—these things being inconsistent with the doctrine of Isa; such as pursued those courses not being really Christians, since Christianity lies not so much in open profession of reverence and worship as in the practice of a holy life.

I shall here insert the opinion of Grotius concerning the Eastern Christians when Mahomet arose that it may appear with how much justice Mahomet did exclude them from the number of Christians:

> Grotius: *De Veritate Religionis Christianæ, liber 6.* The true and simple piety which flourished among the Christians during their oppressions and persecutions began to grow out of fashion and to be disused after that Constantine and his successors had not only indemnified but honored Christianity, the world being as it were crowded into the Church. The Christian emperors ceased not to multiply needless wars, the bishops raised great quarrels and tumults in order to their particular advancement, and as at first, it proved ca-

> lamitous to mankind that the tree of knowledge was preferred before the tree of life, so then was it almost fatal that curiosity of speculations was more valued than true godliness and religion because modeled and methodized into an art. The consequence whereof was that as heretofore in the building of Babel, the erection of too high a structure gave an occasion to the confusion of **<116>** languages, so the elevated disquisitions of Christian doctors produced now a multitude of strange terms and unknown forms of speech, and afterwards discord. The commonalty, being amazed and perplexed with these inexplicable difficulties, and not knowing which to adhere unto or what to believe, and seeing each party establish its opinion upon scriptural interpretations and allegations, they began to complain of the obscurity and ambiguity, and at last turned their indignation into a perfect hatred of the Holy Writ.[6]

Religion now was no longer terminated in the purity of the mind, but in the performance of certain outward ceremonies, as if the law, rites, and Judaism had been only varied not abolished, and men testified their Christianity not so much by amending their lives as by exterior and bodily gestures and humiliations and a zealous adherence to the party they owned insomuch that at last there were few real Christians, notwithstanding the multitude of professors. God did not connive at those sins and enormities but raised up the remote nations in Germany and Scythia to invade Christendom, which overran all like a torrent. And since the damages they did would not serve to instruct and reform the surviving Christians, Mahomet in Arabia began to preach a new doctrine which was directly opposite to the Christian religion, yet did, in words, contain a great part of the Christian practice. He was first credited by the Saracens, who revolted from the Emperor Heraclius, they having carried their conquests in a short time over Arabia, Syria, Palestine, Egypt, Persia, and afterwards into Africa and Spain. With their empire, they propagated their religion.

Nor is it a despicable plea of the Mahometans which is urged by Ismael ibn Ali, a Mahometan historian,[7] that at the Nicene Council in the twentieth year of the reign of Constantine, there were assembled 2,048 bishops, out of which he chose 318 and adhered to their judgment in anathematizing Arius and so published a Christianity different from what had been taught before in the church.[8] It is granted by the oriental historians of the church that such a number of bishops was summoned, as the Mahometans specify. So saith Eutychius and Josephus, an Egyptian presbyter, in his preface to the Arabic version of the councils.[9] And it is confessed that all, excepting the **<117>** 318, did vary from the Nicene faith. Nor is it plain that these 318 were all bishops. Some accounts represent it as if there were but 232 bishops and the rest presbyters and monks. If that council were so managed as it is most likely, the pretences of Mahomet are not despicable. And that Mahomet might with better color deprive the Christians of their honor, powers, and riches, and reduce them to their primitive condition of piety and poverty, it is by these sayings that he and his followers describe Isa.[10]

Isa, the Son of Mary, peace be upon him, said thus: "He that greedily accumulates riches is like him that drinketh much salt water, the more he drinks the more his thirst increaseth and he desists not to drink until he bursts." Isa the Son of Mary said to John the Son of Zachariah: "If any man say anything concerning thee that is true, praise God for it; if he say any untruth, give unto God a greater thanks for that, and He will reward that disposition of mind in thee and add it to the catalogue of thy virtues, and thus, without any trouble, shalt thou multiply thy good actions." The world did once appear unto Isa in the shape of an old decrepit woman unto whom Isa said: "'How many husbands hast thou had?' And she replied, 'The number of them hath been such that I cannot tell them to you.' 'And are they all dead,' then added he, 'and have left thee?' The old woman said, 'Nay they did not leave me. I destroyed them all.' Isa rejoined: 'It is a wonder therefore that any should be such fools as to dote upon thee and not consider how thou hast used all before them to be cautioned thereby against the love of thee.'"[11]

In the time of Isa, three men traveled together who having found a great treasure said: "We want sustenance. Let one of us go and buy food." So one of them went and upon the way reflected also to buy some poison and mix it with the meat and by the death of his companions to render himself sole possessor of the treasure. So he empoisoned the meat. In like manner, those two which stayed behind did purpose to kill him at his return and appropriate to themselves the benefit of their discovery; whereupon they slew him and also died themselves by the poison which he had mingled with the meat. At that **<118>** time Isa came by with his apostles and said: "This is the condition of the world. Behold how these three have suffered by it. These are deceased and left behind what they thought to be owners of. Woe unto him that seeks riches in this world."

These pretenses were first made use of by Julian the Apostate thereby to depress the Christians and, by this stratagem, did Mahomet gain to his party all the ambitious and military who could not satisfy their inclinations unless they embraced the Saracenical religion. And withal, by the same means, he rendered Christianity contemptible and weak and fit only for subjection or slavery. He did also hereby give a just color to the pretense of his followers that they were the *Elmumenin* or true believers, and that their enemies of the Christians were not indeed Christians so that they seem in their wars not to oppose but vindicate Isa.[12]

In reference to him, the Christians were not altogether so candid. You will find as little integrity in the Christian narratives of him as in any before, so that the most dissolute Christians published as great untruths in their times as they who passed for saints. It is acknowledged by all the learned, after a severe inquiry into the Arabian writers, as well Christians as Mahometans, that Mahomet was descended of the principal tribe of the Arabians both by his father's side and mother's side, as I have represented it. Notwithstanding this, "Mahometis Arabis vitam qui descripserunt, multi fuerent qui esse non uno modo illius res tradunt, in eo tamen convenient omnes, (sed male, ut habet Erpen. de Ling. Arab. p. 42.) quod eum à plebejo vilíque genere ortum, pauperibus parentibus, patre Ethnico, matre Judæa affirmant."[13]

It is certain that the Christians which lived under the Mahometans as Elmacin and others do mention Mahomet with great respect as "Mahomet of glorious memory" and "Mahometes super quo pax et benedictio, et cetera." Whereas others have proceeded so far as to say that he was even Antichrist and found out the number of the beast 666 in his name, writing it—than which nothing can be more ridiculous.[14] Is it not mere folly to spell a man's name wrong, and then to imagine mysteries in **<119>** it: some Greeks *Μαχουμέθ* others *Μωαμμέθ,* the Latins *Machumet, Machomet, Magmed, Maomethes,* in Arabic, if rightly pronounced, *Muhammed* or *Mohammed,* which signifies much desired.[15]

I find that his father's name was Abdalla and that, he dying, he was educated by his grandfather Abdolmutleb and, upon his decease, by his uncle Abutaleb; and that he travelled twice to Jerusalem, besides his expeditions into Egypt, Africa, and Spain; that he conversed with the Christians of all sects. And it appears that he understood very well all their tenets and the most solid foundations which they went upon. Nor was he unacquainted with the Jewish principles and Talmudical learning, as is likewise manifest by his Alcoran, the state of Arabia being divided into Jews, Judaizing Arabians, Judaizing Christians (at Cochab there was one of the seats of the Nazarene Christians), Jacobites, Nestorians, Arians, Trinitarians, Manicheans, Montanists, Sabeans, and idolaters. This gave him occasion and opportunity to examine and try all sects and sorts of religions. But the Christians have given him two assistants, one Abdalla a Jew and Sergius a Nestorian monk, and represent Mahomet himself as an ignorant fellow who could not judge of what they instilled into him, which is the reason of such gross errors in his Alcoran.

But I cannot find any Abdalla besides his father who was a Coreischite, nor any tutor or companion of his called Sergius. And if Sergius were a Nestorian, why did not Mahomet adhere to Nestorianism and teach that Isa was true God and true man under a double personality? Why did he not mention Nestorius and Theodorus Mopsuestersis or Diodorus Tarsoris as holy men or saints and condemn Cyril of Alexandria?[16] Neither he nor any of his followers have done this as I know of. Had any such thing been, this would have happened. Nor would he have declined to cajole so great an interest as the Nestorians then were, being so strengthened by the decree of Chosroes and so extended that even the Christians of Saint Thomas in the Indies are of that profession. No, he was undoubtedly a great admirer of Isa as a prophet or apostle of God,[17] and of this he makes so great and **<120>** frequent declarations, and that Isa was his predecessor and taught the same doctrine that it is but justice to style him a Christian.

Nor do I believe that he did cajole or love the Jews at all and consequently would not form his Alcoran so as to please them. It is recorded that he did so detest them albeit out of compliance to the Coreischites he had retained the fast of Ashura on the tenth day of the month of Moharam. Out of hatred to the Jews he would have altered the observation thereof to the ninth day of the same month had he lived but one year longer. I believe that he was a convert to the religion of the Judaizing Christians and did form his religion as far as possible in resemblance of theirs. They and the Arians were his principal instructors, but not any of them had any hand in the penning of the Alcoran. For that was not made before he began his apostleship in any desert, but, published upon several emergencies, most at Medina where that he should have had any such assistance, it is unimaginable.[18] For it would have been suspicious in that city and amongst his followers and so near confidants and secretaries as he there retained about him.

As for the Arians, it is manifest that the Saracens have always retained a veneration for their Saint George, bishop of Alexandria, whom yet they do not allow for a prophet but one of their saints or fathers, and his life is written by Kessaeus a Mahometan as if he were such.[19] And Ahmad Ben Edris, passing over the Nestorians as a foolish sort of Christian heretics, brings in a fable concerning Paul as if he had deluded the world into an opinion of the deity of Isa and given a beginning to the heresy of Eutychius and the Jacobites; and that an Arian, or else a Judaizing Christian, whom he calls an *Elmunim*, or true believer, did anathematize Paul thereupon saying: "We were the companions of Isa, we saw him, we are descended from him, he was the servant of God and his Apostle, he never told us otherwise." Also that Mahomet did meet with thirty of the descendants of this *Elmunim* or orthodox person, they being retired into an hermitage, and that they owned his doctrine and professed Moslenisme.[20]

Let us not then give credit to the aforesaid stories **<121>** but inscribe another original to the Mahometical doctrines. The same Christians say that he was troubled with the falling sickness, that he took advantage from thence to pretend to raptures, and that upon his recovery out of those paroxysms he would repeat the *Bismillah*, "In the name of God, merciful and gracious," and published the *surats* of the Alcoran. I have refuted this story already of which there is no mention among the Arabians nor do they magnify their prophet for any such raptures. I add that the Alcoran was not given out in that manner that each *surat* was penned according to particular emergencies. And it would have been an important piece of intelligence for the Christians to have published the way of contriving epileptic fits according each emergency of his and deferring them at other times. No less vain is the story of Mahomet's pigeon which used to eat peas out of his ear, and therefore, as a representation of the Holy Ghost, would resort to his shoulder and seem to inspire or commune with him. I will not ask whether it be possible to breed a pigeon to that work, so as that it should be kept or fed invisibly (for otherwise it would have bred suspicion in his followers and watchful enemies), or do the feat without prejudice to the drum of the ear, or without discovering what it swallowed or what it sought after.

Nor whether Mahomet did own the Holy Ghost any more than the Arians and Judaizing Christians did. But I would be informed what ground there is for this fable seeing neither Mahomet nor his followers do speak of any such apparition of any pigeon. Nor doth any Christian of the Arabians mention it.[21] Grotius indeed speaks of it, and Doctor Pococke thereupon consulted him desiring to know what grounds he had for such a relation. The reply was that he did not therein follow the narration of the Mahometans or Arabic Christians, but of the European Christians, and particularly of Scaliger (in his notes upon Manilius where this is reported).[22] And this is all that can be said for the relation. But it is to no purpose for any to say that the Mahometans have ever since preserved a veneration or extraordinary respect for **<122>** pigeons. They give another reason for this viz.: because that the prophet Noah did pronounce a blessing upon the pigeon and said she should be forever beloved and regarded by men for returning to the ark with an olive branch, whilst the raven stayed to prey upon the dead bodies, which appeared after the retiring of the waters. I am apt to believe this story concerning the pigeon was by some ignorant person transferred from Athanasius to Mahomet. For it is reported concerning that father how a pigeon in the street flew to him and settled on his shoulder by his ear. This the Trinitarians interpreted as a miracle but the Arians as magical. And indeed, in the legend of St. George, I find Athanasius reputed to be a magician.[23]

I shall add another Christian fable concerning Mahomet: that he privately bred up a bull which was constantly fed out of his hand and thereby accustomed to run to him as soon as he came sight. And to the horns of this bull one day he fastened the Alcoran, and, as he was discoursing to the people concerning his new religion and laws, this bull was contrived into his sight, which immediately rushed through the crowd to the prophet and presented him with the Alcoran, which he received with much ostentation of piety as sent to him by God and read some of it to the Arabians there. And, at the same time, a pigeon came and brought a schedule in which was written: "He shall be king of the Arabians who yoketh this bull." Whereupon Sergius the Nestorian monk brought him a yoke, which he easily put on the neck of the bull aforesaid, and thereupon was saluted as king and the Alcoran received as being of divine authority.[24]

With such stories as these have the Christians represented him to be the vilest imposter in the world and transformed the wisest legislator that ever was into a simple cheat. But neither was the Alcoran written or published all at one time, nor ever reduced into one volume entirely by him, but by Abubacr and Othman as I have shewed.[25] Nor is there any mention of this miracle of the bull in the Saracen records when they speak of the wonders of the prophet. Behold the simplicity of the Christians then who were deluded and thought to delude by such fopperies as these. As little credit is there to be given to that other fable that Mahomet should promise the people of **<123>** Mecca (they demanding a miracle) that he would cause a mountain to remove to him at his sermons. But it, not obeying his call, he briskly said if the mountain will not come to Mahomet, Mahomet will go to the mountain. Was there ever a greater foppery imagined yet in the legends of the Christian saints?

There are such tales that one will not admire if they made no better romances of their enemies. A greater objection is raised against him for his ignorance: this they say is acknowledged by himself in his Alcoran, where he brings in God saying that he had sent to the ignorant a prophet amongst them,[26] that is to illiterate persons an illiterate prophet. Moreover that the inhabitants of Mecca were so illiterate at that time that they could neither write nor read, so that it seems enough to prove him illiterate that it is confessed he was born there. In fine he is generally acknowledged by the Arabians to be *Nabian Ommian*, that is the illiterate prophet.

But none of those arguments are of any validity. Not the first: for though God should say that He had sent to the ignorant a prophet from amongst them, doth it therefore follow that he must be as ignorant as they? Is not the saying verified if it appear that he was of their lineage and country? Not the second: for what necessity is there that every one that was born and lived in Mecca should be illiterate? May there not be an Anacharsis in Scythia?[27] Must the seven sages be as ignorant as the residue of Greece?[28] Must not Ezra be able to read because the people could not (Nehemiah 8:8)? As to his being styled *Nabian Ommian*, though that title be given him by the Arabians generally, yet they do not agree upon the meaning thereof, some of them saying that it was not by reason of his ignorance, but of his being born at Mecca which is termed *Ommal koras*, or the mother city. And how can they call him truly the ignorant prophet since they believe he knew all things, which is acknowledged by Doctor Pococke? The same doctor doth acknowledge that one Warakah, a kinsman (or rather uncle according to Abunazarus), taught him to write Hebrew and the Arabic speech, may be as well penned in that character which was newly propagated at Mecca by one that had married the sister of Abusofian some years before Mahomet pretended to an apostleship.[29] And who will imagine that so subtle **<124>** a man as he and who had framed to himself so vast a design would omit the learning of a thing so important to his ends and so subservient to the promulgation of his doctrine as the writing of Arabic was? I add that since Othman and Ali could write and were his scribes, and so were several of his other followers, why should we think it impossible for Mahomet to write?[30]

It is further considerable that in all this controversy as it is managed the question is only whether Mahomet could write and read the Arabic characters newly introduced there and not whether he were so learned as to understand the religion and rites, customs and histories of his country, the religion and learning of the Jews, and of the several sects of Christians. Concerning this, there can be no question amongst any that know the Alcoran and his constitutions which are such as demonstrate a profound insight into these matters and a knowledge of many minute particularities extending even to legendary stories and fables. And if this be notorious, I should not see any just grounds to conclude him illiterate though it were more demonstrable than it is that he could not write or read the Arabic characters.

Another fable of the Christians against Mahomet is that he should promise his followers to revive again in three days, or some such time, and that they expected his return there so long till his carcass grew noisome, and that they still expect his return, that his body is enclosed in an iron tomb and hangs in the air suspended by the force of two opposite loadstones. But these are such figments as there the Mahometans laugh at and deride the Christians for relating them. Doctor Pococke refutes them more than once.[31] And I will here repeat his words as he delivered them in his speech at Oxford where he excites his scholars to study Arabic:

> Historia quibus curae est ut Arabum eorum monumenta diligentiis evolverent, quam persuasum cuperem; ut ita tollerentur tot ineptæ, quas ignorantia istius linguæ nobis obtrusit, fabulæ. Ita fieret, ut non ultra Mahometis tumulum in aere pendulum somniaremus: nec falsum illius de reditu suo promissum urgentes, Assedis ipsius, quos absurdè haec credere dicimus . . . impingendo veris refutandis ineptos

nosmet redderemus, nec amplius illos Saracenorum appellatione à Sara se oriundos jactare nugaremur. Hujusmodi sexcenta sunt, quibus occurri sine linguarum studio non potest.[32]

This last passage of Doctor Pococke puts me in mind of some other **<125>** forgeries with which the Christians did formerly asperse the Mahometans and proceeded so far therein that they obliged the Saracenical converts in their catechisms to pronounce anathemas against such practices as were never used by the Musulmen viz.: that they worshipped the Morning Star and Venus, by the name of Chabar or Chubar, and that they cried in honor thereto, *Cabar* or *Cubar*, signifying in Arabic the great goddess. Which assertion how great authors so ever it hath as Euthymius Zegabenus,[33] the Saracen catechism, Constantius, Porphyrogenitus, Cedrenus, et cetera, is most false and is rejected by Selden, Pococke, Hottinger, et cetera:[34] this exclamation among the Mahometans, being no other than their usual doxology of *Allah Ekbar Allah* or *Allah Allah Howa Cobar Allah*. God, God the great God. No less false is that report that they worship Venus under the stone called Brachtan, in which stone, if you look exactly, you may see lineaments of that goddess portrayed, though Euthymius Zegabenus relates this: that the Saracens in their catechism are taught to anathematize the worship of it.[35]

Yet it is a great untruth. This stone is no other than the Black Stone I have given an account of, which they do not worship at all, but kiss devoutly as a relic of paradise (or for other reasons alleged by them) which may have been adored perhaps by the old Arabians but not by Mahomet or his sect, nor was it called Brachtan. Our linguists are in as great a perplexity to divine whence the Christians received this appellation (except it be because they kiss it, "tabarracan behi, boni ominis seu benedictionis captandi gratia") as they are to find them place the stone Brachtan on the ground in the middle of the Caaba, which is really raised above two cubits from the ground and fixed in the wall and is a plain stone, having no effigies in it.[36] That which carries the show of any sculpture in it is the other stone (not in the middle of the Caaba but in the midst of the Court or *Almesjad Alharan*) and retaineth the impressions of Abraham's feet, not the face of Venus:

Quod autem à Damasceno, & Euthymio asseritur, si quis accuratiùs inspectet videri in eo figuram capitis scalpro expressam, quod

> Veneris esse volunt, ex Arabum scriptis puto probari non posse. Alius illis lapis est sacer, cui insculptam, vel potius impressam, tradunt figuram, sed tantum à figura capitis quantum caput à pedibus distantem, nisi **<126>** oculi superstitione lippi caput à pedibus distinguere nesciant. Lapis scil quo vestigia pedum Abrahami impressa, cùm vel illis inter aedificandum Caabam insisteret, ut innuit Abulfeda, vel dum ipse caput Ismaelis, quem visum venerat, uxor (ut Ahmed Ebn Yusef, & Safioddinus) laveret. Unde & illi nomen Makam Abrahim Locus (scilicet) Abrahami, vel, quo stetit Abrahamus.[37]

As for the *Τζίτζαφα Μαρουά Τζάφα* mentioned also as idols of the Mahometans by the said Euthymius Zegabenus, these are nothing else but the Safa and Marwa of the Mahometans between which they run in their pilgrimages at Mecca and are said to be two stones into which a man and a woman were metamorphosed for committing adultery together in the Caaba[38] Nor are they the objects of any Mahometan devotion as I have showed. But it is most pleasant to read how Euthymius doth further aggravate the idolatry of the Saracens. "Ibidem esse illis ait - - - - - - Simulacrum Baccha Ismaketh dictum, quod ipse Mohammedes sc. - - - - - - Adoramen observationis appellat, & ut miseri barbari adorarent praecepit."[39] The original of this barbarous idol or rather mistake was that in the Alcoran there is once found the word *Bebecca,* which Beidani, the Arabian commentator, expounds in Mecca, there being a metathesis of B for M.[40] And this *Baccha Ismaketh,* if it be pronounced according to the Arabian manner, signifies now more than *Bacca* or *Becca,* and is the name of Macca or Mecca, and this Mecca called by the said Euthymius - - - - - - is to be explained *adoramen observationis,* or the place towards which the Mahometans pray (or their *Keblah*).[41]

Do not such writers as these, and such were all the Christians that writ of Mahomet (as well the Greeks as Latins), deserve much credit? And can we blame those Mahometans who despise the foolish relations our authors give of their prophet and religion? Certainly no people are more remote from idolatry than the Saracens, and, whatever name you give to their errors and follies, Maimonides (who was scholar to Averroes and traveled through Arabia and Egypt), and Doctor Pococke, will tell you they ought not to be thus stigmatized. That they were once idolaters and until the days of Heraclius did worship the star Venus by the name of *Cabar* or the great goddess is yielded: but Mahomet put an end to all such idolatrous worship and the rites **<127>** which he retained are continued to a different intention than they were first practiced upon. It must be avowed that they adore no other than the true God and err rather in the manner than in the object of their devotion, so that the Emperor Manuel Comnenus seems (in the judgment of Doctor Pococke) to have had good reason to have altered the form of abjuration which was imposed on the converted Saracens viz.: "I do anathematize the God of Mahomet" into another kind of renunciation.[42]

But that we may the better understand the Mahometan religion,[43] I shall give a brief account of the articles of their faith, not of the Alcoran, nor its formal words, but the formal words in which the Mahometans express themselves, as the Christians recite their creed and not the whole scripture, nor a verbal deduction thence. The Mahometans divide their religion into fundamentals and super structures, and though they have a great diversity of opinions in the explication of their law, yet they esteem him orthodox who observes these five articles where to every Musulman is obliged. So Algazali: and Mahomet himself is said to have determined the case.[44]

These are:

> First: The confession, there is no god beside God, and Mahomet is the apostle of God; In a constant saying of the prayers according to appointment; In giving alms; In performing a religious pilgrimage to Mecca; And in observing the fast of the month of Ramadan.

Of these five, two may seem to be established upon prudential reasons: the pilgrimage and the fast of Ramadan. For though Mahomet retained many Arabian usages (pretending only to reform the old and not introduce a new religion), and such I have showed this pilgrimage and fast to have been; yet I believe he wisely discerned that the retaining these two points would be of great use, since he designed a military empire to the support whereof valiant and hardy soldiers were necessary. And nothing could more conduce to the successive generation and education of such than these two institutions. For how active, laborious, and abstinent must the women as well as the men render themselves to be able to endure the pilgrimage and the fast aforesaid. The pilgrimage I have described largely. The fast is moveable, and every year happens **<128>** a month later than before, so that it falls sometimes in summer, other times in winter, in the hottest and coldest seasons, the longest as well as shortest days. The fast is observed so strictly that from daybreak till starlight, not one (except travelers or sick persons) doth eat or drink anything or so much as wash his mouth with a little water.[45] And the most dissolute persons who adventure at other times to drink wine will not then so much as smell to it. It is true that at night, when the *Emaum* or priest declares it to be time to eat, they feed plentifully even to excess. And even this has its reason upon account of health. For this fasting and feasting in such extremes contributes to their health during the whole year. It is recommended by Celsus to the healthy not to live by rule but pursue a variety in diet lest they contract a custom the change whereof would be as dangerous as the continuance inconsistent with daily action and business.[46]

I believe also the third precept concerning alms was political in its original. For having persuaded his followers into such a parsimony as was requisite to the making of them hardy, and to the making of them welcome in their quarters, that they might not lapse from his institutions and be debauched by riches. It was a sort of a Grecian law or leveling to oblige them to so extraordinary alms as he did. Mahomet calls it *Zacot* which signifies as much as increase as if the giving alms to the needy were the principal means to augment their revenue.[47] And this he inculcated to them that they might not grow effeminate through luxury or mutinous by means of their riches. Neither was there less prudence in the precept concerning prayers, for the injunction of the *salah* five times in twenty-four hours obliged them to a diligence and sobriety, which perhaps no other contrivance could have engaged them to, and doth also imprint in them a sense of their religion which, without apostasy, nothing could obliterate. Besides, it is a part of that precept never to mention any prophet or person reverenced by the Mahometans but with this eulogy: "God's peace be with him of glorious memory, et cetera"; or any enemy thereto but thus: "God's curse be upon him, God keep him from hurting us, et cetera"—which sayings did fix them more and more in their religion and estranged them more and more from their adversaries.

AS TO THEIR OPINIONS CONCERNING GOD, PURGATORY, JUDGMENT, AND PARADISE, THEY ARE THESE:

HAT GOD IS ONE GOD; that there is none other; that He hath no equal,[1] no son nor associate; that His eternity hath neither beginning nor end; that it is impossible to explain properly His attributes, and that no intellect can comprehend the extent of His dominion; that contemplative men may conjecture at His being by the daily occurents on earth, but never understand His essence; that the heavens are His throne, the earth His footstool, but that the government of both is no trouble to Him; that He is omnipotent, omniscient, omnipresent, who sits upon the universal throne by His essence, and by His understanding penetrates into all things; that His providence disposeth of all affairs below, neither doth anything fall out, not the corn grow, not the grass wither but according to the decrees of His eternal predestination; that whatsoever man doth ascribe to Him or imagine to be in Him, it is eternal, and those attributes do not argue any composition or distinction in His being; that all things in this world, good or evil, befall us according to His will; that the beginnings, progress, and conclusion of all emergencies depend absolutely upon Him: and that He determined from all eternity whatsoever should come to pass; that His knowledge extends to the deepest secrets; that nothing happens against or not according to His pleasure; that in all matters to think, to will, to do, depends upon Him; that the souls of men are immortal; that those who are preserved by faith and the intercession of the apostles of God—Moses, Isa, Mahomet—from sin do upon death live in happiness until the resurrection and day of judgment;[2] that those who are more or less wicked must in the grave and in a kind of purgatory undergo some torments until the last day, and there with more or less difficulty they shall be saved, but that nothing of evil, how little so ever, shall escape unpunished, nor any thing of good, how small so ever, pass unrewarded.[3]

This is the sum of the Mahometans' religion.

As to the manner whereby the Alcoran doth explicate their purgatory or paradise: it is not to be censured by the Christians. It is evident that the Jews, Judaizing Christians, and other sects of Christians were diffused through Arabia **<130>** and Mahomet, as he continued the ancient usages, so he retained those principles which the nation had imbibed and which he had the Christians and Jews to depose for. Such were those, not only concerning the torments in the grave, praying for the dead, and purgatory, but also of paradise and its joys, as he expresseth in his Alcoran. Doth not Isa (Luke 22:30) speak of eating and drinking at his table in his kingdom and of drinking wine there (Mark 14:25)? I profess that I cannot distinguish betwixt the paradise described by the Jews (and consequently avowed by the Judaizing Christians) and that which Mahomet doth propose to his followers, and if the words be the same I cannot see why they are not as liable to any equitable construction, according as the reason or prejudices of men do sway, as anything delivered by the Jews or Christians.[4] Since all the descriptions we use concerning the senses and nature of glorified bodies are equivocal and deduced from what we are accustomed to upon earth; since God himself in scripture is described with the parts, actions, and passions of a man, I do not comprehend wherein lies the fault or ignorance in giving the like account of paradise.

Much might be said for the Mahometan doctrine of predestination, did I think any doubted but that it was the general tenet of the Jews and primitive Christians. And, in reference to the soldiery, none venture their lives in battle like those who suppose they cannot die before their appointed time, that all the contrivances of men depend upon the sovereign will of God, that there is no such thing as chance or any mistakes in the management of human affairs but are all swayed by destiny. In the late wars of England it was an observation of O. Cromwell's that the best fighters were of this opinion and he gave no encouragement to such preachers as taught the contrary.[5]

As to the rites and ceremonies used in their prayers, pilgrimages, and other occasions: many of them if not all were anciently used by the Arabians and prudentially accommodated. These are not reckoned as fundamentals or principal points of their religion, but as trials of their obedience to the more necessary law they teach.[6] it adds to the majesty of the author of their religion that there be some parts thereof, some institutions, which transcend our reason: that where our intellect doth comprehend and assent to write or command as good **<131>** or wise, albeit our compliance be most exact and ready, yet our devotion is less than when we entirely obey upon the command of God since in the other case, we seem rather to follow our own judgment than that of the legislator.[7] And that as in great empires the reverence to the prince is best secured and established where some capricious and arbitrary decrees intervene and amaze rather than inform the minds of the subjects, so in religion, our obedience becomes more perfect when we know that the divine intellect and will is not subordinate or conformable to ours, but transcends it.

The Mosaical constitutions give much countenance to this plea and an allegorical brain which knows how to dive into mysteries may undoubtedly find out rich mines of knowledge, types, and figures in Mahometanism. Amongst these trials of obedience, they reckon the observation of Friday, circumcision, abstinence from swine's flesh and blood, etcetera. But as to circumcision and those other ceremonies purely Arabian, I take them to be extremely necessary to such an empire as he designed. And, his country not yielding numbers sufficient for the pursuance thereof, this obliging all to circumcision, et cetera, was no less wisdom than old Rome practiced in denizening foreigners or the Jews in their proselytes. And Mahomet, by prohibiting his Alcoran to be translated into other languages, did (as far as in him lay) oblige all his followers to an unity of language. And, certainly, an unity of language, religion, and customs conduceth very much to the strength and peace of a monarchy.[8]

Concerning some particular institutions of Mahomet, it may not be amiss to treat because they seem to evince his great prudence as a legislator. One is the permission of polygamy. The Alcoran gives liberty to each Musulman to take to himself as many wives as he pleaseth: two, three, four, or more, except he fear he is unable to render all due benevolence.[9] Neither is there any positive restraint in their law to a determinate number, wherein the doctrine of Mahomet doth exactly agree with the Law of Nature as Grotius, St. Austin, and all the Jewish rabbins even to Maimonides, whose saying exactly agrees with Mahomet's. As to **<132>** the Law of Nature, I do aver, as you may see in Selden.[10] But what the Law of Nature doth so indefinitely permit, the Mosaical Law hath somewhat moderated, for the kings of Israel are forbidden to multiply unto themselves wives (Deuteronomy 17:17). It is evident that David had several wives besides his concubines, even to the number of six or eight,[11] and the rabbins tell us that the Jewish king might have eighteen wives, notwithstanding that precept. And that David did not sin therein doth appear hence, that God upbraideth him as with a particular favor that he had done him in giving him sundry wives (2 Samuel 12:8). And where his sins are reckoned up, it is said that David turned not aside from all that the Lord had commanded him, except in the case of Uriah's wife (1 Kings 15:5). As to private persons, there are rules fixed in the Levitical Law concerning such as have two wives how to demean themselves (Deuteronomy 21:15). And the precept of the brother marrying with his brother's wife is believed generally to conclude married persons also,[12] so that we cannot imagine polygamy to be interdicted to the Jews.

If we consult Christianity, whether polygamy be thereby prohibited to all or only to bishops, who ought to be the husband of one wife (1Timothy 3: 2) may be a question. The Emperor Valentinian made a law that any man might have two wives and married two himself.[13] It doth not seem to be a part of the ceremonial law, nor politically confined to the Jews only. How then comes it to be abrogated? Besides it was indubitably practiced by the Judaizing Christians, from whom Mahomet derived much of his religion and is practiced by the Jews in the east to this day: "Judei orientales plures ducunt uxores; occidentalibus quidem licet, sed honoris gratia non faciunt. Paulus noluit Christianos plures ducere et praecipue episcopos, ut sic Judaeis os obturaret qui Christianis hoc objiciebant. Judaeis non praecipit ut cum tres habeant, duas repudient, unam servent."[14]

So that we may conjecture that Mahomet was led by the Judaizing Christians that polygamy was not prohibited by their gospel, and that he esteemed that tenet to be a corruption in the vulgar gospels and inconsistent with his doctrine who came not to abolish but to fulfill the law (Matthew 5:17), being rather **<133>** a paganical tenet derived from the Roman constitutions and complied with by the degenerate Christians. It is indeed remarkable that the Mahometans do upon tradition permit but four wives, and since this tradition is conformable to the Jewish doctrines, why may we not think it consonant to that of the Judaizing Christians?[15]

As for concubines, it seems they are not repugnant to the Law of Nature since Abraham, Nachor, Jacob, Eliphaz retained them; nor to the Mosaical Law since Gideon had one and Saul, David, Solomon, and Rehoboam many.[16] It was not held inconsistent with Christianity in the days of Justinian for a single Christian to have a concubine, nor is it prohibited by the Canon Law.[17] By the Mahometan laws and usages a Musulman hath no stint as to concubines, but they must not be other than slaves (between which a Musulman, by their civil law, no marriage can intervene).[18] Upon inquiry, I find that polygamy and the use of concubines were most ancient and inveterate practices of the ancient world. And Mahomet might thereupon comply with them: they were both exceedingly subservient to the multiplying of subjects which is the sinew of empire and therefore prudential. They were requisite upon another score because that in the east and south it is observed that there are far more women than men: and he who pretended to be a prophet and a follower of Abraham, Moses, Isa, et cetera had their precedents and the Law of Nature to justify him in the allowance.

I do not find that polygamy is a piece of sensuality in the Mahometan religion or any argument thereof, nor one sentence in their whole religion, either Alcoran or traditions, tending that way. You may sooner hope to find such suggestions in the Old and New Testament. Yet there is as much luxury in the discipline of their prophet as in the constitutions of Lycurgus.[19] I have in the embassy of Ali represented the sense of the Mahometans concerning the pleasures of this life. As to those of the future, I know not why he should be so blamed for representing the joys of paradise by sensual delights. For if our souls must rise with the same bodies which we have here, excepting that our mortality shall put on immortality (for pleasure ariseth as **<134>** knowledge doth from our senses), and though the stoical and Christian (I add and Mahometan) arguments are conclusive against placing of happiness in sensuality here on earth, yet if we imagine our bodies to be of the same kind and only glorified, the state of the question varieth, and they all come to nothing. The four rivers of paradise of pure water, excellent milk, rich wine, and pure honey are the same with those of the Jews, saving that the rabbins would have their wine spiced, and that they think the Leviathan and Behemoth will make as good dishes there as caviar and botargo or sturgeon here. And they will have a river of oil and balsam, also viands of fruit, and bread, and butter, and thirty-seven tables made of pearl. And the description of the New Jerusalem (Revelation 21:22) doth so much resemble the paradise of Mahomet that one would hardly imagine that any should condemn the latter as ridiculous and gross and yet approve the former as spiritual truth. And the condemnation of the wicked to a lake of brimstone fire hath as much of folly as the paradise of Mahomet.[20]

But this is a digression.

If I may conjecture another reason besides what policy suggested to Mahomet, I would deduce it from hence: that he held (as did the Jews and Judaizing Christians) that all men were absolutely obliged by that first precept of increasing and multiplying which could not be fulfilled by the sterile or those who left no issue behind them.[21] And as the Mahometan marriages have an aspect this way, so there is nothing therein or in their divorces (which last were allowed by the ancient Christian emperors and the laws of the Goths and Franks in several cases) which the Jews and other oriental nations will not justify, as you may read in Selden's treatise concerning an Hebrew wife.

Another prudent law of Mahomet was that whereby he prohibited usury to his Musulmen. It was an ancient Arabian law that every man ought to improve his estate and that every one that did should be honored and who did not should be punished.[22] This prudent legislator, knowing of what importance it was to an empire that was to be great and lasting, that the subjects be not **<135>** too poor and needy, lest that incline them to rebellion and revolt against their prince, nor exasperated against each other (whence arises revenge, unjust self-preservation, and all its evil consequences) as frequently happens upon usury, amended this former law. And, besides his general obligation to deeds of charity, he did enjoin all his Musulmen to follow some trade or vocation whence he desired this other benefit, that his people had their thoughts and bodies perpetually employed (which is a great secret in government and which perhaps was the reason of the public shows among the Romans, et cetera) and the poorer tradesmen were the better satisfied, their employments not being accounted dishonorable.

Since the prince and the basket maker were of one trade (behold another political mystery), and to prevent any inconvenience that his Musulmen might not hold usury as lawful as trade and object that the bartering and exchange of goods was a sort of usury, he declares in a *surat* that God had permitted the one but not the other. By his law it is prohibited any Musulman to practice usury not only with a Musulman but with any Christian living under the protection of their monarchy. Nay, if he comes out of any territory not subject to them, usury with him is unlawful.[23] Any man that considers the civil laws of Mahomet will find perpetual reasons to admire his subtlety and wisdom. It was a secret of Moses that no Israelite should practice usury with an Israelite: and this was very well, considering that Moses did not design to enlarge the Jewish empire but to preserve his people entire and unanimous in their narrow precincts.

But Mahomet, proposing vaster designs, prohibits it to all strangers living under the protection of the Musulmen. For, had this been permitted, there being such a multitude of Christians and others among them, this *questuosa segnities* (as Pliny calls it),[24] the facile way of growing rich by usury would have effeminated the Mahometans. The frequent and great quarrels and tumults arising upon usury would have endangered their empire and rendered the government odious and oppressive to the stranger subjects: whereof he prohibited all usury with them. But yet it is a rule in their law that a Musulman may practice usury with a Christian living in a foreign territory and, by such means, extort or cheat out of him his estate,[25] the reason of which is because such persons **<136>** are, as it were, in a perpetual hostility with them, and where a war is always deemed lawful against them, usury may be put in execution. The Mahometan reason: "Quia facultates eorum patent veluti ad praedam et direptio earum licita est quacunque via" is the same which St. Ambrose gives: "Cui jure inferuntur arma, huic legitime indicantur usure: quem bello vincere potes, de hoc [cito] potes [centesima] vindicare te. Ab hoc usuram exige, quem non fit crimen occidere. Sine ferro dimicat qui usuram flagitat. Sine gladio se de hoste ulciscitur qui fuerit usuraruis exactor inimici. Ergo ubi jus belli, ibi etiam jus usuræ."[26] Let then that please censure Mahomet as ignorant and brutish. Some discourses of politics, considering what evils arise from the Levitical permission of usury with strangers, would prefer the wisdom of Mahomet before that of Moses.

This puts me in mind of another Mahometan constitution against gaming and accumulating riches by any kind of lottery,[27] which he prohibits, as also wine, as introducing discord and poverty and a neglect of their duty to God. From this law it appears how prudently Mahomet did weigh the least and most remote consequences and would not allow of those distinctions betwixt abuse and use or those sophisms by which the Christians delude themselves into practices that terminate at last in the ruin of their commonwealth. He knew how much it imported a Musulman to pray to God and have him reverentially before his eyes always. He foresaw that such as were given to gaming and engaged by the hopes of further winning or sense of losing would be apt to forget their *sallah* or daily prayers and so lapse into irreligion. He foresaw that gaming and the profits arising thence would induce men to cheat each other and that the first principle of cheating was a contempt of God, a disregard of other men, and an inordinate desire of wealth. It was his usual saying that he that was professed with a vehement thirst after riches and temporal advantages is in a fair way to commit all manner of wickedness. He knew that private quarrels often occasioned public damages and involved families, towns, and kingdoms in an universal ruin. Nor did the inconveniences seem less which follow private losses, which not only include the small detriment of a few, but many, and excite the desperate and needy to the highest and most pernicious attempts in which the public suffers. He knew that the examples of some gamesters infect others, **<137>** that men are naturally more prone to hope than fear, to be idle than work, to neglect than attend the service of God, to desire trials of enriching themselves suddenly though with great hazards, rather than stay the tedious procedure which industry and wisdom puts them on, and therefore made this severe prohibition, the strictness whereof is such that he permits them not so much as to draw lots who shall pay a shot.[28]

Whether it were his great prudence or care for the worship of the true God, I shall not determine. But certainly his legislative care extended far when he prohibited all observation of omens and all divination by lots, as debates to do or forbear an action by opening the Alcoran as the Romans did Virgil, or shooting an arrow into the air, or drawing an arrow out of the sheaf wherein should be written: "It is not the pleasure of God." This great prophet would not suffer his Musulmen to employ anything but reason in their debates. He imprinted in their minds that there is not any such thing as chance, no mistakes in providence whereby that befalls one which God intended for another;[29] and that it was a sort of atheism to imagine that God would reveal that by the flight or cry of a bird which He would conceal from human prudence; or to conceive that a man's hand could discover more than His judgment; that the Alcoran and conduct of prudence were less available to our direction than the blind drawing out or shooting up of an arrow.

It were an endless task to descant upon the particular motives upon which depends the excellency of his laws. What a discourse might be made upon his uniting the civil and ecclesiastical powers in one sovereign, upon his rejecting all the Christian scripture rather than decide amidst so great uncertainty of books and so difficult rules to judge of the right and to reconcile the different sects and tenets. Was it not prudently foreseen that it would be more easy to introduce a new religion than to reform such a one, and well conjectured that all interested parties would more willingly submit to a novel doctrine than yield themselves to have been all in an error except one party?

It may perhaps be urged as an argument of Mahomet's ignorance that he denies all contagion in the pest and other diseases in man or beast. But if we consider that Hippocrates speaks nothing thereof,[30] and that much may be said for it out of physic and the doctrine of predestination, this objection will have less force than is usually imagined and in reference to the wisdom of it and the successes which his followers have **<138>** gained by that opinion, whilst the Christians yield up their towns, break up their camps, and upon contrary apprehensions these things plead highly for it.

Alcoran—As to the Alcoran, I have shewed that it was not all written at one time but by parcels and upon several occasions. And it was no small obstacle to his progress that for want of paper the prophet was forced to write the scattered *surats* at first upon the bones of sheep and other cattle from which occasion perhaps some *surats* received their appellations, as that of "The Cow." It was never reduced into one volume by Mahomet, but by the care of Abubacr,[31] his immediate successor, who made a collection of all that had been scatteredly written by the Prophet upon the bones or skins of animals, or leaves of palms, or preserved in the memory of his auditors, and deposited this entire copy with Hapsa, the daughter of Omar and wife of Mahomet.[32]

And, after him, Othman, the third successor of the caliphs, suppressed all the spurious copies which either the ignorance or malice of men had diffused and ordered all for the future to be transcribed out of the copy of Hapsa.[33] This Alcoran is written in Arabic verse. It is not one continued poem, but a collection of sundry *surats* or poems which Mahomet published occasionally,[34] the language, the numbers, the style are all so exquisite, inimitable, that Mahomet himself doth frequently urge this as the ground authentic testimony of his apostleship, that the Alcoran doth surpass all human wit and fancy, and offered to be counted an impostor if any man could but write ten verses equal to any therein. The Mahometans esteem each line of it as an entire miracle and say that, if miracles do attest to the reality of a prophet, the author of the Alcoran brought three thousand demonstrations of his legislative power; that other miracles, being once performed in the sight of a few, lose much of their evidence and certainly when they are communicated to posterity. But God by Mahomet took a better course by leaving to mankind one lasting miracle, the truth whereof should in all ages be satisfactory and convincing.

This is the assertion of Bredani and of Ahmed Ben Edris and the words of Algazali are these:[35]

> The Alcoran, a transcendent miracle, and which is more, one that is permanent, from generation to generation. Nor is there any lasting miracle of the prophet, excepting that whereunto he appealed, challenging all the wits of Arabia (and Arabia did then abound with thousands whose chief study was eloquence and poetry) to make one chapter or more that might compare therewith **<139>** and thereby demonstrated to the most incredulous, the truth of his prophesy. And God said concerning it, that if all men and angels should combine to write anything like it, they should fail in their enterprise.

I do not find any understanding author who doth controvert the elegancy of the Alcoran, and it hath this advantage over the Christian Bible, that being a poem there is a greater liberty allowed to fiction, figurative expressions, and allegories than is allowed of in prose. Also defects in chronology and errors in history are here tolerable, though, for my part, I believe that many of the incoherencies and chronological and historical defaults are voluntary, partly because the vulgar, being prepossessed with them (in many cases this is evident to have dissented thereform) would have been prejudicial to his aims, the universal credit of the errors being likely to overbear the real truth of things, partly because it was a received tradition among the Jews and Judaizing Christians (and it is now made use of as an apology for our scripture) that the Spirit of God in the prophets is not confined to the grammatical rules' ordinary methods.

It is further observable that the Alcoran, being such a poem, is not to be judged of by any translation into prose, much less such as is formed in

Christendom. Our English doth follow the French, and the French is very corrupt, altering and omitting many passages.[36] There are so many stories alluded unto: such idioms of Arabic poetry and of the Arabian tongue that it is impossible to explicate it without the help of the Arabic, Persian, and Turkish commentaries, which our translators, not knowing (or for their interest) not regarding, they have obtruded to the world such figments as Mahomet never uttered.[37] I have often reflected upon the exceptions made by the Christians against the Alcoran and find them to be no other than what may be argued with the same strength against our Bible, and what the Christians say for themselves will fully justify the Alcoran. Therefore I will not excuse him by comparing the errors of Mahomet with those of the Talmud and our ecclesiastical history, or the popish legends or the fables recorded in our Fathers and believed by the primitive Christians.

As for miracles, I do not find but that Mahomet constantly rejected their authority as impertinent and unnecessary since so many were obtruded on the world (especially by the Christians) that he scorned the pretense. And he had this further reason: that true miracles and **<140>** false cannot be distinguished by any human test, that the wicked may do real miracles, that the original of miracles might be derived from magic, or are the effect of some celestial constellation ruling the nativity of particular persons. This last opinion was common among the Arabians and Chaldeans and the oriental astrologers so that for him to have insisted on miracles among them would have been to little purpose or advantage. Whatsoever of miracles befell him was ascribed to magic by the Coreischites.[38] And yet did they importune him to transfer mountains, raise the dead, produce an angel visibly, to all which he replied that the greatest of miracles was the Alcoran,[39] that such was their unbelief that they would be obstinate even against miracles and evade them by sundry pretensions.

That miracles were the works of God, not of man, that they never were arbitrary to the prophets, but God wrought them when, where, and how He pleased, and not only to confirm the truth, but sometimes to try His people; and that some prophets never wrought any: the Protestants in the beginning of the Reformation excused themselves handsomely as to this point. It is written of John Baptist expressly that he did no miracles nor do we read that Amos and others did any, that Antichrist may do some, and that the Papists have some real miracles. It would be tedious to transcribe their defense. Yet do I find those miracles recorded of Mahomet though it were his modesty or policy not to insist on them:

First. That he showed the people publicly the moon so cleft into two parts that a mountain was visible in it.[40] Whether he had the use of any telescope or by what chance such an aperture discovered itself in the moon, I know not. But of this miracle there is no mention in the Alcoran, but it is said that before the end of the world such a rupture shall happen, and it bears a resemblance with the predictions of Christ concerning the end of the world. I find that some Mahometans do relate this miracle as if it had happened, but others deny it to have been done. And the Christians needed not to have spent themselves in refuting as impossible what is not pretended to have been done and what it is possible to have seen without the help of our modern glasses.

Secondly. That he, being afflicted with scorching heat, did once cause two trees to remove together thereby to shade him. **<141>**

Thirdly. That the stones saluted him in the streets and cried: "Peace unto thee O Apostle of God," and it is reported of Mahomet that he should say that to his remembrance no stone saluted him in Mecca until God commissioned him for His prophet.

Fourthly. That twice when his army was in great distress for want of water, the prophet putting his hand into a little vessel of water, it issued thence betwixt his fingers in so great a quantity as to supply all their necessities.

Fifthly. That he fed multitudes with a little food, as eighty persons once with four measures of barley and one kid; at another time, also eighty persons with a little bread which multiplied as he brake it into pieces.

Lastly. That he relieved his whole army with a few dates which a damsel brought him in her hand, and there remained many after they were satisfied.

Sixthly. That an old beam or tree did groan audibly as loud as any camel when he removed his station where he preached (which was near to it and made use of a pulpit) and that when he returned to his usual place it desisted to groan.

Seventhly. That a camel came to him and complained of his master that he put him upon hard work and yet made slender provision to feed him.

Eighthly. That the sheep spake to him when he was eating the impoisoned shoulder of mutton and bid him beware to eat it because it was impoisoned.[41]

These are the miracles which are related concerning him whereupon the Mahometans do not much rely. Yet do they say that though they were not done but once or seldom, yet is the concurrent testimony of so many miracles joined together a pregnant evidence of the truth of his apostleship since they are related by credible witnesses who would not conspire to cheat mankind in such a matter; which is also the plea of the Christians and therefore not to be rejected lightly. But the most judicious of them do principally insist upon the Alcoran as a standing miracle, since many persons of singular eloquence did attempt to write the like but never could equal it.

As to the pretenses out of our scripture which were urged in his behalf by his followers, they are those: that God (in the law) is said to have come from Sinai, to have appeared in Seir and manifested himself in Paran: that is, the Mosaical Law came from Mount Sinai, the Gospel from Seir, which are mountains adjacent to **<142>** Jerusalem, and Paran are the mountains about Mecca where Mahomet arose.[42]Also in the Psalms: it is said that God did manifest in Sion *Ectilan Mahumidan*, which words import in the Syriac version a glorious crown, but they mystically or by way of allusion to Mahmud and Mahomet did accommodate to their prophet. Lastly whereas it is said in the Gospel, "Except I go hence, the comforter shall not come," this they interpret about Mahomet, and it is one of the names of Mahomet among the Saracens viz., the Comforter.[43]

They say also that the Christians have corrupted their gospels and expunged many passages which gave credit to Mahomet, and that a Christian priest showed them in a true copy to that purpose and said there was another unsophisticated preserved at Paris.[44]

FINIS[45]

Other arguments which the Turks make use of against the Christians are such as follow: that whereas the Christians believe in one God, they also believe that He is the Father, the Son, and the Holy Ghost, which opinion is so contradictory in itself that it wants no other refutation.

For no human intellect can comprehend how one and the same can be Father, Son, and Holy Ghost, in one sole essence, and at one and the same time. And God did never desire a man to believe what he cannot understand or conceive, but rather adapted man's understanding to assent to and conceive what is necessary and possible to deny, and not conceive what is impossible. This distinguishing faculty, being its excellency, without which can be no true understanding, nor can a man form a right judgment of anything, to be obliged to anything anymore than a newborn child. It is to be confessed that there are many abstruse and hidden things of which our understandings cannot have a perfect notion, of which we can nevertheless judge whether they are possible or impossible and repugnant. We do not perfectly understand the future state, the joys of heaven and pains of hell: we cannot comprehend the methods of the almighty in the working of miracles, nor even His government in the ordinary course.

NOTES

INTRODUCTION

1. The title continues: *ac doctrina omnis, quae & Ismahelitaru, lex, & Alcoranvm dicitur, ex Arabica lingua ante CCCC annos In Latinam translata.* That same year witnessed the publication in Paris of Guillaume Postel's *Alcorani seu legis Mahometi et Evangelistarum concordiae liber,* which, notwithstanding its title ("concord"), stated that Islam was a heresy similar to Protestantism that could easily be defeated. See, however, Nancy Bisaha, who argues that Renaissance humanists examined Islam from a cultural and political rather than a religious perspective: *Creating East and West: Renaissance Humanists and the Ottoman Turks* (Philadelphia, 2004). See also Matthew Dimmocle, *Mythologies of The Prophet Muhammad in Early Modern English Culture* (Cambridge, 2013).

2. John Tolan, "European Accounts of Muhammad's Life," in Jonathan E. Brockopp, ed., *The Cambridge Companion to Muhammad* (New York, 2010), 226–250. See also Gunny, *The Prophet Muhammad,* ch. 1.

3. Shireen Khairallah, "Arabic Studies in England in the Late Seventeenth and Early Eighteenth Centuries" (Ph.D. diss., University of London, 1972), 82.

4. P. M. Holt, "The Study of Arabic Historians in Seventeenth-Century England," in *Studies in the History of the Near East* (London, 1973), 37, in 27–49.

5. All folio references are to the University of London manuscript. I have retained the spelling of the manuscript in the course of this introduction.

6. The only biography and study of Stubbe remains Jacob, *Henry Stubbe.* See also Wood, *Athenae Oxonienses*; Hill, *The Experience of Defeat,* 252–277; and Feingold, "Stubbe, Henry (1632–1676)," in *ODNB.*

7. G. J. Toomer, *Eastern Wisedome and Learning: The Study of Arabic in Seventeenth-Century England* (Oxford, 1996), 224. Judging from their transliterations of Arabic words and phrases, neither Stubbe nor Prideaux knew Arabic. For a biography of Prideaux, see Khairallah, "Arabic Studies," 132–157.

8. BL MS 32553, Letters from Stubbe to Hobbes, fols. 5 and 25v (8 July 1656 and 13 January 1657 respectively). The first letter in the collection is dated 8 July 1656 and the last is 6 May 1657. See also Nicastro, *Lettere di Henry Stubbe a Thomas Hobbes.* In that same year, 1657, Stubbe wrote in defense of Hobbes against Wallis, *A Severe Enquiry into the late Oneirocritica; or,An Exact Accovnt of the Grammatical Part of the Controversy betwixt Mr. Hobbes and J. Wallis D.D.* (London, 1657). Either

Stubbe did not finish the translation or he never sent a copy to Hobbes, who, in 1668, translated and published a condensed version of *Leviathan* in Latin.

9. Thomas Hobbes, *The Correspondence*, ed. Noel Malcolm (Oxford, 1994), 2:782; Wood, *Athenae*, 3:1069.

10. Ibid., 3:1071.

11. Stubbe, *The Common-wealth of Israel*, 3.

12. Wood, *Athenae*, 3:1071.

13. See the preface to *An Essay in Defence of the Good old Cause* and *A vindication of that most prudent and honourable knight*, 1. This treatise was welcomed by John Locke, who wrote a letter to Stubbe in which he discussed the latter's views on toleration. See Locke, *Two Tracts on Government*, 242–244.

14. Cook, "Physicians and the New Philosophy," 251.

15. Stubbe, *Legends no histories*, 1—the second part. See the essay by Cook (in the previous note) on this confrontation.

16. Ibid., 154.

17. Stubbe, *Campanella revived*, 17.

18. In May 1670 he wrote to Secretary of State Arlington hoping that his quarrel with the Royal Society would not "displease your lordship or any other English patriot, since it has no other design than to support the monarchy, the Protestant religion, and the peace and welfare of the nation; and to vindicate the two universities and my own family," *Calendar of State Papers Domestic Series, Charles II, with Addenda, 1660 to 1670*, 10:224.

19. Stubbe, *Campanella revived*, 62.

20. Ibid., 10.

21. Samuel Butler's "The Elephant in the Moon," in John Wilders and Hugh de Quehen, eds., *Hudibras Parts I and II and Selected Other Writings* (Oxford, 1973), 206, l.431. Because of these attacks, Westfall, in *Science and Religion in Seventeenth-Century England*, unfairly describes Stubbe as "a wholly venal scoundrel," 23*n*17.

22. Stubbe, *Campanella revived*, 7.

23. Ibid., 13.

24. See my study of Ross in *Islam in Britain* (Cambridge, 1999), ch. 3. For the earlier Latin translations of the Qur'ān, see Hartmut Bobzin, "Latin Translations of the Koran: A Short Overview," *Der Islam* 70 (1993): 193–206.

25. Henry Stubbe, "To the Reader," in *A justification of the present war against the United Netherlands*.

26. John Spurr, *England in the 1670s: "This Masquerading Age"* (Oxford, 2000), 34.

27. For a detailed discussion of these two treatises and Stubbe's political stance, see chapter 6 in Jacob, *Henry Stubbe*.

28. The Edict of Milan, AD 313, in *A further iustification of the present war against the United Netherlands*, 34, 43.

29. Ibid., 83.

30. Stubbe, *Rosemary & Bayes*, 4–5. See also James R. Jacob, "The Authorship of 'An Account of the Rise and Progress of Mahometanims,'" *N&Q* 26 (1979): 10–11.

31. Wood, *Athenae*, 3:1071.

32. Even nonconformist contemporaries recognized the difference between the two: see the manifesto of fifteen nonconformists, including Richard Baxter, *The Judgment of Non-conformists, of the Interest of Reason in matters of Religion* (London, 1676), especially 6: "We deny not but some Non-conformists, and Conformists did cast out their suspitions of two very Learned rational Men, Mr. Hales, and Mr. Chillingworth, as if they had favoured Socinianisme, because they so much used, and Ascribed to Reason, in Judging of matters of Religion."

33. Stubbe uses the new English term, *Islamism,* in a positive sense. Contrast its use with Thomas Warmstry's *The Baptized Turk; or, a Narrative of the happy Conversion of Signioer Rigep Dandulo* (London, 1658), 117. See also Thomas Bedwell who used "Alesalem," in "The Arabian Trudgman," in *Mohammedis Imposturae: That is, a Discovery of the Manifold Forgeries,Falshoods, and horrible impieties of the blasphemous seducer Mohammed* (London 1615).

34. The National Archives (TNA): SP 29/275/276. See also the reference to two other short pieces on Queen Elizabeth and in defense of the king's suspension of the "laws against conventicles by his declaration of March 15, 1672," *CSPD Charles II, October, 1672, to February, 1673,* 14:350.

35. See Stubbe's letter to Williamson on 8 July 1672 describing what he plans to write against the Dutch, *CSPD, Charles II, May 18th to September 30,* 1672, 13:319. But Stubbe was so eager to proclaim his royalism that he aligned himself with Samuel Parker—who, like him, had conformed to the Anglican Church after the Restoration and become a mouthpiece for the monarchy.

36. James and Mary were married by proxy in a Catholic ceremony on 20 September 1673. Stubbe's piece argued against marriage by proxy and wondered "What benefits may accrue, or be justly expected from the Farreigner with whom such Alliance and Marriage is to be Contracted."

37. Actually, a few months earlier, in *A further justification,* he had praised the "prudence of His Royal Highness" and criticized those "Inferiours" who "foment even just quarrels or resentments against their Suepriours" and "Men in Authority," 83–85 (irregular pagination).

38. *CSPD Charles II, March 1st to October 31st, 1673,* 15:599.

39. Wood, *Athenae,* 3:1082.

40. BL MS 35835, 18 July 1674, fol. 276r in a cluster of fols. 269–276.

41. "This day there came in A Tun of Madeira wine, which I think will be excellent for your Lady: I have tasted it & presume to prescribe a pipe of it for physick for her Stomach. It is not hot in the mouth, but warm in the Stomach, it is as of good a body as Sack, and better tasted than Bourdeaux, but paler coloured, it is two years old. It will come for about 12 d a bottle. It is good at Meal, but not for a Debauch. It bears 272v water in a general proportion and so will be better for her than Beer. It is an excellent Table Wine, & will seem extraordinary in the Country. My Lord of Ossery hath half a Tun & Sir Hugh Cholmly a Tun. This wine seldom or never comes into England, but in the West Indies they could not live without it, or digest any meat." BL MS 35835, fol. 272r–v.

42. BL Sloane 35 is a posthumous inventory of his books.

43. Joseph Glanvill, "To the Reader," in *A further discovery of M. Stubbe* (London, 1671).

44. Volunteers at the abbey kindly showed me the recent and "comprehensive" inventory of all the names on memorials and gravestones inside the church (26 July 2012). There was no record of Henry Stubbe.

45. For studies of Stubbe, see Jacob, *Henry Stubbe*; Kaplan, "Greatrakes the Stroker; Champion, "Legislators, Imposters" and *The Pillars of Priestcraft Shaken*, ch. 4; Kontler, "'Mahometan Christianity'"; Birchwood, "Vindicating the Prophet"; Rose, "Royal Ecclesiastical Supremacy and the Restoration Church"; Garcia, "A Hungarian Revolution in Restoration England" and *Islam and the English Enlightenment.*

46. Jacob, *Henry Stubbe*, 2.

47. Ibid., 6, 129, and 139–160.

48. Hill, *The Experience of Defeat*, 263.

49. Champion. *The Pillars of Priestcraft Shaken*, ch. 4. See also idem, "'I remember a Mohometan Story of Ahmed ben Idris'," which focuses on Stubbe and Toland.

50. See also Garcia, *"Islam and the English Protestant Imagination, 1660–1830"* (Ph.D. diss., University of Illinois at Urbana-Champaign, 2007).

51. Holt, *A Seventeenth-Century Defender of Islam*, 29.

52. See my "A Note on Alexander Ross and the English Translation of the Qur'ān," *Journal of Islamic Studies* 23 (2011): 76–84.

53. For a study of Milton's familiarity with Islam, see Eid Abdallah Dahiyat, *John Milton and the Arab-Islamic Culture* (Amman, 1987), revised as *Once Upon the Orient Wave: Milton and the Arab Muslim World* (London, 2012). See also William G. Kenton III, "English Liberty and Turkish Tyranny: The Symbolic Function of the East in Milton's Poetry and Prose" (Ph.D. diss., New York University, 2005), 119–134 ("Satan as Sultan").

54. In so doing, Stubbe advanced the Islamic interpretation, which Johann Hottinger had called "errore plane intolerabili," *Historia Orientalis* (Tiguri, 1660), 38.

55. See C. Edmund Bosworth, "The Prophet Vindicated: A Restoration Treatise on Islam and Muhammad," *Religion* 6 (1976): 11 in 1–12.

56. H. John McLachlan, *Socinianism in Seventeenth-Century England* (Oxford, 1951), 55. As he continues, Chillingworth and other Laudian clergy were accused of Socinianism as early as 1643, 164. See also John Marshall, *John Locke, Toleration and Early Enlightenment Culture* (Cambridge, 2006) for a discussion of Chillingworth and anti-Trinitarianism in ch. 7.

57. Champion, *The Pillars of Priestcraft Shaken*, 107, 110.

58. Quoted by Christopher Hill, *Milton and the English Revolution* (London, 1977), 295, from *A Censure upon Certain Passages Contained in the History of the Royal Society* (1670). See also Hill's discussion of "Anti-Trinitarianism," ibid., 285–296.

59. Jacob, *Henry Stubbe*, 75.

60. See the English translation, Giovanni Paolo Marana, *The eight volumes of letters writ by a Turkish spy*, trans. Daniel Saltmarsh (London, 1694).

61. Cited by Jacob, *Henry Stubbe* 159. Humerto Garcia states that Stubbe's work was "implicit" in John Toland's *Nazarenus* because Magney compared Toland's "'Mahometan Christianity' to *The Rise and Progress of Mahometanism*." Garcia, *Islam and the English Enlightenment*, 52. Magney mentions the "Physician of some note" (Stubbe), but he does not quote him at all, relying instead on Hottinger, Warner, and

Reeland, the first two of whom were widely used by Stubbe. The reason he ignores Stubbe is because the latter had praised Muḥammad, while Hottinger and Warner had not. And, of course, Magney is vitriolic in his description of the Prophet and of Islam, as that chapter shows.

62. Jacob invokes this episode in support of his view of Stubbe's "Socinian" leanings. Jacob, *Henry Stubbe*, 155. But there is no evidence that Stubbe belonged to the group that, five years after the death of Stubbe, approached the ambassador. See my discussion of this episode in *Britain and Barbary, 1589–1689* (Gainesville, 2005), 158–159.

63. Wood, *Athenae*, 3:1071.

64. Quoted by Humberto Garcia, "Islam in the English Radical Protestant Imagination, 1660–1830," 52.

65. Ibid., 51. The view had been advanced by Jacob, *Henry Stubbe*, 139–142, and repeated by Hill, *The Experience of Defeat*, 277.

66. Jacob, *Henry Stubbe*, 121.

67. For a general discussion of Restoration theological arguments, see Gerard Reedy, S. J., *The Bible and Reason: Anglicans and Scripture in Late Seventeenth-Century England* (Philadelphia, 1985). See the sermon by Barrow, "Of the Impiety and Imposture of Paganism and Mahometanism," *Theological Works of Isaac Barrow*, 8 vols. (Oxford, 1830), esp. 5:24–31. Interestingly, his Latin treatise on "Epitome fidei et religionis Turcicae, a Muhameto Kureischita, arabum propheta" is less hostile. Barrow uses the term *Islam* rather than *Mahometanism*, ibid., 8:145 ff.

68. He actually lumped the Socinians with "Atheists" and "Papists": *A Specimen of some animadversions upon a book entituled, Plus ultra* (London, 1670), 13.

69. None of these names appear in Jacob's study. Stubbe kept a 1649 copy of Salmasius's *Defensio Regia, pro Carolo I* till the day he died (BL MS Sloane 35, fol. 18r). See also Champion, who counted the number of references to some of these writers in Stubbe's 1701 manuscript: Hottinger, thirty-six times and Pococke fifty-six times: "'I remember a Mahometan Story of Ahmed Ben Edris,'" 464 and note 59.

70. See G. J. Toomer, "John Selden, the Levant and the Netherlands," in Alastair Hamilton, Maurits H. Van Den Boogert, and Bart Westerweel, eds., *The Republic of Letters and the Levant* (Leiden, 2005), 53–76.

71. Hobbes, *The Correspondence*, 2:759–763.

72. Gunny believes that Prideaux may have intended his account as a refutation of Stubbe (*The Prophet Muhammad*, 51). The propinquity between Stubbe's and Prideaux's accounts lies in the common sources that they used, especially Hottinger, Pococke, Rycaut, and Erpenius/al-Makīn. For references to Stubbe after his death, see Jacob, *Henry Stubbe*, ch. 8.

73. See my discussion of this treatise in *Europe Through Arab Eyes, 1578–1727* (New York, 2009), 96–98. See also Adrian Reeland, *A Defence of the Mahometans from Several Charges fully laid against them by Christians* in *Four treatises concerning the doctrine, discipline and worship of the Mahometans* (London, 1712), 185, note c.

74. Rijk Smitskamp, *Philologia Orientalis: A Description of Books Illustrating the Study and Printing of Oriental Languages in Sixteenth- and Seventeenth-Century Europe* (Leiden, 1992), 287.

75. As Loop shows, in his "Johann Heinrich Hottinger (1620–1667) and the *Historia Orientalis*," Hottinger used his extensive study of the Qur'ān and of various Arabic manuscripts to present a Protestant interpretation of church history. Jan Loop, *Church History and Religious Culture* 88 (2008): 169–203.

76. In *The Present State of the Ottoman Empire*, Rycaut stated that as "Mahometanism" was first revealed, "it found a great part of the World illuminated with Christianity, endued with active Graces, Zeal and Devotion, and established within it self with purity of Doctrine, Union, and firm profession of Faith," *The Present State of the Ottoman Empire* (London, 1668), 98.

77. G. J. Toomer's *Eastern Wisedome and learning: the Study of Arabic in Seventeenth-Century England* remains the most important book on the subject. See also the Panizzi Lectures of 1996 by Charles Burnett, *The Introduction of Arabic Learning into England* (London, 1997) for a detailed discussion of the medieval period; and Karl H. Dannenfeldt, "The Renaissance Humanists and the Knowledge of Arabic," *Studies in the Renaissance* 2 (1955): 96–117.

78. *The first printed Catalogue of the Bodleian Library, 1605: a facsimile* (Oxford, 1986).

79. William Bedwell, "To the Christian Reader," in *Mohammedis imposturae: that is, A discovery of the manifold forgeries, falsehoods, and horrible impieties of the blasphemous seducer Mohammed* (London, 1615). For the Arabic manuscripts at Oxford, see Colin Wakefield, "Arabic Manuscripts in the Bodleian Library: the Seventeenth-Century Collections," in G. A. Russell, ed., *The "Arabick" Interest of the Natural Philosophers in Seventeenth-Century England* (Leiden, 1994), 128–146.

80. The Hartlib Papers, Sheffield University, Great Britain: Samuel Hartlib Electronic Project, CD-ROM, 29/3/64 A. I am grateful to Professor Donald Dickson for his help.

81. Mordechai Feingold, "Oriental Studies," in Nicholas Tyacke, ed., *The History of the University of Oxford* (Oxford, 1997), 4:481, 490.

82. Quoted by Toomer, *Eastern Wisedome*, 108.

83. Leonard Twells, *The Theological Works of the Learned Dr. Pocock*, 2 vols. (London, 1740), 1:35.

84. Brian Walton, *Polyglot* (London, 1657), 1:95. Their topics, he explained, ranged from mathematics to Aristotle's physics and Ptolemy's geography, with collections, in the library of Fez alone, reaching thirty-two thousand volumes.

85. Bodleian MS Or 298, 1. See also the 1669 *Lexicon Heptaglotton* of Edmund Castell, professor of Arabic at Cambridge. In the *History of the Royal Society* (1667), Thomas Sprat praised "the Learned Age of the Arabians" and mentioned how "some worthy and industrious Men of our Nation, who have search'd into their Monuments" believe the Arabians "almost compar'ed to Rome, and Athens." Thomas Sprat, *History of the Royal Society*, ed. Jackson I. Cope and Harold Whitmore Jones (London, 1959), 45.

86. Peter Rietbergen, "A Maronite Mediator Between Seventeenth-century Mediterranean Cultures," *LIAS* 16 (1989), 25 in 13–41.

87. Cited in Adrian Reeland, *A Defence of the Mahometans from Several Charges fully laid against them by Christians* in *Four treatises*, 61.

88. *Synodikon, sive, Pandectae canonum ss, apostolorum, et conciliorum ab ecclesia Graeca receptorum* (Oxford, 1672).

89. *Purchas his Pilgrimage* (London, 1617), 284. It is not clear whom Purchas had in mind, but Nicholas of Cusa had mentioned that a Christian Arab had refuted a Muslim who had tried to convert him, "Prologues to the Examination of the Koran" (1461) in *Toward a New Council of Florence: "On the Peace of Faith" and Other Works by Nicolaus of Cusa*, trans. with introd. William F. Wertz (Washington, DC, 1993), 387. For a full translation of *Cribratio Alkorani*, see Jasper Hopkins, *Nicholas of Cusa's De Pace Fidei and Cribratio Alkorani: Translation and Analysis* (Minneapolis, 1990). As Hopkins observes, the Christian Arab is al-Kindī.

90. See Edward Pococke's translation of Abū al-Faraj, *Historia Compendiosa Dynastiarum* (Oxford, 1663), 93. For other early Christian Arabic views on Muḥammad, see Samir K. Samir, "The Prophet Muhammad as Seen by Timothy I and Some Other Arab Christian Authors," in David Thomas, ed., *Syrian Christians Under Islam: The First Thousand Years* (Leiden, 2001): 75–106. For Arabic scientific material, see Francis J. Carmody's critical bibliography of *Arabic Astronomical and Astrological Sciences in Latin Translation: A Critical Bibliography* (Berkeley, 1956), part 2.

91. *Geographia nubiensis id est accuratissima totius orbis in septem climata divisi descriptio* (Paris, 1619).

92. This treatise later appeared separately in a small volume about *Arabia, seu Arabūm vicinarumq[ue] gentium orientalium leges, ritus, sacri et profani mores, instituta et historia* (Amsterdam, 1630), 1–90. It is not likely that Stubbe bothered with the translation of a summary of "De Nonnvllis Orientalivm Vrbibvs," which was published by Samuel Purchas in the *Pilgrimes* of 1625 as "Mosleman superstitions and rites." Purchas explained that he had used the "Arabicke Bookes, by the said Maronites Gabriel and John," *Purchas His Pilgrimes* (Glasgow, 1905), 9:162. Indicative of Purchas's hostile attitude to Islam is his selective translation of Sionita's text, his focus on the negative passages, his omission of the chapter on Christian sects in the East, and, most significantly, his contraction of the section on "Viri illustres qui Arab: lingua scripserunt," mentioning only a few of the names that the two Maronites had proudly included. Most egregiously, he omitted the last chapter in which Sionita had shown, by reference to the Qur'ān, how much Mary was venerated in Islamic belief—a celebration that Sionita's Catholic readers would have appreciated. It bears noting that Purchas referred at the end of the translation/adaptation to "my learned Friend Master Bedwell [and his book] called Mahomeds imposture" (9:118). As the title shows, the book was deeply hostile to Muḥammad.

93. *Geographia nubiensis*, 55 (the second part).

94. Ibid., 41.

95. Having been trained at the Maronite College in Rome, the two priests had been exposed to numerous Arabic texts: see the list of books at the college: Nasser Gemayel, *Les Échanges culturels entre les Maronites et l'Europe: Du Collège Maronite de Rome (1584) au Collège de 'Ayn Warqa (1789)*, 2 vols. (Beirut, 1984), 1:180–190.

96. As Camille Aboussouan noted, the aim was to show Europeans "la connaissance du monde des Arabes," *Exposition: Le livre et le Liban jusq'à 1900* (Paris, 1982), 254.

97. Gemayel, *Les Échanges culturels*, 1:326–327.

98. See A. S. Tritton, *The Caliphs and Their Non-Muslim Subjects* (London, 1930), 5–17, and an extended discussion in Maher Y. Abu Munshar, *Islamic Jerusalem and Its Christians* (London, 2007), chs. 2 and 3.

99. Twells, *The Theological Works of the Learned Dr. Pocock*, 1:18.

100. A collection of geographical writings in Arabic by John Gagnier shows how, even in the first half of the eighteenth century, Idrīsī was still used, and how Gagnier was collating the Arabic of al-Idrīsī with the manuscript translation of Idrīsī by Pococke; see Bodleian MS Or 318.

101. The title page of *Purchas his Pilgrimage* mentions that an account of "the Saracenicall Empire Translated out of Arabike by T. Erpenius" is included in the fourth edition. But there is no mention of al-Makīn anywhere in the account about Islam. In 1657 a French translation appeared in Paris: *L'histoire mahometane; ou, Les qurante-neuf chalifes dv Macine*, trans. Pierre Vattier. See also Rijk Smitskamp, *Philolgia Orientalis* (Leiden, 1992), entry 85a.

102. It is interesting that Ibn Khaldūn, who used al-Makīn in his *Kitāb al-'ibar*, consulted the first part that dealt with Jewish and early Christian history and not the part on Islam, which Erpenius translated. See Ayman Fu'ād Sayyid, "Maṣādir Ibn Khaldūn 'an tarīkh ghayr al-Muslimīn fī *Kitāb al-'ibar*," in Muḥammad Zakariya 'Anāni, ed., *Dirāsāt adabiya wa lughawiya* (Cairo, 2011), 539–550. I am grateful to Professor Wadad Kadi for this reference.

103. Edward Pococke, *Specimen Historiae Arabvm* (Oxford, 1650), 383.

104. For John Gregory's Arabic studies, see my "Some Notes on John Gregory and Islam," *Discoveries* 14 (1997): 1–2, 6–7.

105. See P. S.Van Koningsveld's discussion of its use in Muslim Spain, "Christian Arabic Literature from Medieval Spain: An Attempt at Periodization," in Samir Khalil Samir and Jørgen S. Nielsen, eds., *Christian Arabic Apologetics During the Abbasid Period (750–1258)* (Leiden: 1994), 216–217.

106. *Historia Saracenica, qua res gestae Muslimorum* (Leiden, 1625), 2.

107. "Erat autem optimae indolis, voce suavi, visitans &excipiens suos ut ipsum visitabant, &excipiebant, pauperis munerans, Magnates laudans; conversans cum infimatibus; & petentem à se aliquid, non repellens sine eo, aut sermone facili." *Historia Saracenica*, 10.

108. "Cumque venisset ad eum magnus quidam Christianus; surrexit honorem ei exhibens qua de re cum cum alloquerentur quidam, respondit; Cum venerit ad vos Primarius populi alicjus, honorate eum: Atque hic vir maximus est in populo suo. Dixit quoque: Benefacite Cophitis Aegypti: sunt enim vobis genere &affinitate juncti. Item: Qui Christianum opprimit, adversarium cum habebit die Juidicii. Et, Qui Christiano nocet, mihi nocet." *Historia Saracenica*, 11.

109. *Eutychii Agyptii, patriarchae orthodoxorum Alexandrini . . . Ex ejusdem Arabico nunc primùm typis edidit ac versione & commentario auxit Ioannes Seldenus* (London, 1642). For a study of Selden's Eutychius, see Toomer's magisterial *John Selden*, 2:600–614.

110. Twells, *The Theological Works of the Learned Dr. Pocock*, 1:53.

111. This latter edition included a picture of John Selden along with the following explanation on the title page: "Illustriss: Johanne Seldeno" and "Interprete Edwardo Pocockio."

112. Humphrey Prideaux wrote that Selden was thought to be the translator, but that it was Pococke who had done the work, although Selden had "born the Expences of this Chargeable Edition, the most Worthy and Learned Author of that Version acknowledged it by those words in the Title-page, which several having mistaken to the robbing him of the honour of his Work, as if Mr. Selden had begun the Translation, and Dr. Pocock finished it." Prideaux, *The True Nature of Imposture* (London, 1697), 165.

113. Cited in Toomer, *John Selden*, 2:606.

114. "Vita Auctoris," *Contextio Gemmarum* (Oxford, 1658).

115. Selden, *Eutychii Agyptii* (1642), 70–76.

116. See Eutychius of Alexandria, *The Book of Demonstration*, ed. Pierre Cachia (Louvain, 1960), 1:12–13.

117. See, for instance, Pococke, *Eutychii Patriarchae Alexandrini* (Oxford, 1654), 1:307–309.

118. Ibid., 2:279.

119. Ibid. 2:284: "In nomine Dei misericordis, miseratoris, Ab Omaro Ebnil Chetabi, urbis AEliae incolis. Securos fore ipsos quod ad vitas suas, & liberos, opes, & Ecclesias suas; illas scil. nec dirutum iri, nec habitatum: testęque adhibuit." It is not clear if Stubbe knew that al-Makīn had relied on Ibn al-Baṭrīq.

120. Ibid., 2:295.

121. *Arabicae Linguae Tyrocinium id est Grammatica Arabica* (1656), 250–263.

122. Edward Pococke, "Prefatio ad Lectorem," in *Specimen*, 3v. The original Arabic version was an abridgement of a Syriac version—but Pococke worked from the former version. See Lawrence L. Conrad, "On the Arabic Chronicle of Bar Hebraeus," *Parole de L'Orient* 19 (1994): 319–378, especially part A. For the discussion of Islam, see 338–339.

123. Prideaux, *The True Nature of Imposture*, 153.

124. It is interesting that John Gagnier, the French-born orientalist who lived in England until his death in 1740, copied from Pococke's translation of Abū al-Faraj as he compiled general geographical information: Bodleian MS Or 318, 239–266. For the importance and influence of Pococke's translation, see Hans Daiber, "The Reception of Islamic Philosophy at Oxford in the Seventeenth Century: The Pococks' (Father and Son) Contribution to the Understanding of Islamic Philosophy in Europe," in Charles E. Butterworth and Blake Andrée Kessel, eds., *The Introduction of Arabic Philosophy Into Europe* (Leiden, 1994), 69 in 65–82.

125. Pococke, *Historia Compendiosa* (Oxford, 1663), 101.

126. "Futurum est (inquit) ab hoc Puero magnum aliquid, cujus fama per Orientem & Occidentem se diffundet, nam cum approprinquaret nube obumbratus apparuit." Pococke, *Specimen*, 9.

127. Ibid.

128. Interestingly, the same verb was used, "azharū al-dīn al-mustaqīm"/manifestabant, by Eutychius (in Selden's edition) to describe the Nicene position on Christology: *Eutychii Agyptii*, 75.

129. Pococke, *Specimen*, 9, 12, 13.

130. Ibid., 14.

131. Stubbe does not state explicitly that Islam was a reformation of Christianity (fol. 137), but, in 1690, Arthur Bury was forthright: "*Mahomet* professed all the articles of the Christian faith, and declared himself not an Apostate, but a Reformer." Arthur Bury, "The Preface," in *The Naked Gospel* (London, 1690).

132. See also Johann Hottinger, *Historia Orientalis quae, ex variis Orientalium Monumentis Collecta* (Tiguri, 1651), 103–107. I will also use the 1660 edition (also published in Tiguri).

133. Reeland, *A Defence of the Mahometans*, 196. See the earlier use of Warner by Thomas Warmstry, who relied on him for the Qur'ānic view of Jesus, *The Baptized Turk*, 101ff.

134. *Compendium Historicum eorum quae Mahammedani de Christo et praecipuis aliquot religionis Christianae tradiderunt* (Leiden, 1643), 15–16.

135. It is not surprising that Daniel writes that Warner's approach was "polemic, but not primarily so." Norman Daniel, *Islam and the West: The Making of an Image* (Edinburgh, 1960), 287. Hadith is the collection of sayings and determinations by the Prophet Muḥammad.

136. Selden, *Eutychii Agyptii*, 59.

137. For the Muslim Jesus, see Tarif Khalidi, *The Muslim Jesus* (Cambridge, Mass., 2001).

138. (Leiden, 1644), 30–31. It was also included in Hottinger, *Historia Orientalis* (1660), 516.

139. Matar, *Europe Through Arab Eyes*, 33.

140. There is a brief mention of Stubbe in Abdelwahab El-Affendi, ed., *About Muhammad: The Other Western Perspective on the Prophet of Islam* (Richmond, Surrey, 2010), xxvi.

141. Marcus Zeuerius Boxhornius, *Historia universalis sacra et profana a Christo nato ad annum usque* (Lugduni, 1652), 397. Hottinger mentions that Muḥammad's parents were poor, "paupers habūit parens," *Historia Orientalis* (1651), 136.

142. One source for this information is found in Bibliander, *Machvmetis Sarracanorvm principis vita,* part 2, "De Haeresi Herachii et Principatu ac Lege Machvmeti."

143. It is interesting that Gibbon in *Decline and Fall of the Roman Empire*, introduction by Christopher Dawson (New York, 1978), compared the Arabs to the "Medici of Florence," 5:217.

144. Sionita, *De Nonnvullis*, in *Geographia nubiensis,* 17.

145. Thomas Erpenius, *Orationes Tres, De Linguam Ebraeae atque Arabicae Dignitate* (Leiden, 1621), 42.

146. See H. R. McAdoo, *The Spirit of Anglicanism* (London, 1965), ch. 5.

147. *The Alcoran of Mahomet* (London, 1649), sig d r.

148. But first published in 1691: *The Works of Sir William Temple* (London, 1720), 2:221–222. See also Lancelot Addison, *The Life and Death of Mahumed* (London, 1679), which appeared three years after Stubbe's death, ch. 9, and p. 52: "the Alcoran is a very rude Poem."

149. For a study of Du Ryer, see Alastair Hamilton and Francis Richard, *André du Ryer and Oriental Studies in Seventeenth-Century France* (London, 2004); and, for the Qur'ān, chapter 3 in my *Islam in Britain, 1558–1685* (Cambridge, 1998).

150. Pococke does not take a stand, although he advances evidence regarding the literacy of the Prophet. Edward Gibbon mentioned a certain "Mr. White" who argued in a sermon for the literacy of the Prophet, but used it to confirm "imposture." I have not been able to identify the *Sermons* to which he alludes, *Decline and Fall*, 5:233, n. 1. See the discussion of "ummiyy" as illiterate in Pockocke, *Specimen*, 156.

151. *Historia Josephi Patriarchae, ex Alcorano* (Leiden, 1617).

152. Edward Pococke, *Porta Mosis* (Oxford,1655), 244. Five years earlier, in *Specimen*, Pococke had stated that Psalm 50:2 referred to Muḥammad, 17. Selden believed that the Qur'ān had been composed by Muḥammad, but, as Toomer notes, more correctly, it was "God speaking to and through Muhammad." Toomer, *John Selden*, 2:749*n*421.

153. Pococke, *Specimen*, 17.

154. See Bibliander, *Machvmetis Sarracenorvm principis vita*, 189–200. It also appears in Purchas, *Pilgrimage* (1626), bk. 3, ch. 5, 259–263, and Boxhornius, *Historia universalis*, 398–399. Another dialogue was translated into English by John Greaves, again between the Prophet and "Abdalla Ebn Salem the Jew," but with different content: Bodleian, MS. Locke c. 27, fols. 3–9.

155. In regard to "Venery": while the manuscript mentions the Prophet's ability to satisfy "forty women" in one night (fol. 67), the BL Harleian 6189 manuscript mentions "two" (fol. 11).

156. Pococke, *Specimen*, 16.

157. Richard Baxter, *The Reasons of the Christians Religion* (London, 1667), 202–203.

158. Hobbes too had used "poem" in his discussion of prophecy, but not in the context of Islam. Thomas Hobbes, *Leviathan*, ed. C. B. Macpherson (Harmondworth, 1971), 457.

159. Pococke, *Specimen*, 274–292 (Arabic and Latin).

160. Although it is not likely that he would have been familiar with it. See the study and the translation of the Morisco "epic" in Ṣalāḥ Faḍl, *Malḥamat al-Maghāzi al-Moriskiyya* (Cairo, 1989).

161. Part 2, ch. 10. The spelling "Hali" had been popular since Bibliander. Stubbe never uses it.

162. As the author of "The Life and Death of Mahomet" in the English translation of the Qur'ān argued, "Haly" sought to inherit the" Power" of Muḥammad. *The Alcoran of Mahomet*, xii.

163. Twells, *The Theological Works of the Learned Dr. Pocock*, 9.

164. Sionita *De Nonnvllis*, 24. Hottinger changes Sionita's words to "primus Moselmannorum" but without applying them to 'Ali, since the words are from Q 6:163. Hottinger, *Historia Orientalis* (1660), 5.

165. Erpenius, *Historia Saracenica*, 43.

166. Pococke, *Historia Compendiosa Dynastiarum, autore Gregorio Abul-Pharjio* (Oxford, 1663), 102–103.

167. Hottinger, *Historia Orientalis* (1651), 370.

168. Petrus Ibn Rahib, *Chronicon Orientale*, ed. P. L. Cheikho (Beirut, 1903), 53

169. Adam Olearius, *The Voyages and Travells of the Ambassadors Sent by Frederick Duke of Holstein, to the Great Duke of Muscovy, and the King of Persia. Begun in the year M.DC.XXXIII. and finish'd in M.DC.XXXIX*, trans. John Davies (London, 1669), 161.

170. Ibid., 276.

171. Ibid., 278.

172. Twells, *The Theological Works of the Learned Dr. Pocock*, 1:9. See also Toomer, "Arabic Learning After the Restoration," where there is mention of Pococke's early lectures on the proverbs, "Proverbia Quaedam Alis" in 1636, and a manuscript with notes on these lectures, 215.

173. P. M. Holt, "An Oxford Arabist: Edward Pococke," in *Studies in the History of the East* (London, 1973), 6 in 1–26.

174. "Alis his Arabick proverbs with my translation," quoted by Toomer, *Eastern Wisedome*, 199.

175. Hottinger, *Historia Orientalis* (1660), 507ff.

176. Ockley, Sentences of Ali (London, 1717), B 2r–v.

177. *The Koran*, 430–431*n*. For a biography of Sale, see Khairallah, "Arabic Studies," 203–263.

178. Gibbon, *Decline and Fall of the Roman Empire*, 5:278.

179. See the section on eastern Christians in chapter 5 of Gerald MacLean and Nabil Matar, *Britain and the Islamic World: 1558–1713* (Oxford, 2011).

180. A3v–A4r.

181. See references to the first two in the notes to the text below. Stubbe owned a London 1669 edition of Blount's travels (BL MS Sloane 35, fol. 19r).

182. Especially after the publication of Bartolomé de las Casas, *The Tears of the Indians: being an historical and true account of the cruel massacres and slaughters of above twenty millions of innocent peoples* (trans. J. P. 1656) as well as William Davenant's *The Cruelty of the Spaniards in Peru* (1658) and John Dryden's *The Indian Emperour, or the Conquest of Mexico* (1667). For an excellent discussion of the difference in imperial policies between Euro-Christians and Muslims, see Anouar Majid, *Freedom and Orthodoxy: Islam and Difference in a Post-Andalusian Age* (Stanford, 2004).

183. William Biddulph, *The Travels of certaine Englishmen* (London, 1609), 84.

184. In 1678 and 1679, after Stubbe's death, Thomas Smith and Paul Rycaut published accounts of the plight about the eastern Christians. Stubbe either did not know, or ignored, Smith's second epistle about the oriental Christians in *Epistolae Quae Quarum altero de Moribvs ac Institvtis Tvrcarvm agit: Altera Septem asiae Ecclesiarvm notitiam continent* (1672).

185. John Selden, *De Jure Naturali et Gentium* (London, 1640), 734.

186. Olearius, *The Voyages*, 158. For a reference to al-Makīn, see 196.

187. Pococke, *Porta Mosis*, 260.

188. Stubbe, *A Further iustification*, 23.

189. See the various references to Stubbe in the introduction to Locke, *Two Tracts on Government*; and a discussion of Stubbe's toleration in W. K. Jordan, *The*

Development of Religious Toleration in England, 4 vols. (Cambridge, MA., 1940), 3:335–340.

190. Hill, *The Experience of Defeat*, esp. 262.

191. See my discussion in "John Locke and the 'Turbanned Nations,'" *Journal of Islamic Studies* 2 (1991): 67–77.

192. For Selden, see Toomer's quotations, *John Selden*, 1:156; Hottinger's Liber II of *Historia Orientalis* (both editions) is about the "Pseudopr."

193. Although it was a merchant who endowed the Thomas Adams Chair of Arabic at Cambridge, the first to fill it was Abraham Wheelock, who held a bachelor of divinity from Cambridge (1624); while the chair at Oxford was endowed by Archbishop Laud, to be filled by the chaplain to the Levant Company, Edward Pococke. The first account of the Ottomans written by an English eyewitness was by the chaplain to the British ambassador to the Porte, Paul Rycaut.

THE PRINTED AND MANUSCRIPT SOURCES

1. For a brief description of the life and political orientation of Hornby, see Justin Champion, "'I remember a Mahometan Story of Ahmed Ben Edris': Freethinking Uses of Islam from Stubbe to Toland," *Al-Qantara* 31 (2010): 449–51 in 443–480.

2. John Gregory, *The Works of the reverend and learned Mr. John Gregory Master of Arts of Christ's Church, Oxon: in two parts* (London, 1665, 1671, 1684). The first works that were published after his death were *Gregorii posthuma* in 1649 (London) and *Notes and Observations on some passages of scripture* in 1650 (London, and again in 1655, 1671). The *Notes* also appeared as part of *The Works*.

3. For Pococke and other English orientalists, see P. M. Holt, *Studies in the History of the Near East* (London, 1973), chs. 1 and 2. Robert Wakefield was the first English scholar to write about the three languages of Hebrew, Arabic, and Aramaic: *Oratio de laudibus & utilitate trium linguarum: Arabicae, Chaldaicae & Hebraicae* (London, 1524). See the translation by G. Lloyd Jones published in 1989, *On the Three Languages* (Binghampton, NY).

4. See, for instance, Hottinger, who discusses the Qur'ānic verses about Jesus and retains "Jesu": Johann Hottinger, *Historia Orientalis* (Tiguri, 1660), 142–144.

THE ORIGINAL AND PROGRESS OF MAHOMETANISM

1. Theodosius died in AD 395.

2. The opening of the *Originall* suggests a dedication that Stubbe may have been preparing for a patron or to the reader, as it echoes the opening of Newton's translation of *A Notable Historie of the Saracens*: "I Am purposed to write an Historie concernyng the Actes of the Saracens, atchieued aswel in the East as in the West partes of the world: first because they were greate and renoumed over the face of the whole Earth and brought all things out of good state into tumultuous broyle and confuse disorder, and also because this power of theirs encreased, through the

discorde and dissention of the Christians." Cello Augustino Curioni, *A Notable Historie of the Saracens,* trans. Thomas Newton (London, 1575), 1.

3. The four empires are mentioned in the book of Daniel: Babylonian, Persian, Macedonian, and Roman (Daniel 2-11). Contemporary with the rise of Islam were the Byzantine and the Sassanid empires.

4. A reference to a German tribe that invaded Gaul—mentioned by Julius Caesar in his *Gallic Wars.*

5. For the description of Muḥammad that follows, see Marcus Zeuerius Boxhornius, *Historia universalis sacra et profana a Christo nato ad annum usque MDCL* (Lugduni Batavorum/henceforth Leiden, 1652), 401. Stubbe sometimes translates word for word.

6. In this paragraph Stubbe borrows from Jirjis ibn al-'Amīd al-Makīn, *Historia Saracenica,* trans. Thomas Erpenius (Leiden, 1625), 10; see also Johann Hottinger, *Historia Orientalis* (Tiguri, 1651), bk. 2, ch. 3. Stubbe owned a copy of the latter. I will also use the 1660 edition, published in Tiguri.

7. In the margin: "Blount has copied this in his Oracles of reason fol. 159," Hand A.

8. Stubbe admired Jean Bodin's *Six Bookes of a Commonweale* (London, 1606). The reference to the change of aristocracy to democracy and vice versa occurs on pp. 421–422. Stubbe owned a copy of the 1597 edition.

9. Ibid., 417.

10. Lycurgus and Solon were the lawmakers in Sparta and Athens, respectively.

11. See Virgilio Malvezzi, *Discovrses upon Cornelius Tacitus,* trans. Sir Richard Baker (London, 1642). But Stubbe differs in his interpretation of political change from Malvezzi, especially in "The second Discourse" where there is a discussion of the reasons for the political changes in Rome. Stubbe owned a copy of this edition.

12. See Christopher Hill, "The Word 'Revolution,'" in *A Nation of Change and Novelty* (New York, 1990), 82–102. In BL Harleian 6189, the word is replaced by "Resolutions," fol. 5.

13. A reference to Antiochus IV (reg. 175–164 BC), who, in reaction to a revolt by the Jews, sacked Jerusalem, imposed the worship of Zeus, and gave support to the Hellenized Jews (who, as Stubbe suggests, later became the Sadducees) over the traditionalists (later the Pharisees). For the history of the revolt and its aftermath, see the fifth and sixth books of 2 Maccabees, and Josephus, *Antiquities,* trans. William Whiston *The Life and Works of Flavius Josephus,* intro. H. Stebbing (Philadelphia, n.d.), bk. 13, ch. 3.

14. BL Harleian 6189 has "justify" instead of "honest," fol. 6, which also appears in BL Harleian 1876, fol. 5. Sadoc and Baithos were influenced by Epicureanism (denying the resurrection and reward and punishment). Their disciples became the Sadducees. Eleazar was the son of Moses (Exodus 18:4). According to Maimonides, the Kabbalah was secretly revealed to Moses and his son: see Walter Farquhar, *A Church Dictionary* (Philadelphia, 1854), 78.

15. Stubbe used the King James Bible.

16. See John Lightfoot, *In Evangelium Matthæi, Horæ Hebraicæ et Talmudicæ* (Cambridge, 1658), 31–32. Stubbe owned a copy of this edition.

17. BL Harleian 6189 has "Rights," fol. 7, where BL Harleian 1876 has "Rites," fol. 6. The reference is to Antiochus IV. See Isaac Casaubon, *De Rebus Sacris et Ecclesiasticis, exercitationes XVI: ad Cardinalis Baronii prolegomena in annales et primam eorum partem* (London, 1614), 6–22, where there is a discussion of the great calamities that befell the Jews.

18. A numerology used to interpret the Hebrew scriptures.

19. BL Harleian 6189 has "indifferently" instead of "indefinitively." There is the following note in BL Harleian 1876: "Concerning the weeks of Daniel & the visions in him yt they contain but the same thing repeated four times over; & terminate in the destruction of Jerusalem by Antiochus Epiphanes, & that they are but Tipicall & by way of parode accomodated to the last destruction of Jerusalem, See Jo. Masham's chronolog. Diatribe," fol. 6. I am unable to locate this text.

20. Pompey conquered Palestine in 63 BC. BL Harleian 1876 has "possesseth," fol. 7, while BL Harleian 6189 has "possessed" and a note "*or possessed*," fol. 9.

21. Acts 2:11.

22. Lightfoot, *In Evangelium Matthœi*, 21–22. Born in Babylonia, in the late first century BC, Hillel went to Palestine where he was instrumental in the development of the Talmud and the Mishnah.

23. Archelaus was the son of Herod the Great and was banished in AD 6.

24. It is possible that Stubbe is thinking here of Sabbatai Sevi who proclaimed himself a messiah in Izmir, and assembled a large following, until he converted to Islam. See John Evelyn, *The history of the three late famous impostors : viz. Padre Ottomano, Mahomed Bei, and Sabatai Sevi* (Savoy, 1669), 41–103.

25. Both *asinego* and *intrado* were new words in English, used by Thomas Herbert in *Some Years Travels into divers parts of Africa and Asia the Great* (London, 1665). See *OED* entries.

26. Claudii Salmasii/Salmasius, *De Hellenistica Commentarius, Controversiam De Lingua Hellenistica dicidens, & plenissimè pertractans Originem & Dialectos Graœae Linguœ* (Leiden, 1643), 199–200. Stubbe owned a copy of this edition.

27. In the margin: "thus far Blount," Hand A. Charles Blount, *The Oracles of Reason* (London, 1693), 164, the letter to Rochester.

28. Caius Caligula, Roman Emperor (reg. AD 12–41); Herod Agrippa (reg. AD 33–44). See Solomon Zeitlin, "Did Agrippa Write a Letter to Gaius Caligula?" in the *Jewish Quarterly Review* 56 (1965–66): 22–31.

29. The Land of Onias was near Heliopolis in Egypt, where a large Jewish community lived. The temple was destroyed ca. AD 73. See the reference to Philo in *Evsebii Pamphili, Rvffini, Socratis, Theodoriti, Sozomeni, Theodori, Evagrii, et Dorothei Ecclesiastica Historia* (Basel, 1570), 18–19.

30. See for these terms *Eusebii Pamphili Ecclesiasticœ Historiœ Libri Decem. Ejusdem de Vita Imp. Constantini, Libri IV . . . Henricus Valesius* (Paris, 1672), 27, in *Annotationes*.

31. In Ezra 1:11, there is mention of the vessels of gold and silver that were taken from Babylon to Jerusalem.

32. See John Lightfoot, *Horae Hebraicœ et Talmudicœ Impensœ in epistolam primam S. Pauli ad Corinthios* (Cambridge, 1664), 125–127. Stubbe owned a copy of this edition.

33. Followed by "~~in his Jewish Antiquities gives this relation of the Condition of the Babylonish Jews at the Ascent of Esdras to Jerusalem & the remaining party, even in his days.~~" The reference is from Josephus's *Antiquities*, bk. 11, ch. 5.

34. Stubbe read Manasseh ben Israel's *The Hope of Israel*, which appeared in London in 1650 (rep. 1652) and described the various Jewish communities around the world.

35. The Epistle of James is a Christianization of Jewish wisdom literature, which is why Stubbe associated its recipients with the Jews. See Lightfoot, *Horæ Hebraicæ et Talmudicæ*, 130.

36. The reference is to the Septuagint.

37. Benjamin of Tudela traveled in the twelfth century. His account was published in Latin in 1633, but Stubbe derives his information from Edward Brerewood, *Enqviries Tovching the Diversity of Langvages, and Religions throughout the cheife parts of the World* (London, 1614), 105. Stubbe owned a copy of the 1622 edition by Brerewood. Salmonasar (reg. 731–713 BC) was a Persian ruler mentioned in 2 Kings 17:6.

38. In the right margin, Hand A: "[. . .]ad Chro. 11. 16th that many of the Israelites came to Jerusalem with the Levites upon the [. . .] in the time of Rehoboam," 2 Chronicles 11:16.

39. Cf. John Selden, *De Iure Naturali & Gentium, Iuxta Disciplinam Ebraeorum, libri septem* (London, 1640), 239–248, esp. 244. "Soria" is Selden's spelling of Syria; Nehardea and Pumbeditha are in Iraq and are mentioned by Benjamin of Tudela.

40. Salmasius, *De Hellenistica Commentarius*, 241.

41. Josephus, *Antiquities*, bk .13, ch. 9.

42. Under the Hasmonean ruler Hyracnus (reg. 134–104 BC), the Idumeans had been forcibly converted. Selden mentioned Nero as a convert in *De Iure Naturali*, bk. 2, ch. 3.

43. *Funus Linguæ Hellenisticæ sive Confutatio Exercitationis de Hellenistis et Lingua Hellenistica* (Leiden, 1643), 72 ff. This book was a refutation of Salmasius. Stubbe owned a copy of this edition.

44. Salmasius, *De Hellenistica Commentarius,* 230. The Bar Kokhba revolt occurred in AD 132–136.

45. Stubbe's use of the phrase "universal monarchy" in the early 1670s may be in reference to the French monarchy of Louis XIV. See his *A further iustification*, 18.

46. Acts 11:26.

47. In BL Harleian 6189, the scribe adds after this word: "There is a Blank" fol. 19. BL Harleian 1876 has "Hobs Leviathan" in that space, fol. 14.

48. In the margin: "here Blount go's on again in this same letter," Hand A.

49. In the margin: "thus far" in regard to Blount's copying of the letter to Hobbes, Hand A.

50. Joseph Mead (1586–1639) was author of the influential interpretation of the Book of Revelation, *Clavis Apocalyptica* (1627), which had a tremendous influence on the millenarianism of the civil wars and the Interregnum. See Brian Ball's classic study, *A Great Expectation: Eschatological Thought in English Protestantism to 1660* (Leiden, 1975). Stubbe may have been drawn to the writings of the Great Tew

circle by Thomas Barlow, who visited there in the early 1640s: see Noel Malcolm, ed., *Thomas Hobbes, The Correspondence* (Oxford, 1994), 2:785. Stubbe dedicated his *Deliciæ poetarum Anglicanorum in Græcum versæ quibus accedunt elogia Romae & Venetiarum* (Oxford, 1658) to Barlow. William Chillingworth (1602–1644) was the chaplain of Lord Falkland and published his celebrated *The Religion of Protestants a Safe Way to Salvation* (London, 1638): see ch. 3. The *Discourse of Infallibility* by Lord Falkland, Lucius Cary (1610–1643), was published in 1646 (with frequent reprints). Cary showed how the millenarian tradition was rejected by the early church, ch. 4, and in "The Lord of Faulklands Reply," he focused on the history of early Christian heresies (including millenarianism and chiliasm). Stubbe owned a copy of Falkland's book.

51. "Concluded" in the sense of "enclosed," as in Romans 11:32.

52. This paragraph draws on Selden, *De Iure Naturali*, bk. 2, ch. 7.

53. Cf. Romans 1:16.

54. Salmasius, *De Hellenistica Commentarius*, 71.

55. From the Greek, δεσπόσυνοι (the ones belonging to a master), but here referring to the relatives of Jesus. See Eusebius, *Ecclesiastica Historia*, 10. Stubbe was using the Greek text of Eusebius (bk. 1, ch. 7); in the Latin, it is bk. 8. Sulpicius Severus was a Christian historian, ca. AD 363–425.

56. "All these things which are handed down in the Gospel in regard to the rites of the Jews are taught in the same way without any discrepancy." Jospeh Scaliger, *De emendatione temporum* (Frankfurt, 1593), where in bk. 6, Scaliger examines the differences in calculating the dates of the birth, baptism, and other events in the life of Christ.

57. Johann Buxtorf (1564–1629), author of *De Synagoga Judaica* (Hanover, 1604, English translation by A.B. in London, 1663) was professor of Hebrew at Basel. Chapters 20 and 21 describe the feast of Reconciliation, to which Stubbe refers. Stubbe owned a copy of the 1604 Latin edition.

58. BL Harleian 6189 has "procreation" instead of "generation," fol. 18. See John Lightfoot, "Utcunque Iudæi Filium Dei negant eo sensu," in *In Evangelium Matthæi*, 316. See also Buxtorf, *The Jewish Synagogue*, ch. 36, for the Jewish understanding of the Messiah.

59. The paragraph draws on Selden, *De Iure Naturali*, 260–266.

60. Thebeth is the tenth month in the religious year: see the reference in Claudii Salmasius, *Ossilegium Hellenisticæ sive Appendix ad Confutationem Exercitationis de Hellenistica* (Leiden, 1643), 337.

61. *Funus Linguæ Hellenisticæ*, 89ff. There is no paragraph or unit division in this book and the discussion continues for pages about hellenized synagogues. For Tertullian, see 92.

62. Also known as the Palestinian Talmud. In BL Harleian 1876, there is the following note: "Dr. Lightfoot (in addend. ad 1. Cor. c. 14 v.10) saith they did not there in Cæsarea read ye Scripture, but repeat yrr Phylacteries in Greek: which is as inconsistent with yr tenets as the other," fol. 20. See Lightfoot, *Horæ Hebraicæ et Talmudicæ* , 145.

63. The first entry in the *OED* for "sophisticated" as falsified appears in Dryden's 1673 comedy, *The Assignation*.

64. For the "Gospel of the Nazarenes" and the "Gospel according to the Hebrews," see the texts in Bart D. Ehrman and Zlatko Pleše, *The Aporcyphal Gospels: Texts and Translations* (New York, 2011). Both gospels are apocryphal and belong to the second and third centuries. Epiphanius was bishop of Constantia (ca. 310–403) and author of *Contra Octaginta haereses opus Panarium*, trans. F. Williams, in *The Panarion of Epiphanius of Salamis, Book 1*, 2d ed. (Leiden, 2009): see his reference to these texts, 131. Stubbe's reference to the apocryphal gospels coincides with the "discovery" and publication of various other books of the apocrypha such as the *Protoevangelion and the Epistle of Barnabas*. The *Codex Alexandrinus that* was given to King Charles I by Cyril Lucaris included the (apocryphal) *First Epistle of Clement to the Corinthians. Archbishop James Ussher and Gerard Vossius printed some of the letters of Ignatius in Oxford (1644) and Amsterdam (1646) respectively.*

65. Acts 17:10–15. It is interesting that Stubbe uses the name "Cephas" instead of "Simon Peter." Epiphanius describes the Nazarenes of Pella in *Panarion*, 123–130.

66. In BL Harleian 1876 there is the following note: "It is said yt some of ye Corrinthians were of Christ: those were like ye disciples of John at Ephesus. Act. 19 who believed a Messiah, but not yt Jesus was he. See Dr. Lightfoot on yt place," fol. 21. John Lightfoot, *The Harmony, chronicle and order of the New Testament the text of the four evangelists* (London, 1655), 107.

67. The *aurum coronarium* was mentioned in the Theodosian Code (*CTh*.16.8.14) and was in "process of time a mere tribute in gold or in silver, which the Roman potentate received from those placed under his government." http://www.forumancientcoins.com/numiswiki/view.asp?key=aurum%20coronarium. (accessed 26 February 2012). See also Walo Messalinus, *De Episcopis et Presbyteris contra D. Petavium Loiolitam Dissertatio Prima* (Leiden, 1650), 381. It is not clear if Stubbe recognized Messalinus as a pseudonym used by Salmasius.

68. Ibid., 379–383.

69. In BL Harleian 1876: "spectibiles, as the other grand Patriarchs Illustres, and Clarissimi, as also Primates," fol. 31/ notables, as the other grand illustrious patriarchs, most renowned.

70. In BL Harleian 1876, there is a reference to "Dr. Thorndike's treatise of the service of God of religious assemblies," fol. 22: See Herbert Thorndike, *Of religious assemblies, and the publick service of God: a discourse according to the apostolicall rule and practice* (Cambridge, 1642). The discussion of church offices is in chapter 7, from where Stubbe borrows "Sacredotes, Presbyteri, Antistites."

71. See Leo Modena (1571–1648), *History of the rites, customes, and manner of life, of the present Jews, throughout the world*, trans. Edmund Chilmead (London, 1650). Stubbe owned a copy of this edition and may have been thinking of the opening words of the treatise: "The Rites which are at this day observed, and in Use, among the Jewes, are not all of them of equall Authority, nor equally practiced by all, after one and the same Manner," 1. See also Selden, *De Iure Naturali*, 365 ff. The 1650 Modena text was bound with *The Hope of Israel* (see note 34).

72. Ioannes Drusius, *De Sectis Ivdaicis commentarii . . . Iosephi Scaligeri I.C.F. Elenchus Trihaeresii ejusdem* (Arnheim, 1619), 341.

73. In BL Harleian 1876, there is the following note: "That there were Sadducee-Christians appears out of Justin Martyr's discourse with Tryphon: & such were Hymenæus & Philetus, who denied ye resurrection: tho' their names be Greek, they might be original Hebrews, or Jews, & have also Hebrew names, as Dr. Lightfoot shews upon 1. Cor. 1.1," fol. 23. The reference to Lightfoot is from *Horæ Hebraicæ et Talmudicæ*, 1; Hymanæus and Philetus are mentioned in 2 Timothy 2:17–18.

74. The first part of Epiphanius's *Panarion* includes description of twelve heretical groups of Jewish Christians.

75. In BL Harleian 6189 "Ceremoniall" and "certaine" are corrected over "criminal" and "coercive," fol. 33.

76. See Buxtorf, *The Jewish Synagogue*, 188. "Succedaneous" means substitute, a medical term first used by Sir Thomas Browne in 1646 (*OED*).

77. *Origen against Celsus*, trans. James Bellamy (London, 1660), chiefly bks. 2 and 5.

78. The Latin quotations are corrected and added at the bottom of the page by Hand A. The verse from Ovid is translated in L. P. Wilkinson, *Ovid Recalled* (Cambridge, 1955), 287: "Ah, men too lax, who think that the gloomy crime of murder can be washed away by river-water." The quotation from Virgil is from the *Aeneid*, 2: "Now you, Father, take up the gods of our ancestral home, our holy symbols. I cannot touch them without sin, until I have washed my hands in a living spring, for coming as I do straight from the fury of war, I have fresh blood still on them." Virgil, *Aeneid*, trans. W. F. Jackson Knight (Penguin, 1958), 72.

79. Gerard Vossius, *De baptismo disputationes XX* (Amsterdam, 1648), 24, from where "aspersione."

80. In BL Harleian 6189, the following sentence comes after "scripture" and is crossed out: "any more than [for these words follow again the next line but two] and not condemned in the Greek Church." In the margin, and in the same hand: "The words are interlined by the Corrector, over the words & *not condemned by the Gr. Ch.*," fol. 35. See 1 Corinthians 15:29 and Tertullian (ca. AD 160–225). Ernest Evans, ed. and trans., *Homily on Baptism* (London, 1964), section 18.

81. Sozomen in *Evsebii Pamphili, Rvffini, Socratis*, 549. Vossius wrote about Gregory of Nazianzen (325–389) and the baptism of blood, *De baptismo*, 24.

82. Vossius, *De baptismo*, 27, thesis 2.

83. BL Harleian 1876 has the following note: "Or from ye use of Baptism in some pagan-worships. In multis Idolarum sacrilegis sacris baptizari himines perhibentur. Augustinni de baptism.adu.Donat.lib. 6.c.25," fol. 25.

84. L Harleian 1876 has the following note: "Montacut.orig.sacri. part. 1.p.103.104. ye Days were called Nominalia or dies lustrici," fol. 25. See Richardi Montacuti (Richard Montague), *Episcopi Cissacestriensis, De originibus ecclesiasticis* (London, 1636), 103: "Romani Nominalia appellabant . . . Lustrici dies infantium appellantur," and then citing Macrobius, "Nundina Romanorum Dea." The application to Christian children comes a page later, 104.

85. BL Harleian 6189 has "Ember Week and days" after "previgils," fol. 36.

86. " & μύσται & ἐπόπται into Paganos Græcos," in the margin, Hand A/ catechumens to petitioners and then to the faithful/believers.

87. BL Harleian 1876 has the following note: "See this largely illustrated by Casaubon. exercit. adu. Baron. exercit. 16.§.43," fol. 26. The reference is to Casaubon's *De Rebus Sacris et Ecclesiasticis*, 541–566.

88. Imperial meal—"paganical" meals.

89. Common meals, feasts/confraternities, meals/festivals, solemn feasts.

90. Congregation and community.

91. Lordly meal and community. BL Harleian 1876 has the following note: "This is further confirmed in yt Pliny, by comand from Trajan, prohibited Christian meetings as ἑταιρεῖαι"/congregations, fol. 27.

92. 1 Corinthians 13.

93. Followed by "fellowship," in BL 6189, fol. 39.

94. BL Harleian 1876 adds "dis" above "honour" as a correction, fol. 28.

95. Both are mentioned by Epiphanius in the *Panarion*.

96. Discussion.

97. Justin Martyr, *Dialogue with Trypho*, ed. Michael Slusser, trans. Thomas B. Falls (Washington, DC, 2003), ch. 80.

98. See John Selden, *De synedriis & praefecturis iuridicis veterum Ebraeorum* (London, 1655), bk. 1, ch. 8. In BL Harleian 6189, "Decision" is followed by "*aut nescio quid*," and in the margin, "Interlined by the corrector of the Or.," fol. 41. Stubbe owned the 1653 edition of Selden's book. For a detailed study of Selden and Stubbe, see ch. 8 in Rosenblatt, *Renaissance England's Chief Rabbi*.

99. Selden, *De Iure Naturali*, 844.

100. The discussion by Paul of idolatrous food occurs in 1 Corinthians 8:9–10 and 1 Corinthians 10:1–11. A marginal note in BL Harleian 1876 refers to Johann Heinrich Heidegger (1633–1698), "libert a lege. c.7. l. 3," fol. 29. I was unable to locate this text, but Stubbe owned a copy of Heidegger's *Rashi aboth, sive, de historia sacra patriarcharum. Exercitationes selectae* (Amsterdam, 1667).

101. In BL Harleian 6189, "paramount" is followed by "vel nescio," and in the margin, "Interlined by the Corrector," fol. 44. The story of Cornelius is in Acts 10.

102. Selden, *De Iure Naturali*, 180–181.

103. See the discussion of this Trinitarian conundrum in Pliny and Tertullian: http://fosterheologicalreflections.blogspot.com/2010/03/lightfoot-and-tertullians-mention-of.html; accessed September 30, 2012.

104. Artemon was a third-century Antitrinitarian in Rome; Pope Victor (AD 189–199); Pope Zephyrinus (AD 199–217). Stubbe is drawing on bk. 5, chs. 27 and 28 (Greek version) of Eusebius, *Ecclesiastica Historica*, 73–74 (chs. 24 and 25 in the Latin version).

105. See this discussion in Casaubon, *De Rebvs Sacris et Ecclesiasticis*, 477–499.

106. The Apostles' Creed contains nothing about the controversies regarding the human-divine nature of Christ—which is why it was acceptable to the Arians.

107. St. Athanasius (AD 296–372), bishop of Alexandria, upheld the doctrine of the Incarnation against the Arians.

108. In the margin, BL Harleian 1876, fol. 33: "In Ecclesia πολιτεία ita ordo à plebe vel Laicis olim distinguebatur, ut in civili gentium, ordo & plebs. Ordo est magistratus vel senatus. Walo Messalin. P.388." See Messalini, *De Espiscopis*, 388.

Waldonis Messalin was a pseudonym that Salmasius used: *De Episcopis et Presbyteris* (Leiden, 1641).

109. Stubbe is reading Buxtorf, *The Jewish Synagogue*, 314–315. The story of Balaam and his prophecy to Balak appears in the book of Numbers, ch. 22.

110. Rabbi Akiva (fl. early second century AD), whose writings furnished the basis for the Mishnah. See the discussion of Casaubon on Akiva and Bar Kochba in Anthony Grafton and Joanna Weinberg, with Alastair Hamilton, *"I have always loved the Holy Tongue": Isaac Casaubon, the Jews, and a Forgotten Chapter in Renaissance Scholarship* (Cambridge, 2011), 319–320.

111. BL Harleian 6189 has "four hundred," fol. 48.

112. Followed by *"Idolls"* in BL Harleian 6189, fol. 49, and a note, *"Interlined by the Corrector."*

113. "The worshippers of Serapis are Christians, and those are devoted to the god Serapis, who (I find) call themselves the bishops of Christ. There is here no ruler of a Jewish synagogue, no Samaritan, no Presbyter of the Christians, who is not either an astrologer, a soothsayer, or a minister of obscene pleasures. The very Patriarch himself, should he come into Egypt, would be required by some to worship Serapis, and by others to worship Christ." From the letter of the Emperor Adrian in AD 134, translated in Robert Taylor, *Diegesis*, 3d ed. (London, 1845), 386.

114. BL Harleian 1876 includes the following note: "Tho' ye dignity of a Patriarch was not settled in ye Church till long after ye Nicene Council, is certain: yet yt ye word Patriarch was analogically used in ye Church. & yt ye Alexandrine was such: See Valles. in Socrat. Hist. Eccles.l.5.c.8 Hottinger. Hist. Orient. Pag.101," fol. 35. See *Evsebii Pamphili, Rvffini, Socratis*, 311; and Hottinger, *Historia Orientalis* (1651), 102.

115. See the discussion of Eutychius/Ibn al-Baṭrīq in the introduction.

116. The name given to Christians who offered incense to idols in order to escape persecution.

117. "It follows that the eagles are the gods of the legions," Tacitus, *Annals*, 2:17.

118. Labarum was the military standard used by Constantine with the first two letters of the Greek spelling of "Christ."

119. Office of chief priest.

120. *CTh*.12.1.112: Florentio praefecto Augustali. In consequenda archierosyne ille sit potior, qui patriæ plura praestiterit nec tamen a templorum cultu observatione christianitatis abscesserit. Quippe indecorum est, immo ut verius dicamus, illicitum ad eorum curam templa et templorum sollemnia pertinere, quorum conscientiam vera ratio divinæ religionis imbuerit et quos ipsos decebat tale munus, etiamsi non prohiberentur, effugere. Emissa XVI kal. iul. Constantinopoli Honorio n. p. et Evodio conss. (386 iun. 16). http://ancientrome.ru/ius/library/codex/theod/liber16.htm#8; accessed September 30, 2012.

121. Quintus Aurelius Symmachus (ca. AD 345–402). The pontifices maximi occupied the highest position in Roman religion.

122. "Hathur" is the third month of the Coptic year: see Selden, *De synedriis*, where, in chapter 15, there is a detailed description of Coptic feasts and fast days, along with the story about Alexander, 345. The story was told by Eutychius in

Contextio Gemmarum (Oxford, 1658), 435. BL Harleian 6189 has "Captives" for "Coptites," fol. 53.

123. Amandus and Ælianus were insurgents in France, ca. AD 285.

124. Aemilius Papinianus (AD 142–212), a Roman jurist.

125. *Eusebii Pamphili Ecclesiasticæ Historiæ Libri Decem.*, 251–252, in *Annotationes.*

126. Selden, *De synedriis*, 342ff.

127. BL Harleian 1876 includes the following note: "Cod. Theodos. lib.16. tit.8.leg.29 cum notis Gothofredi, " fol. 42. The code describes "the annual tribute that is to be collected from rulers of Jewish synagogues." *Imperial Laws and Letters Involving Religion, AD 395–431* (Fourth Century Christianity, Wisconsin Lutheran College), http://www.fourthcentury.com/index.php/imperial-laws-chart-395; accessed September 30, 2012.

128. "Jews will be restricted in their ceremonies; let us, meanwhile, follow the ancients in the preservation of their privileges, by whose law and the assent of our divinity it is ordained that those who are subject to the authority of the illustrious patriarchs (i.e. the archsynagogues, the patriarchs, the elders, and the rest who are involved in the sacrament of that religion) shall preserve those privileges which were conferred upon the first clerics of the venerable Christian law. The deified emperors Constantine, Constantius, Valentinian, and Valens decreed this with a divine order." Stubbe elaborates on the code: 1 July 397, *CTh* 16.8.13, Arcadius, Honorius: "Jewish clergy are allowed to retain their own laws and rituals and are exempt from service as in municipal senates. They are to have the same privileges as Christian clergy." *Imperial Laws and Letters Involving Religion, AD 395–431* (Fourth Century Christianity, Wisconsin Lutheran College), http://www.fourthcentury.com/index.php/imperial-laws-chart-395; accessed September 30, 2012.

129. "Ethnic" is used to refer to Gentile, specifically Greek. BL 1876 has "Metaphysicks" instead of "Mathematicks," fol. 42.

130. BL Harleian 1876 has "two hundred," fol. 44.

131. In *A further iustification* Stubbe thinks of "Mahometanism" immediately after discussing the Donatists, 65. Justinian reigned until AD 565 and therefore, appropriately, leads Stubbe to Muḥammad, born a few years later.

132. Novatus (ca. AD 200–258); Maximinus Thrax (reg. AD 235–238); Diocletian (reg. AD 284–305).

133. BL 6189 has "remitted" instead of "ruined," fol. 65.

134. See the same use in *A further iustification*, 41. Andrew Marvell also used this analogy in *A Short Historical Essay Concerning General Councils, Creeds, and Impositions, in Matters of Religion* (1676), in *The Prose Works of Andrew Marvell*, ed. Annabel Patterson (New Haven, 2003), 2:129.

135. A church historian of the fifth century.

136. Denius Petau/Petavius (1583–1652), Jesuit theologian and historian.

137. Contrast Stubbe's treatment of this choice of bishops in *A further iustification*, 39, where the tone is favorable.

138. See Bodin, *Six Bookes*, 537 where the marginalia state: "Religion not to be enforced," and "How a prince wel assured of the truth of his religion is to draw his subiects thereunto, being the fore diuided into sects and factions."

139. The other sites which Stubbe does not mention were Milan, Seleucia, Nice, Tarsis/Tarsus, and Ariminum/Rimini. In BL Harleian 6189 and 1876, the number is 600, fols. 67 and 48 respectively.

140. Salvian, Bishop of Marseilles, fifth-century author of *De gubernatione Dei* (Oxford, 1629), especially bk. 5. Hilary was bishop of Poitiers (d. AD 368).

141. In the margin: "Blount has copied this in a letter to Hobbs and ye 2 pages & a half Next," Hand A. Blount made a few changes in copying from Stubbe: see especially Malcolm's notes 31 and 40, *Thomas Hobbes*, 2:763–766.

142. BL Harleian 6189 has a note: "f. layd aside the Exercise of the Power," fol. 70.

143. Curiously, the title nostrum numen was applied to Constantine. Circensian relates to circus.

144. Eutychius of Constantinople (ca. AD 512–582); Dioscorus of Alexandria (d. AD 454); Severus of Antioch (AD 465–538); Jacob Baradaeus (ca. AD 500–578), bishop of Edessa; Nestorius (ca. AD 386–451).

145. Followed by "part" in BL Harleian 6189, fol. 73.

146. Council of Jerusalem (described in Acts 15), AD 48; (First) Council of Ephesus, AD 431; Council of Chalcedon, AD 451.

147. "It is Greek, and therefore not understood," in Guillaume Ranchin, *A Review of the Councell of Trent*, trans. G. L. (Oxford, 1638), 152. Stubbe owned a copy of this edition. The pope is Gregory the Great (ca. AD 540–604).

148. Valentinus (reg. AD 364–375), Justinius II (reg. AD 565–578), Mauritius Tiberius (reg. AD 582–602). Phocas, Byzantine Emperor (reg. AD 602–610); Heraclius, Byzantine Emperor (reg. AD 610–641).

149. Martianus/Marcian/Marcianus (AD 390–457), was emperor of the Eastern Empire.

150. Brerewood, *Enqviries Tovching the Diversity of Langvages*, 140–141.

151. Chosroes I (reg AD 531–579); King Hormisdas (reg. AD 579–590); Chosroes II (reg. AD 590–628).

152. "unimaginable" is followed by "effects, and" in BL Harleian 6189, fol. 57.

153. See David Blondel, *Treatise of the sibyls, so highly celebrated, as well by the antient heathens, as the Holy Fathers of the Church*, trans. J. D. (London, 1661), 3. Stubbe owned a copy of this edition. *Evsebii Pamphili, Rvffini, Socratis*, 22, from which Stubbe borrows the phrase "Simoni Deo Sancto."

154. Antoninus Pius, one of the "Five Good Emperors" (reg. AD 138–161). Justin was beheaded in AD 165 during the reign of Marcus Aurelius.

155. The battle was between Emperor Marcus Aurelius and the Quadi in AD 174. Appolinaris was an apologist (fl. ca. AD 170).

156. Cf. Casaubon, *De Rebvs Sacris et Ecclesiasticis*, 70–87; *Eusebii Pamphili Ecclesiasticæ Historiæ Libri Decem.*, 225, in *Annotationes*; and the earlier reference to Blondel.

157. In both Bodleian 6189 and 1876, the word "postnate" precedes "authority."

158. It is significant that Stubbe does not mention Anglicans, obviously thinking them the only true Christians: "I defend Truth, and the Church of England," he wrote to the dean of Christ Church, John Fell (*A Censure* (Oxford, 1670), dedication. Nor does he mention the Quakers whom, in 1659, he had mildly defended *A*

light shining out of darknes: . . . with a brief apologie for the Quakers, that they are not inconsistent with a magistracy (London, 1659). BL Harleian 1876 has the following note: "The Lieflanders are so ignorant, that it may be said Baptism excepted, they have not any character of Christianity. See Olearius, *The voyages*, p. 30," fol. 60: *The voyages and travels of the ambassadors sent by Frederick, Duke of Hostein, to the Great Duke of Muscovy and the King of Persia*, trans. John Davies (London, 1669), 32. Stubbe copied word for word about the inhabitants in Livonia. He owned a copy of this edition.

159. Cf. Casaubon, *De Rebvs Sacris et Ecclesiasticis*, 6–21.

160. In the margin, Hand A: "v. Blunt fo. 104." John Dale was the author of *The analysis of all the Epistles of the New Testament: Wherein the chiefe things of every particular chapter are reduced to heads, for the memory* (Oxford, 1652).

161. *Eusebii Pamphili Ecclesiasticæ Historiæ, Libri Decem.*, 34–36 in *Annotationes*. See also Philo on *The Contemplative Life* in which he describes the *therapeutae*, trans. Frank William (Bloomington, 1922), 3–26.

162. *Evsebii Pamphili, Rvffini, Socratis*, 23. The Latin uses the term *cultores*; therapeutae appears in the margin, in Greek, in association with the Essenes, 55. Epiphanius relied heavily on Eusebius.

163. Salmasius, *De Hellenistica Commentarius*, 181: "Inde etiam Hebrœ lingua appellate est Syriaca." BL Harleian 1876, fol. 62, adds in the margin: "That Mark was also such is most probable." Eusebius wrote that Mark's gospel was written in Egypt, *Evsebii Pamphili, Rvffini, Socratis*, 23.

164. Salmasius, *De Hellenistica Commentarius*, 254, 258, 250: "It must be rightly understood for a truth that nearly all of Christ's disciples and Apostles, being uneducated and common, evidently fishermen, sailors, and boatmen, understood no other language than the vernacular, that is, the Galilean and Syrian parlance which prevailed in that region. For even if many in Syria and Judea knew Greek, it did not reach at all the men of the basest class who knew only the vernacular and were entirely ignorant of Greek. . . . Therefore the Apostles wrote in their own idiom and the tongue and in the vernacular that was familiar to them, which was immediately translated into Greek by either hellenized Syrians or Greeks, who spoke Greek and who rendered it faithfully, and who were with the preaching Evangelists as supporters and assistants. In certain cases, this has been verified for a fact; in others, it is not known, since it is not apparent: nevertheless, concerning all of them, there is the resemblance of truth, since there is truth in some of them. For there is no difference between these men, who were equals in respect to tribe and station, as well as vocation and function. . . . This is a thing which holds for the books of the New Testament; for this reason it is also possible to convey why it is that they are written in a manner greatly different from the more elegant and pure type of spoken Hellenism. As you see, one may say that they were composed partly by the uneducated, partly by translators, who were even themselves not entirely familiar with Greek speech." In the margin of the manuscript, there are the following words: "Predicare non scribere precepti fuere."

165. BL Harleian 1876 has "carry age" instead of "carriage," fol. 64.

166. Lactantius, rhetorician who converted to Christianity (ca. AD 250–325); Annobius the Elder was his teacher; Minicius Felix, Christian apologist (fl. ca. AD

160–300). The Third Council of Carthage, AD August 397, specified the books of the Old and New Testaments: see B. F. Westcott, *A General Survey of the History of the Canon of the New Testament,* 5th ed. (Edinburgh, 1881), 440, 541–542. Pope Clement's (alleged) letter was published in 1647: *Clement, the blessed Paul's fellow-labourer in the Gospel, his first epistle to the Corinthians* (London, 1652 [1647]), 2–3.

167. Stubbe may have been thinking of Pococke's *Specimen Historiæ Arabica,* where Avicenna is associated with "Philosophiam Saracenicam recte inscripseris, non quod Barbara." Edward Pococke, *Specimen Historiæ Arabica* (Oxford, 1650), 35. As a physician, Stubbe read the works of Avicenna, whose *Canons* had been published as early as 1555 in Paris, *Avicennae Arabis Medicorvm.* Stubbe owned a copy of the Louvain edition of 1658.

CHAPTER 3

The title is written in the margin, Hand B: "A Breif Account of Arabia and the Saracens." Henceforth, all odd-numbered pages have "CHAP 3" in the upper left corner. In BL 1876, the title "The History of ye Saracens and of Mahomet " is followed by a blank page and then, in large letters: "A generall Preface to the account of the originall & progress of Muhammadanisme," fol. 57.

1. Scribal variants include "Hagarens," "Hagarites," and "Agarens."

2. See Gabriel Sionita, *De Nonnvullis Orientalivm Vrbibvs* (Paris, 1619), 2, which is bound with the translation of al-Idrīsī's *Geographia Nubiensis.* Stubbe owned a copy of this edition. Edward Pococke, *Specimen Historiæ Arabica* (Oxford, 1650), 33. The second part of Pococke's *Specimen* consists of *Notæ in quibus aliqvam mvlta qvæ ad historiam orientalivm apprimè illustrandam faciunt,* which had been printed in Oxford two years earlier, 1648, by the same printer.

3. Pococke, *Specimen,* 76–78, probably from Abū al-Fida who had mentioned that the Arab clan of Ṣālih was the first to establish a kingdom in Syria. In BL Sloane 1709 there is "Banu Salih filis Salhi" in the margin, fol. 94r.

4. The Ghassānid Arabs (Banū Ghassān) were Christians from the tribe of Azd.

5. Julius Solinus's third-century AD *De memorabilibus mundi* was published frequently and translated into English by Arthur Golding as *The worthie work of Iulius Solinus Polyhistor: containing many noble actions of humaine creatures* (London, 1587). But Stubbe is borrowing directly from Johann Hottinger, *Historia Orientalis* (Tiguri, 1660), 211: "Solino & aliis Ayman dicitur." The scribe uses "Yaman."

6. See Johann Hottinger, *Historia Orientalis* (Tiguri, 1651) on "De Mvhammedis parentibvs," 134–137.

7. Pococke, *Specimen,* 150–152.

8. Sionita, *Nonnvllis,* 2. Joktan is the biblical name for Qaḥtān, Genesis 10:25–29. Stubbe copied "Mota-Arabes"/Mostaarabs from Pococke, *Specimen,* 39; p. 45 has "Most Arabes." In the translation of *Eutychii Patriarchæ Alexandrini Annalium,* the term is "Most Arabibus" (Oxford, 1654), 2:272. The first use of "Mozarab" appears in 1615 (*OED*). The manuscript has "the Son of Heber the Son of Saleh" with "of Heber" crossed out. In BL Sloane 1709, it is not, fo. 94v. Sionita has "Heber," 2.

9. This use of "Coreischites" is very early in English. The variants in the manuscript are "Koreischites" and "Coreishites."

10. Pococke writes Jorham/Jorhamum in *Specimen*, 38. The *OED* records the first use of "Coreis"/Quraysh by Alexander Ross in his English translation of the Qur'ān (1649).

11. Pococke, *Specimen*, 4, 150–51. Pococke's spelling is "Hamyar," which Stubbe uses. Ḥimyar was a tribe in southwestern Arabia. "Ismailites" had been used as early as 1571 (*OED*).

12. Pococke, *Specimen*, 40.

13. Ibid., 138. See also Hottinger, *Historia Orientalis* (1660), "Henoch, qui vocatur Adris," 30.

14. The scribe wrote, "Maimonides apud Hottinger.hist.or.l.1.c.8." In *Historia Orientalis* (1651), bk. 1, ch. 8, there is discussion of the religions of the Sabeans and the Nabateans, along with other religions of "veterum Arabum." There are numerous references to Maimonides.

15. Pococke spelled the name, "Abulfeda," ignoring its patronymic construction. There was no published edition of Abū al-Fida's geography covering the Arabian Peninsula, although as Toomer states, Selden owned a manuscript of the geography (*John Selden*, 2:619 and also "Arabic Learning after the Restoration," in *Eastern Wisedome*, 227). John Gregory mentions a manuscript of Abū al-Fida at Cambridge, in *The Works of the Reverend and learned Mr. John Gregory* (London, 1665), 73 margin, but later adds: "For the Arabick-Nubian Geographie, translated into Latine by the Maronites, though otherwise of a rare and pretious esteem, yet it is not commended for this, That the Distances of Places are there set down by a gross Mensuration of miles: and John Leo's Africa is not so well. But when the Learned and long-promised Geographie of Abulfeda the Prince shall come to light, there can be nothing done there without this Meridian," 266. It is unclear what is meant by "long-promised," unless Gregory had known (before his death in 1646) about John Greaves who published in 1650 an Arabic and Latin selection by Abū al-Fida about the region "extra fluvium Oxum," *Chorasmiae et Mawaralnahrae* (London, 1650). There may well have been a longer manuscript by Greaves that was circulating since in 1712 John Hudson published the earlier account by Greaves with a unit on Arabia, specifically describing the Islamic holy cities and many other locations, *Geographiae veteris scriptores Græci minores Accedunt Geographica Arabica* (Oxford, 1712), 3:1–66, new pagination. At the same time, there are twelve manuscripts of Abū al-Fida's *Taqwīm al-buldān* in the BnF, one of which is a copy made by G. Schikhart, professor of Hebrew at Tubingen: see MS Arabe 2241 in *Catalogue des Manuscrits Arabes*, M. Le Baron de Slane (Paris, 1883–1895).

16. God almighty.

17. From Pococke, *Specimen*, 108.

18. Ibid., 139–140.

19. Claudii Salmasius, *De Annis Climactericis et Antiqua Astorlogia diatribœ* (Leiden, 1648), 578–579, where there is a discussion of the Greek origin of the Arabic word, ṭalṣam, "vulgo Talisman." Stubbe owned a copy of this edition. See also the discussion of "Tilsemat" in Hottinger, *Historia Orientalis* (1660), 284–289.

20. Pococke, *Specimen*, 140–141.

21. Ibid., 148–149.

22. All these passages, from "They say that Noah" until here, follow Pococke, *Specimen*, 144. Manuscript variants for 'Ka'ba and Mecca are the following: "the Caab," "Alcaab," "Caaba," "Kabe," 'Cabea," and "Meccah," "Mecha," "Macca," "Mecca."

23. For references to the Sabians/al-Ṣābi'a in the Qur'ān, see 2:62; 5:69; 22:17.

24. Pococke, *Specimen*, 274. The reference is to the Nabateans, whose kingdom included the trading center in Petra.

25. Thomas Erpenius, *Orationes tres, de linguarum Ebraeœ, atque Arabicœ dignitate* (Leiden, 1621), 41; Hottinger, *Historia Orientalis* (1651), bk 1, ch. 4.

26. Pococke, *Specimen*, 39.

27. 'Adnān and Qaḥṭān are the two ancestors from whom western and central Arabs and eastern Arabs are respectively descended.

28. Hottinger, *Historia Orientalis* (1651), 142–143.

29. The tribe of Khuzā'a.

30. Pococke, *Specimen*, 42 where he writes, "akhsar min abi Gabshan." Pococke writes "Chozaah," which Stubbe borrows.

31. Ibid., 114, 115.

32. Ibid., 115. Stubbe borrows the translation of "Domum interdictam" from Pococke.

33. In BL Harleian 1876, there is the following note: "It was always a part of Arabick devotion, to go about, & compass ye temple where they worshipped: to some such devotion perhaps David alludes when he says ps.77. so shall the congregation of ye people compass thee about. & Ps.26:6 so will I compass thine Altar," fol. 112.

34. The references are to the tribe of Khuzā'a, and to King 'Amr ibn Luḥay.

35. As'ad abū Karib was a Ḥimyarite king.

36. Pococke, *Specimen*, 80, 60, 81.

37. Ibid., 98 ff.

38. Ṣafā and Marwā are the two mountains between which Hagar ran to find sustenance for her son.

39. The names are taken from Pococke, *Specimen*, 118: "Abu Kobau," and 128 "Koaikaban." The latter might be a reference to Kawkaban in northern Yemen.

40. The tribes of Ṭayy and Qaḥṭān; Al-Ḥārith ibn Ka'b. Stubbe lifts this name from Pococke's notes, *Specimen*, 109, where it refers to "Bani Hareth."

41. Ibid., 60–64. Yūsuf Dhū Nuwās (reg. ca. AD 517–525), the last king of Ḥimyarite Yemen, converted to Judaism.

42. Maḥmūd.

43. Pococke, *Specimen*, 63–64, where the whole episode, along with the Qur'ānic verse about it, is described.

44. Pococke's spelling, *Specimen*, 71. Anū Sherwān, king of Persia (reg. AD 488–513).

45. Al-Nu'mān and al-Mundhir. Stubbe's spelling is from Pococke, ibid., 72.

46. *Evsebii Pamphili . . . Ecclesiastica historia*, 544, "De Mauia Saracenorum regina." For Mavia and the Christian Kings of Arabia, see Glen W. Bowersock, "Mavia, Queen of the Saracens," in *Studies on the Eastern Roman Empire* (Goldbach, 1994), 127–140.

47. Pococke, *Specimen*, 85.

48. There is a note referring to "Evagrius bk 4, ch. 12," the same words that appear in Pococke, *Specimen*, 85.

49. Al-Mūsil in Iraq.

CHAPTER 4

The title is written in the margin, Hand B. Henceforth, all odd numbered pages have "CHAP 4" in the upper left corner.

1. The date 580 appears in Thomas Erpenius, *Orationes tres, de linguarum Ebraeæ, atque Arabicæ dignitate* (Leiden, 1621), 42, but there is a discussion of other dates in Johann Hottinger, *Historia Orientalis* (Tiguri, 1660), 217–218.

2. 'Abdallah and Amīna.

3. Roderici Ximenez, *Historia Arabum*, ed. Thomas Erpenius (Leiden, 1625), 2. The treatise is bound with Jirjis ibn al-'Amīd al-Makīn, *Historia Saracenica*, trans. Thomas Erpenius (Leiden, 1625).

4. There is a note in BL Harleian 1876, fol. 117, to "Gregor.Abūlfarai.p.101," but it does not correspond with any of the three editions that had been published of Abū al-Faraj. Johann Hottinger, *Historia Orientalis* (Tiguri, 1651), bk 2, ch. 1, writes about "Muhammedis Educatione, Itinere Syriaco," but there is no mention of travel beyond Syria "& alia loca," 210.

5. BL Harleian 1876: "Others say yt he was an Hermit, & yt he cry'd out, having view'd Mahomet well: There is no God, but God & Mahomet , ye Apostle of God" (fol. 117). See Hottinger, *Historia Orientalis* (1651), 203, where there is mention of a hermit who exclaims: "Non est Deus, nisi Deus, & Muhammed, Apostolus ejus."

6. The month of Muḥarram. Stubbe is borrowing from Edward Pococke, *Specimen Historiæ Arabica* (Oxford, 1650), 174–176, but the imperfect spelling of the month is the scribe's.

7. Abū Bakr al-Ṣiddīq was not Muḥammad's uncle (d. AD 634), but he was the father of one of the Prophet's wives. In Arabic, however, a father-in-law is also an "uncle." The name is also spelled "Abubecr" in the manuscript.

8. In the seventeenth century, "obnoxious" meant "exposed to harm" (*OED*).

9. The words in parentheses are in the margin, BL Harleian 1876, fo. 118, with a sign after "Princes" to add them into the text.

10. Hottinger, *Historia Orientalis* (1651), bk 2, ch. 1.

11. Pococke, *Specimen*, 170.

12. Gaius Julius Priscus, born in Syria, rose from soldier to brother of Emperor Philip the Arab in the third century AD; Pertinax, Roman Emperor who started his life as a teacher and later as a soldier (AD 126–186); Don Ambrogio Spinola Doria (1569–1630), Italian aristocrat who served the Spanish crown. See also André Tiraqueau, *Commentarij de nobilitate, et ivre primigeniorvm, hac postrema editione ab autore ipso diligentissimè recogniti, & tertia ampliùs parte locupletati* (Venice, 1574), chapter 33, "An mercatura derogit Nobilitati," especially paragraph 17 where there is a discussion of emperors and kings who were "mercatores."

13. Boxhornius mentions the travels of Muḥammad to Egypt and Palestine, but not Spain. Marcus Zuerius Boxhornius, *Historia universalis sacra et profana a Christo nato ad annum usque MDCL* (Leiden, 1652), 397. King Ricaredus was the first king of the Goths who was not Arian.

14. Purchas repeats this story about rice, "Foolish and blasphemous traditions." *Purchas his Pilgrimage* (London, 1626), 232. Purchas relied on the introduction of Sionita's 1619 translation of al- Idrīsī.

15. Khadīja bint Khuwaylid, d. AD 619. Another variant: "Chadijah."

16. Pococke, *Specimen*, 170–171.

17. Hottinger, *Historia Orientalis* (1651), 206, for the dream.

18. Tiraqueau, *Commentarij de nobilitate*, chapter 25, "An nobilitas perdatur ob paupertatem," but the emphasis is on the poverty of Graeco-Roman, rather than biblical, figures.

19. Waraqa ibn Nawfal, the paternal cousin of Khadīja, is mentioned in Bukhāri's rendition of the Hadith, narrated by 'Āisha (I, 1, 3): "Khadija then accompanied him [Muḥammad] to her cousin Waraqa bin Naufal bin Asad bin 'Abdul 'Uzza, who, during the pre-Islamic period became a Christian and used to write the writing with Hebrew letters. He would write from the Gospel in Hebrew as much as Allah wished him to write. He was an old man and had lost his eyesight." He died a few days after Muḥammad received the first revelation of the Qur'ān. There is no reference in the Hadith that he was a teacher to the Prophet. Toward the end of *Originall* the name is transliterated correctly as "Warakeh."

20. Ibn Muqla (AD 886–940), Persian calligrapher in Abbasid Baghdad; and, probably, al-Qāsim ibn Abī al-Bazza (d. AD 741), an exegete.

21. Pococke, *Specimen*, 157.

22. Ximenez, *Historia Arabum*, 2.

23. Pococke, *Specimen*, 169–170, 153.

24. Another variant in the manuscript is "Aly."

25. Al-Makīn, *Historia*, 43.

26. Genethlia is birthday celebration.

27. The reference to al-Makīn is from Hottinger: "Undoubtedly Muhammad was born at the end of the night, when Libra was in the middle of the sky; in the middle of the night, to be sure, the constellation Taurus had crossed the meridian, for otherwise the prophet and leader would not have been able to coincide with it." Hottinger, *Historia Orientalis* (1651), 146. Abū Ma'shar (AD 787–886) was an astrologer.

28. Another variant of the Qur'ān is "Alkoran." I shall retain both of Stubbe's spellings as they appear in the manuscript.

29. As Purchas shows, the term derives from Strabo, "Scenites vel Nomades," *Pilgrimage*, 224. See J. Spencer Trimingham, *Christianity Among the Arabs in Pre-Islamic Times* (London, 1979), appendix A, "Greek and Latin Terms designating Arab Nomads," for a discussion of the term.

30. In AD 626.

31. BL Harleian 1876 has "miserably" while BL Harleian 6189 has "universally," fols. 125 and 110 respectively.

32. 'Umar ibn al-Khaṭṭāb (d. AD 644) and 'Uthmān ibn 'Affān (d. AD 656), second and third of the Righteous Caliphs. Other variants for "Othman" in the manuscript

are "Otsman," "Otsmin," and "Osman." The spelling of "Omar" was consistent throughout the manuscript although there is a later variance in reference to "Ibn Omer."

33. Pandects: a unit of laws in Justinian jurisprudence.

34. Pococke, *Specimen*, 158–161, esp. 160.

35. The reference is from Nicholas Fuller, *Miscellaneorum Theologicorum*, 2d ed. (Strasbourg, 1650), 448, but to a pseudo prophet, and not specifically to "Mahomet." See also Pococke, *Specimen*, 374.

36. Purchas makes this point, but without citing a source for it, *Purchas*, 232. In BL Harleian 6189, the number is "two," fol. 111.

37. See Bodin, *Six Bookes*, 500–501.

38. Geronimo Cardan (1501–1576), mathematician, and his father Fazio Cardan.

39. Ximénes de Cisneros (1436–1517), Spanish statesman and scholar. See William Hickling Prescott, *History of the Reign of Ferdinand and Isabella the Catholic* (London, 1885), 436.

40. Pococke's spelling, *Specimen*, 121.

41. Sūrat al-An'ām (the Cattle) is one of the early Meccan revelations. The spelling *surat* is taken from Pococke. The first *OED* entry, however, is from Robert Boyle in 1661.

42. Pococke, *Specimen*, 108–109.

43. The Qur'ānic 'Ozayr (9:30), revered by the Jews as "son of God." For the veneration of Mary, see Epiphanius, *The Panarion of Epiphanius of Salamis, Book 1*, trans. F. Williams, 2d ed. (Leiden, 2009), 30.3.7, p. 122 and the discussion in Hottinger, *Historia Orientalis* (1660), 343, and for 'Ozayr 334–36.

44. Luqmān al-Ḥakīm/the Wise, after whom it is very likely that Sura 31 in the Qur'ān is named. Erpenius had translated "Fabūlae Locmani Sapientis" which appeared in *Arabicae Linguae Tryocinium, id est Grammatica Arabica* (Leiden, 1656), 1–172. The book was edited by Jacob Golius. See also Hottinger, *Historia Orientalis* (1660), 101–103, where there is a discussion of the sura. The association with Aesop is in *Historia Orientalis* (1651), 69.

45. He died in 619, the same year as the Prophet's wife, Khadīja.

46. 'Aws and Khazraj were two tribes of Yathrib with connections to Jewish communities.

47. Stubbe borrows "Muslimin" from Hottinger, *Historia Orientalis* (1660), who uses it early on in the book, 4, "Moslemin."

48. "Specious" used in its Latin derivation: beautiful, plausible.

49. The previous four paragraphs are from al-Makīn. The material in the last paragraph was also developed from al-Makīn by Hottinger, *Historia Orientalis* (1660), 424–425.

50. Abū 'Abdallah Muḥammad al-Idrīsī, *Geographia Nubiensis*, trans. Gabriel Sionita (Paris, 1619), 44–45.

51. BL Harleian 6189 has "evince" instead of "revive."

52. Stubbe takes some liberty with his source (as he does on numerous other occasions): al-Makīn does not state that the Prophet had favored Jesus, but had asked that the message of all "Prophetarum & Apostolorum" be accepted. Al-Makīn, *Historia*, 3.

53. Q 3:45.

54. Most likely Khālid Abū Ayyūb (al-Anṣārī).

CHAPTER 5

The title is written in the margin, Hand B. Henceforth, all odd numbered pages have "CHAP 5" in the upper left corner.

1. Other variants are "Islanisme," "Islanism," and "Islamisme."

2. Sionita, *Geographia Nubiensis* (Paris, 1619), ch. 1.

3. See *Purchas his Pilgrimage* (London, 1626), 231, where there is a similar description.

4. BL Harleian 6189 has "two," fol. 122.

5. See al-Makīn, *Historia*, bk. 1, ch. 1.

6. In the sense of a grammatically complete sentence (*OED*).

7. Fātima.

8. Other variants are "Moslemin" and "Mosslemin."

9. The noun is used in the singular and in the plural with "Mossleman," "Mussulman," "Mosleman," and "Mussulmen," as variants. The emphasis that Stubbe places on it is important since he challenged seventeenth-century misusages. In 1611 John Floria stated that "A Pagan beleeuer is a Mussulman," *Queen Annas New Worlde of Words* (London, 1611), 195, and toward the end of the century, in 1695, and during his controversy with John Edwards (1637–1716), Locke ridiculed his opponent's ignorance of Arabic and the use of "Musselmen" instead of "in plain English, the Mahometans." Locke, *The Reasonableness of Christianity* in *Works* (London, 1963 [1833]), 7:282.

10. Verbatim from Johann Hottinger, *Historia Orientalis* (Tiguri, 1660), 438. Bilāl ibn al-Ḥārith, Suhayl ibn'Ammār, possibly Ṣuhayb al-Rūmi, and Khabbāb ibn al-Aratt. It is difficult to identify the others.

11. The paragraph is from Edward Pococke, *Specimen Historiæ Arabica* (Oxford, 1650), 102.

12. The scribe split the noun in two. It should be *al-Muhajirūn*.

13. Paranomasia is pun.

14. 1 Chronicles 5–18 describe the wars between the Hagarites and the Reubenites.

15. Nicholas Fuller, *Miscellaneorum Theologicorum*, 2d ed. (Strasbourg, 1650), 255.

16. In BL Harleian 6189, there is "**victory*" rather than "history," but the asterisk reads: "**f. History*," fol. 129.

17. Trajan, Roman Emperor (reg. AD 98–117); Severus, Roman Emperor (reg. AD 193–211). See also Pococke, *Specimen*, 53.

18. Olearius, *The voyages and travels of the ambassadors sent by Frederick, Duke of Hostein, to the Great Duke of Muscovy and the King of Persia*, trans. John Davies (London, 1669), 196.

19. In BL Sloane 1709, the words are "ostentation but courage," fol. 102r.

20. BL Harleian 1876 has the following note: "The Arabians amongst ye blessings God bestowed on ym reckon these: yt instead of Crowns each of ym hath his Tulipant: & yt yr swords are to ym what walls & bulwarks are to others," fol. 140.

21. Stubbe takes liberty with the episode of "Arbitration," during the battle of Ṣiffīn when the slogan was first raised. It was described by al-Makīn, *Historia*, 39.

22. Fuller, *Miscellaneorum Theologicorum*, bk. 1, ch. 13, on "De Astroarchæ & Vrania apud Herodianum: De Astarte: Deque Lunæ imaginæ in Saracenorum insignibus."

23. Shahoronim: chains around the camel's neck with small moon-like or crescent-like ringlets, Judges 8:26; Isaiah 3:18. Stubbe's use of "lunulets" is before the first 1826 entry in *OED*. Stubbe is borrowing from Selden, *De Dis Syris*, Syntagma II, 289.

24. BL Harleian 1876 has the following note: "These are all Mahometan sayings, & some ascribed to Ali," fol. 141. The note also appears in BL Sloane 1709, fol. 102v.

25. Verbatim from Olearius, *The voyages*, 279. The note also mentions Lancelot Addison, *West Barbary, or, A short narrative of the revolutions of the kingdoms of Fez and Morocco* (Oxford, 1671), 160, where there is another version of the Sura.

26. In BL Harleian 1876, there is the following note: "Keblah is ye place of Heaven or Earth towards wch they praied: wch was Jerusalem, till Muhammad changed it to ye Caab," fol. 143. The scribe in MS 537 wrote "Reblah" instead of Pococke's "Keblah." Pococke, *Specimen*, 113. In BL Sloane 1709, "Keblah" is replaced by "Kaabah," fol. 103r.

27. John Selden, *De Dis Syris Syntagmata* (Leipzig, 1662), 292, 294.

28. In the margin, Hand A: "v. Selden de Dii Syrii in venere."

29. Selden, *De Dis Syris Syntagmata*, 291: "It was not established but related by Muhammad that the Guimia [Friday] feast seemed to have flowed from the rites of horned Urania and the ancient effigy of little moons near to them..it seemed to have flowed."

30. See Fuller, *Miscellaneorum Theologicorum*, bk. 1, ch. 13.

31. In BL Harleian 1876, there is the following note: "This story is in the Alcoran: Dr. Pocock ubi supra. p. 87," fol. 145. In BL Harleian 6189, there is the following alteration: " . . . escaping in the Ark [**that besides the Introduction of a multitude of Associate Gods]* that this . . . " The asterisk points to the following note: "**Sic. This seems to be misplaced. It follows in the next page*," fol. 139. For the Prophet Ṣālih, see Q 7:73.

32. The tribe of Thammūd. See Hottinger's discussion of Ṣālih and the episode on which Stubbe elaborates, *Historia Orientalis* (1660), 44–48.

33. In BL Harleian 1876, there is the following annotation: "This is avowed by Sharestanius, in Dr. Pocock ubi supra. p.54" (fo. 146).The reference to Shahrastānī is in Pococke, *Specimen*, 53.

34. Ibid., 119.

35. Ibid., 118–121.

36. Ibid., 120. See Hottinger, *Historia Orientalis* (1660) who quotes the same passage, 356–357.

37. The scribe wrote "fund a Mentall." BL Harleian 1876 has the following note: "Olearius & others give another reason for its blackness, & how it come there: but

'tis not strange amongst the Muhammadans to find many reasons for ye same thing," fol. 147.

38. In BL Harleian 1876, there is the following note: "Selden, Syntag bk 2, ch. 14," fol. 148. There is a discussion of Mercury/Merkolis and the throwing of stones in chapter 15. Selden, *De Dis Syris Syntagmata,* 353–354.

39. Another variant is "Muslimittical."

40. Stubbe relies on Olearius, *The voyages*, 173, from where he borrows "scei-than." "that it should be soe" is underlined, but is omitted in BL Sloane 1709, fol. 104r.

41. Genesis 17:23–27.

42. Genesis 16:10.

43. BL Harleian 1876 has this note: "Ahmed Ben Edris in scripto Elenetic.l.c.38," fol. 151, which Stubbe copied from Hottinger, *Historia Orientalis* (1660), "Ahmed ben Edris, scripti sui, Elenchitici l. 1, c. 38," 12.

44. Pococke, *Specimen*, 110. In BL Sloane 1709 the sentence starting "crying Allah" and ending "turned into Cobar" is in the margin, fol. 105r. Is the scribe of the University of London manuscript copying from Sloane and integrating material into the text proper? Or was there another (lost) manuscript?

45. There is "man" in Sloane 1709, fol. 105r, and in the other manuscripts.

46. In BL Harleian 6189, "objects" replaces "projects," fol. 154.

47. Pococke, *Specimen*, 105–107. "Ismaelism" is followed by "which God was now resolved to put an end unto," BL Sloane 1709, fol. 106r.

48. In BL Sloane 1709, "paradise" is followed by "& if it is lawfull to drink it there why not here," fol. 106r.

49. See Marcus Zeuerius Boxhornius, *Historia universalis sacra et profana a Christo nato ad annum usque MDCL* (Leiden, 1652), 398, for this dialogue. BL Sloane 1709 continues: Abdias replyed There is very good reason for it. "The Agareans . . . " fol. 106 r. There were numerous versions of this story: J. Kritzeck, *Peter the Venerable and Islam* (Princeton, 1964), 89.

50. In BL Harleian 1876, there is the following note: "All ys discourse at wine is alleged by me upon supposal yt in Arabia they had wine: wch is probable from yr worship of Bacchus: but if they had none, as Amianus Marcellinus (who was amongst ym) says he met with none that knew wt wine was: then did Mahomet comply with the constitution of ye Saracens in forbidding it: wisely foreseeing yt yir conquests & travells would acquaint them with it: & so he by those stories endeavoured to prevent the inconveniences of drinking it. But I believe they had wine in some places," fol. 157. The use of "apologue" is the first before the 1699 entry in the *OED*.

51. *Augerii Gislenii Busbequii d. Legationis turcicae epistolae quatuor* (Frankfurt, 1595), 106–107.

52. The first use of "complacent" in this manner had appeared in 1660 (*OED*).

53. Pococke, *Specimen*, 52–53, but the earlier part is taken from the Qur'ān.

54. A note in BL Harleian 1876 reads: "This was written on Muhammad's seal: In duplex testimonium," fol.160.

55. Also spelled "Melchite" in the manuscript.

56. Gratian (AD 359–383) was a Roman emperor who continued the fight against the Arians. His father was Valentinian I, and his mother was Marina. His uncle was Valens.

57. Justin I (reg. AD 518–527), Byzantine emperor and founder of the Justinian dynasty; Sozomen, in *Evsebii Pamphili, Rvffini, Socratis, Theodoriti, Sozomeni, Theodori, Evagrii, et Dorothei Ecclesiastica Historia* (Basel, 1570), 544, "Saraceni cū Romanis federe conjuncti." There is mention of Palestine, Phoenicia, and Egypt, but not Syria.

58. A note mentions "Abu al faraj 93," which corresponds to the same page in Edward Pococke, *Historia Compendiosa Dynastiarvm* (Oxford, 1672).

59. Fuller, *Miscellaneorum Theologicorum*, 314. See also Pococke, *Specimen*, 74.

60. "Aretas" derives from the Arabic, Ḥāritha: al-Mundhir ibn al-Ḥārith was the king of the Ghassānid Arabs from AD 569 to ca. 581. It is not clear whom Stubbe had in mind in regard to "Aretas," unless it is to the NT reference, 2 Corinthians 11:22.

61. BL Harleian 1876 has "Emperour" instead of "Empire," fol. 162. Philip the Arab (reg. AD 244–249). The reference to "Bostra" could be to Busra in Syria, since Philip was born in the province of Arabia.

62. Odenatus and his wife Zenobia ruled Palmyra and fought the Romans in the third century.

63. Sozomen in *Evsebii Pamphili, Rvffini, Socratis,* 545. Another variant, rare, for Hagar is "Agar."

64. Fuller, *Miscellaneorum Theologicorum*, bk. 2, ch. 12, "De nomine Saracenorum, De Ismaëlitis, Cedrais, & Agarenis"; Pococke, *Specimen*, 33; Hottinger, *Historia Orientalis* (1651), 4–9.

65. Hottinger, *Historia Orientalis,* 7–8. For a discussion of the term *Saracens* in English seventeenth-century usage, see Katharine Scarfe Beckett, *Anglo-Saxon Perceptions of the Islamic World* (Cambridge, 2003), ch. 9. See especially her references to Thomas Newton, 205–207.

66. BL Harleian 1876 has the following note: "This saying is related to have been ye most frequent of any in the mouth of Ali: Hottinger.hist.or.l.2.c.5," fol. 167.

67. BL Harleian 1876 has the following note: "That ys is ye Muhammadan tenet concerning praier, see L. Addison of Westbarbary.c.9," fol. 167, Addison, *West Barbary*, "Of the Moresco Church Government," 155–165.

68. BL Harleian 1876 has the following note: "These are all Muhammadan sayings," fol. 168.

69. Another example of Stubbe taking liberties with his sources. The episode is from *Augerii Gislenii Busbequii d. Legationis turcicæ epistolæ quatuor,* 107–108, but it has nothing to do with 'Ali.

70. BL Harleian 1876 has the following note: "Orotal ye Great God: Alilia ye Associate Goddess of ye Arabians," fol. 168.

CHAPTER 6

The title is written in the margin, Hand B. Henceforth, all odd numbered pages have "Chap 6" in the upper left corner. This chapter division is absent from BL Sloane 1709 where there is just a new paragraph.

1. Edward Pococke, *Specimen Historiæ Arabica* (Oxford, 1650), 172.

2. See Acts 8:27ff. Henceforth the scribe used "Abyssines" instead of "Abyssinians."

3. Edward Brerewood, *Enqviries Tovching the Diversity of Langvages, and Religions throughout the cheife parts of the World* (London, 1614), 155.

4. BL Harleian 1876 has the following note: "Gregor.Abulfarai.p.93. say's ye Arabian Christians were Jacobites," fol. 170, Edward Pococke, *Historia Compendiosa Dynastiarum* (Oxford, 1663), 93–94. Also repeated in BL Sloane 1709, fol. 110v.

5. Pococke, *Specimen*, 63–64.

6. John Selden, *Uxor Ebraica* (Frankfurt, 1673), 395–396. Stubbe closely followed Selden, but he spelled the names differently. In BL Harleian 1876 there is the following note: "I am sorry yt Selden did not publish the letters entire," fol. 170.

7. Johann Hottinger, *Historia Orientalis* (Tiguri, 1660), 461. But Stubbe was confused about the names: Ja'far ibn abī Tālib went on the migration to Abyssinia; Zayd ibn Ḥāritha was the adopted son of the Prophet. There is no record of 'Abdallah ibn 'Umar.

8. Jirjis ibn al-'Amīd al-Makīn, *Historia Saracenica*, trans. Thomas Erpenius (Leiden, 1625), 4.

9. The title of this section is written in the margin, Hand A.

10. Al-Makīn, *Historia*, 5. The reference is to "Abusofianum f. Harithi," Abū Sufyān ibn al-Ḥarith, a cousin of the Prophet and one of the Companions. Another variant in the manuscript is "Abusophian."

11. The Battle of Badr—AD 624.

12. Hottinger, *Historia Orientalis* (1660), 329, "Phinhas, filius Azura," Finḥās, a rabbi in Medina. See also p. 358 where Hottinger contrasts the trustworthiness of the Christians with the deceit of the Jews.

13. The title is written in the margin, Hand A.

14. Hottinger, *Historia Orientalis*, 328.

15. Most probably 'Utba ibn Waqqāṣ at the battle of Uḥud in AD 625.

16. The paragraph is from al-Makīn, *Historia*, 4–5. The references are to "Ka'baum fil. Alasrafi"/Ka'b ibn al-Ashraf, "Ochas filius Abumugidi"/'Uqba ibn abī Mujīd, and "Abdalla quoqs filius Sjehabi"/ 'Abdallah ibn Shihāb.

17. The reference is to "Naimus f.Masudae Gatfanites"/Na'īm ibn Mas'ūd al-Ghatfani.

18. The title is written in the margin, Hand A.

19. Al-Makīn, *Historia*, 6–7, Hudaybiyya.

20. The Treaty of Hudaybiyya, AD 628.

21. Edward Pococke, *Historia Compendiosa Dynastiarvm* (Oxford, 1672), 102.

22. The title is written in the margin, Hand A.

23. Pococke, *Specimen*, 98, "AlJannabium."

24. Ibid.

25. The image of "vulgar heads" recalls Sir Thomas Browne's *Psuedodoxia Epidemica* (London, 1646), ch. 5, where Browne is denouncing the Muslims for their credulity. Stubbe owned a copy of "Brown's vulgar Error et Religio Medici London 1672," BL MS Sloane 35, fol. 8r.

26. Al-Makīn, *Historia*, 8, "Melicum filium Aufi"; Hottinger, *Historia Orientalis* (1651), 271. The tribes are Thaqīf and Hawāzin.

27. The opposition of the Hawāzin tribe to Muḥammad was led by Mālik ibn 'Awf al-Anṣārī. "Taiph" is Ṭā'if, the city of the tribe of Thaqīf. "Horam" is Ḥunayn.

28. Erpenius, *Orationes Tres, De Linguam Ebraeae atque Arabicae Dignitate* (Leiden, 1621), 42ff.

29. Hottinger, *Historia Orientalis* (1651), 271–272.

30. Qur'ān 9:25.

31. Al-Makīn, *Historia*, 8–9.

32. The title is written in the margin, Hand A.

33. Sihan ad-Dauma, in Yemen.

34. Pococke, *Historia Compendiosa Dynastiarvm*, 103. In the margin, there is "Mosaleima" which is similar to Pococke's "Mosailema." In this manuscript another variant is "Moseilina." Musaylima ibn Ḥabīb claimed to be a prophet in the ninth year after the *hijra*.

CHAPTER 7

The title is written in the margin, Hand B. Henceforth, all odd numbered pages have "CHAP 7" in the upper left corner.

1. Quoting verbatim from Olearius, *The voyages and travels of the ambassadors sent by Frederick, Duke of Hostein, to the Great Duke of Muscovy and the King of Persia*, trans. John Davies (London, 1669), 172.

2. Edward Pococke, *Specimen Historiæ Arabica* (Oxford, 1650), 315–316. The place is "al-'Aqaba."

3. Gabriel Sionita, *De Nonnvullis Orientalivm Vrbibvs* (Paris, 1619), 20.

4. Olearius, *The voyages*, 172.

5. "Daroga" is a word that Stubbe must have taken from Olearius, 1662 (*OED*). The passage continues in BL Sloane 1709, "giving him many blows on ye head neck & heart," fol. 114r.

6. Pococke, *Specimen*, 114.

7. See Olearius, *The voyages*, 173; Pococke, *Specimen*, 120, 121. In BL Sloane 1709 the sentence is different: "advanced from the ground about 7 handfulls or 2 cubits & an half," fol. 114r.

8. Pococke describes the pilgrimage, *Specimen*, 310–316.

9. Both are Moabite deities. See Judges 11:24, Numbers 25:3.

10. The celebration of Eid al-Aḍha takes place between 10–12 of the month of Dhul Ḥijja.

11. "Ashura" is 'Āshurā', the tenth day of the month of Muḥarrahm. The Jews fasted on that day in remembrance of the exodus, and so the Prophet instituted it as a fast day, as Stubbe notes.

12. Ibn al-Athīr (1160–1233) was a historian, frequently mentioned by Pococke.

13. For "accquests," BL Harleian1876 has "conquests" and BL Harleian 6189 has "acquaintance," fols. 188 and 209 respectively. In BL Sloane 1709, "power" is followed by "nor his inauguration to be Xerirriffs," fol. 114r.

14. The scribe was careless. In both BL Harleian 1876 and Harleian 6189, the word is "dignity."And "broils" should be "brawls."

15. Stubbe anglicized the name from Hottinger, *Historia Orientalis* (1660), 416–417, "Firus, Dailamatia," Fayrūz al-Daylamī. In BL Sloane 1709, "prophet" is followed by "in Yaman, & multiplied his followers, & possessed himself of power, provinces," fol. 114v.

16. Pococke, *Specimen*, 189–190.

17. Ibid., 189.

18. Ibid., 178. Stubbe misunderstood (his memory failed him?) the reference in Hottinger, *Historia Orientalis* (1660), where the quotation reads as follows: "the Prophet had received what none other had received, over 3,000 verses ('éaque varia ad tria millia, et amplius'). Had he received only the Qur'an, it would have been a sufficient demonstration of the miraculous" (488).

19. BL Harleian 1876 has the following note: "The Muhammadans believe, & so he told ym, yt Isa was not crucify'd, but conveyed to heaven, & an imaginary body crucify'd in his stead," fol. 191. The reference is to Q 4:157. In BL Sloane 1709 the note reads: "Muhammadans believe {or so he told ym}[added above the line] yt Isa was not crucified but conveyed to heaven & an image . . . crucified in his stead," fol. 115r.

20. Pococke, *Specimen*, 14. See also 179–180, where Pococke cites al-Shahrastanī.

21. Edward Pococke, *Historia Compendiosa Dynastiarvm* (Oxford, 1672), 103.

22. Sionita, *De Nonnvullis*, 19. BL 6189 has "double Stone" instead of "tombstone," fol. 214.

23. "Pretend" as in "offer, present, or put forward for consideration" (*OED* 1655 entry).

24. The first entry of "Indostan" in the *OED* refers to language rather than country, as with Stubbe (*OED*, E. Terry, 1655).

25. In the margin: "Vide Blue Book 123 Chap. 8eg," Hand B.

CONCERNING THE JUSTICE OF THE MAHOMETAN WARS

In the margin, "fo. 158," Hand A.

1. At the beginning of the second century AD, Hyrcanus forced the Idumeans to convert to Judaism. Stubbe had made the same point earlier.

2. BL Harleian 1876 has the following note: "There are a multitude of decrees in ye Theodosian Code, for ye enforcing men to turn Christians ye like occur in the German & Spanish Chronicles," fol. 196.

3. BL Harleian 1876 has a note about the work of Francisco de Vitoria, which contained a long section on "De Indis" immediately followed by a section on "De Indis, siue de iure belli Hispanororum in barbaros." The first title in this section is about "Christianis licet militare, & bella gerere," 129–173, 174–199: Francisco de Vitoria, *Relectiones undecim* (Salamanca, 1565).

4. BL Harleian 1876 has the following note: "This practise of his in yt Arabia, had ys political ground, yt whosoever will rule a diversity of nations, & religions,

must somewhere have an united force to overballance any opposite power; & a few being unanimous will retain many, if divided sufficiently in subjection," fol. 196.

5. Jirjis ibn al-'Amīd al-Makīn, *Historia Saracenica*, trans. Thomas Erpenius (Leiden, 1625), bk. 1, ch. 1 where there is a description of Muḥammad's friendship with the Christians.

6. Ibid., 28. Al-Makīn uses "Ælia" for Jerusalem.

7. 'Amr Ibn al-'Āṣ conquered Gaza from the Byzantines in AD 634. The paragraph draws on al-Makīn, *Historia*, 19–20.

8. Cf. John Selden, *De Iure Naturali & Gentium, Iuxta Disciplinam Ebraeorum, libri septem* (London, 1640), 732. Selden presents numerous verses from the Qur'ān about the security that was afforded the Christians, 732–734.

9. The reference is to al-Makīn, *Historia*, 3. The reference to "Mahomet Ben Achmed" is very likely to Muḥammad ibn Jarrīr al-Ṭabari, the historian on whom al-Makīn relied in writing his chronicle.

10. Ibid., 11.

11. Hugo Grotius, *Epistolæ ad Gallos* (Leiden, 1648), 239–240. Stubbe owned a copy of this edition. For Selden's view, see Toomer, *John Selden*, 2:620.

12. Paul Rycaut, *The Present State of the Ottoman Empire* (London, 1670), 99–102.

13. "Wars of sovereignty against other peoples, so that he might expand the borders of his realm and augment its greatness alone with fame." Wilhelm Schickard, *Jus regium hebraeorum, E tenebris Rabbinicis erutum, & luci donatum* (Leipzig, 1674), 112.

14. Cf. Selden, *De Iure*, bk. 6, ch. 14: "De Federis ineundi ratione & captibus, ubi hostes se dederent."

15. BL Harleian 1876 has the following note: "The principles of a narrow Monarchy, such as yt of Moses, do not become a great one, like unto yt of Muhammads," fol. 200.

16. BL Harleian 1876 has the following note: "The Saracens have for yr rule of faith ye Alcoran: then ye Assonnah, or Tradition, wherein ye sayings & actions of yr prophet are recorded, as examplary & directive: then ye decrees & actions of his four Successours: & then lastly Reason. So Gregor Abulfaraj de mosr. Arab Sect.ult. cum notis Pocockii. p. 298," fol. 200. Cf. Pococke, *Speicmen*, 298ff.

17. Selden, *De Iure*, 744.

18. Ogier Gislain Busbecq, *Augerii Gislenii Busbequii d. Legationis turcicæ epistolæ quatuor* (Frankfurt, 1595), 67r–68r.

19. Hugo Grotius, *De Jure Belli ac Pacis* (Amsterdam, 1631), 443.

20. In the margin, "fol 164," Hand B.

21. Jean Bodin, *Six Bookes of a Commonweale* (London, 1606), "The disposition of the people is greatly to be obserued in the gouernment," 560.

22. *Augerii Gislenii Busbequii d. Legationis turcicae epistolae quatuor*, 66r–66v.

23. BL Harleian 6189 has "explicable" instead of "despicable," fol. 229.

24. BL Harleian 6189 has "never" instead of "ever," fol. 230.

25. In margin: "h . . . usq Cap. 10," in Hand A. Under it at the bottom of the page, "to fol 165 Wanting here from fol 165 to fol 169. in blew book" in Hand B. BL Harleian 6189 has "performed" instead of "inform'd," fol. 230.

CONCERNING THE CHRISTIAN ADDITIONS

1. Epiphanius, *The Panarion of Epiphanius of Salamis, Book 1,* trans. F. Williams, 2d ed. (Leiden, 2009), 131, "Khokhabe in Hebrew."

2. James Windet, *Minhah belulah, sive, Stromateus epistolikos* (London, 1664), 222. Stubbe owned a copy of this edition.

3. See Johann Hottinger, *Historia Orientalis* (Tiguri, 1651), on the status of Christians (and Jews) at the time of Muḥammad, 212–238, although the section on the Christians focuses on early schisms, 228ff. The reference to Christians and money draws on al-Makīn and on Q 3:75.

4. In margin: "fo. 135," Hand A.

5. John Selden, *De Iure Naturali & Gentium, Iuxta Disciplinam Ebraeorum, libri septem* (London, 1640), 238. Muḥammad ibn Aḥmad was a Qur'ānic exegete (d. 1459). Selden cites him often in his *Uxor Ebraica.*

6. Hugo Grotius, *De Veritate religionis Christianæ* (Amsterdam, 1662), 375–376. Stubbe did not use the English translation of 1632 and avoided the anti-Islamic emphasis in that chapter (and all the rest of the treatise). In margin: "fo. 166," Hand A. It is not clear what these references by the hands mean: there is a bracket from "that no man" until "universally" next to which is "fo. 135"; and from "demolish" to "confusion of" next to which is "fo. 166."

7. Abū al-Fida.

8. John Selden, *Eutychii Ægyptii, Patriarchæ Orthodoxorum Alexandrini* (London, 1642), 74.

9. Ibid., 16 "per totum." The reference is to Yusuf al-Misrial-Gibti's introduction in *Synodikon, sive, Pandectae canonum ss, apostolorum, et conciliorum ab ecclesia Graeca receptorum* (Oxford, 1672), xix–xxi, where there is mention of "Arabicam Josephi Ægyptii." The Arabic accounts of the councils are 681–727.

10. In the margin, an asterisk.

11. The story appears in Levinus Warner, *Proverbiorum et sententiarum Persicarum Centuria collecta* (Leiden, 1644), 30, and in Hottinger, *Historia Orientalis* (1660), 515.

12. Both BL Harleian 1876 and BL Harleian 6189 end with this reference to "Isa," although they differ in the ordering of the chapters. See the tables of contents in the discussion of the "Printed and Manuscript Sources: Editorial Policy," this volume.

13. "There have been many who have described the life of the Arab Muhammad, which they relate in this manner; on this however all agree. But it is a bad thing that Erpenius, de Lingua Arabica p. 42 holds, that they affirm that he was born from a plebian and base stock, from impoverished parents—a pagan father and a Judean mother." Stubbe copies verbatim from Hottinger, *Historia Orientalis* (1651), 136. Erpenius mentions that the Prophet's parents were "obscuris." Thomas Erpenius, *Orationes tres, de linguarum Ebraeæ, atque Arabicæ dignitate* (Leiden, 1621), 42, but it was Boxhornius who mentioned that the parents were idolaters and that the mother was "gente Iudaea." Marcus Zeuerius Boxhornius, *Historia universalis sacra et profana a Christo nato ad annum usque MDCL* (Leiden, 1652), 397, 401.

14. Hottinger discusses this number, *Historia Orientalis* (1651), 146. BL Harleian 1876 has "Μαομέτις" in the blank space, fol. 66.

15. Ibid., 9. It is interesting that Prideaux also refers to the correct spelling and enunciation of the name, but then retains "Mahomet." Humphrey Prideaux, *The True Nature of Imposture* (London, 1697), xxii.

16. Theodore of Mopsuestia (ca. AD 350–428); Diodorus of Tarsus (d. AD 392).

17. In the right margin: an asterisk.

18. BL Harleian 6189 has "undeniably false" instead of "unimaginable," fol. 258.

19. "Kessaeus" is Muḥammad 'Abdalla al-Kisā'ī, mentioned by Henrys Sike in his 1697 edition of an apocryphal gospel, "The Gospel of Thomas," the manuscript of which had formerly been in the possession of Jacob Golius, "Praefatio ad lectorem," *Evangelium Infantiae*, 2v. There must have been another manuscript by al-Kisā'ī about the lives of the prophets, *Qisas al-anbiyā'*, which was heavily used by Hottinger in his *Historia Orientalis*. While the reference to "Casus Effendus in his Commentaries upon the Alcoran" suggests that John Gregory, *The Works* (London, 1665), 9, may have seen a manuscript by this Muslim scholar, the reference by Stubbe points to his indebtedness to Hottinger.

20. See Hottinger, *Historia Orientalis* (1660), 352–354 from the manuscript by Ibn Idrīs al-Qarafī, *Al-Ajwiba al-fākhira 'ala al-as'ila al-fājira*, ed. Bakr Zakī 'Awaḍ (Cairo, 1986), 318–322. See also Champion, " 'I remember a Mahometan Story of Ahmed ben Edris.' "

21. BL Harleian 1876 has "Arrians" instead of "Arabians," fol. 70. Actually, there is mention of it in Gabriel Sionita, *De Nonnvullis Orientalivm Vrbibvs* (Paris, 1619), 21.

22. Edward Pococke, *Specimen Historiæ Arabica* (Oxford, 1650), 186, 187. The Scaliger reference is to the improvement on Marcus Manilius: *M. Manill Astonomicon a Iosepho Scaligero ex vetusto codice Gemblacensi infinitis mendis repurgatum* (Leiden, 1600).

23. In BL Harleian 1876, fo. 70, there is the following note: "See the prodigies of Ægypt lately translated." The reference to Noah's pigeon is from the medieval text by Murtaḍā ibn al-'Afīf, *The Egyptian history: treating of the pyramids, the inundation of the Nile, and other prodigies of Egypt, according to the opinions and traditions of the Arabians. Written originally in the Arabian tongue by Murtadi, the son of Gaphiphus, rendered into French by Monsieur Vattier, Arabick professor to the king of France. And thence faithfully done into English by J. Davies of Kidwelly* (London, 1672), esp. 86–87. For Stubbe's reference to Athanasius and his pigeon, see Champion, "Legislators, Imposters, and the Politic Origin of Religion," 346.

24. There is a note referring to "Wierus de præstig. Dæmonum.l.1.c.19." See Johann Veyer, *De praestigiis daemonum, et incantantionibus ac ueneficijs, Libri V* (Basel, 1564). But there is no direct mention of Muḥammad in that chapter.

25. Henceforth, the scribe uses "Osman." Was he or the scribe correcting the earlier mistake?

26. Pococke, *Specimen*, 156, 157.

27. Anacharsis was a Scythian philosopher who, after training in Athens, returned to his own people. According to Herodotus, he was killed because of his foreign ways.

28. The seven pre-Socratic philosophers, seventh to sixth centuries BC.

29. For "Abunazarus," see Hottinger, *Historia Orientalis* (1651), 205.

30. Al-Makīn, *Historia*, 10, where there is reference to letters sent to the Prophet.

31. Pococke, *Specimen*, 180–181.

32. "For those to whom history is a concern, I would desire that they pursue their Arabic works diligently, rather than persuasively; so that many foolish stories might be removed, which our ignorance of this language throws in our way. Thus it would come about that we might no longer dream that Muhammad's tomb is a pendulum in the air: nor would we continually propagate the falsehood of his promise concerning his return to his followers, whom we absurdly believe. . . . We might pay back those fools by striking against them with truths aimed to refute them; nor would we any longer talk nonsense in saying that the Saracen people boast descent from Sarah by way of their appellation. There are six hundred such things which are impossible to oppose without a study of their languages." Edward Pococke *Lamiato'l Ajam* (Oxford, 1661), "Oratio in Auditorio Arabica habita," B4v. See also an excerpt from his oration "in auditorio Arabico 10. Augusti, 1636," 234.

33. Euthymius Zigabenus (fl. 12th ca.), Byzantine theologian.

34. John Selden, *De Dis Syris Syntagmata* (Leipzig, 1662), 286; Pococke, *Specimen*, 120–21; Hottinger, *Historia Orientalis* (1651), bk. 1, ch. 7. But, as Toomer points out, Pococke disagreed with Selden's view that "Cobar" was the name of a goddess. Toomer, *John Selden*, 1:241.

35. Stubbe took this reference to Venus from Selden, *De Dis Syris Syntagmata*, 216. Selden, citing Euthymius, concurred, unlike Stubbe who disagreed. See also Hottinger, *Historia Orientalis* (1651), bk. 1, ch. 7, for discussion of the stone.

36. Pococke, *Specimen*, 114, 118 /for the sake of good omens or for obtaining blessing.

37. Ibid., 120. "This is a thing, however, asserted by the Damascene and the Euthynian. If anyone should inspect more carefully the apparent figure of a head carved out with a scraper, which they want to be Venus's, I think it impossible to prove it by Arab carvers. Another of these [claims is] that the stone is a holy one, to which they offered the carved, or rather imprinted, figure, but it is as distant from the figure of the head as the head is from the feet, unless their eyes were so blurred by religious awe that they did not know how to distinguish the head from the feet. Of course, there is the stone in which the footprints of Abraham were imprinted when he stood on it during his building of the Ka'ba , as Abū al-Fida assents to, or (as Aḥmad ibn Yusef and Safioddinus say), when Ishmael's wife washed his head, which she revered when she saw it. Thence the place takes its name, the Maqām Ibrahīm, that is, the Place of Abraham, or where Abraham stood." The reference to the "Damascene" is probably to St. John of Damascus who wrote about this topic: D. J. Sahas, *John of Damascus on Islam: The 'Heresy of the Ishmaelites"* (Leiden, 1972), 132-41.

38. Professor Perale was unable to decipher the Greek word before Safa and Marwa. The spelling of "Marwa" is the accurate transliteration, unlike the "Meriah" of earlier pages.

39. Pococke, *Specimen*, 111. The scribe did not copy the Greek. "Elsewhere he says to these that it is. . . . called the likeness Baccha Ismaketh, which Mohammed himself named the Adoramen observationis [object of their prayer], and he instructed that the wretched barbarians adore it."

40. 'Abdalla ibn 'Umar al-Bayḍāwi (1126–1160), a major commentator on the Qur'ān.

41. Pococke, *Specimen*, 112–113. The scribe did not copy the Greek names: Μάκε and Μάκχε.

42. See Pococke, *Specimen*, 128–129.

43. In the margin:" Mahometan Religion w." Hand A.

44. Pococke, *Specimen*, 301. BL Harleian 6189 has "Originals, and" before "religion," fol. 273.

45. Ogier Gislain Busbecq , *Augerii Gislenii Busbequii d. Legationis turcicae epistolae quatuor* (Frankfurt, 1595), 105r–106r; and Paul Rycaut, *The Present State of the Ottoman Empire* (London, 1670), 160–161. The note in BL Harleian 1876, fol. 79, mentions "Bartholom. Georgivita Peregrin. de morib. Turcar.c. de quadragesim": there is no title that includes the two words, "peregrin." and "quadrogesim." But see the two accounts by Bartolomej Georgijević published in 1598 and 1671, each of which includes one of the two words in the title. The account was very popular and reprinted regularly. English translations appeared in 1569 and 1661. Stubbe owned a copy of the latter edition.

46. Aulus Cornelius Celsus (ca. 25 BC–ca. AD 50) was a Roman encyclopedist.

47. Zakāt. The first use in English occurs in 1802, "zecchat" (*OED*).

AS TO THEIR OPINIONS CONCERNING GOD

1. In the right margin: "fol 144," Hand B.

2. BL Harleian 6189 has "Holy Ghost" before "apostles," fol. 278.

3. Johann Hottinger, *Historia Orientalis* (Tiguri, 1651), 255.

4. Johann Hottinger, *Dissertationem miscellanearum pentas: De abusu patrum* (Tiguri, 1654), where there is a discussion of Muḥammad in comments by Maimonides and Gedaliam, 302–334.

5. Because of the war against Holland, in *Further justification*, Stubbe quietly praised Cromwell for having faced up to the naval rival. Although he described him as "HYPOCRITE" and mere "Oliver," he also showed how Cromwell defended England's right to the seas, 79. See the discussion of article 15.

6. Paul Rycaut, *The Present State of the Ottoman Empire* (London, 1670), 98, quoted verbatim by Stubbe. BL Harleian 1876 has "types" instead of "trials," fol. 83.

7. Edward Pococke, *Specimen Historiæ Arabica* (Oxford, 1650), 312–313.

8. In the right margin: "nolitic institutions," Hand A. In BL Sloane 1786, "mysteries" is followed by "as an Indian into ye sea for pearl," fol. 181r.

9. Wilhelm Schickard, *Jus regium hebraeorum, E tenebris Rabbinicis erutum, & luci donatum* (Leipzig, 1674), 179–180.

10. Hugo Grotius, *De Jure Belli* (Amsterdam, 1667), bk.2, ch. 9, parags. 8 and 9; John Selden, *De Iure Naturali & Gentium, Iuxta Disciplinam Ebraeorum, libri septem* (London, 1640), 564–565. For the agreement between Maimonides and Muḥammad, see p. 565. A note refers to Johannes Frischmuth (1619–1687), but the title of the work is not clear, BL Harleian 1876, fol. 85.

11. Schickard, *Jus regium hebræorum*, ch. 3, theor. 9, "Sed non tot a) uxores quot placebant," 173, where there is a reference to the verse in the Qur'ān about polygamy from the Sura on "Women," 4:3. In BL Sloane 1786 the sentence starts with "not so as that they were confined to one, for not to mention Solomon who is notorious," fol. 181v.

12. Deuteronomy 25:5.

13. Socrates in *Eusebii Pamphili, Rvffini, Socratis, Theodoriti, Sozomeni, Theodori, Evagrii, et Dorothei Ecclesiastica Historia* (Paris, 1672), 306. Stubbe accepts this view, while Selden had doubted its authenticity: Toomer, *John Selden*, 2:651*n*181.

14. "Eastern Jews take many wives; indeed it is permitted to western ones, but they do not do so out of respect. Paul did not want the Christians to take multiple wives and especially bishops, so that in this way he might silence the mouths of the Jews who were using it as an insult toward Christians. He did not warn the Jews that when they had three, they should repudiate two, and keep one." The quotation is translated in an article by Henk Jan de Jonge, "Scaliger's De LXXXV Canonibus Apostolorum Diatribe," *LIAS* 2 (1975): 115–124, where de Jonge writes in n. 25: "A somewhat different Interpretation of Tit. i.6 (and I Tim. iii.2/12) is preserved in the *Secunda Scaligerana* ed. Des Maizeaux, p. 402." Pierre Desmaizeaux was born a few years before Stubbe died and published two volumes of *Scaligerana* (Amsterdam, 1740).

15. John Selden, *Uxor Ebraica* (Frankfurt, 1673), bk. 1, ch. 9 on "Polygamia; Monita & Consilia de uxorum numero Quaternario non excedendo."

16. Selden, *De Iure*, 570. In BL Sloane 1786, Saul is omitted and Samson is added, fol. 182 r.

17. François Hotman, *De Castis incestisve nvptiis disputatio* (Basel, 1594), 327, mentions Hagar, Bala, Zilpa "& illa Gedeonis, quæ non nominator."

18. Selden, *Uxor Ebraica*, 46.

19. Lycurgus of Sparta was the legendary lawgiver.

20. Pococke contested the view that Muslims place the supreme happiness of the afterlife in bodily pleasures: *Porta Mosis*, 301. BL Sloane 1786 has "the Musselmans" instead of "Mahomet," fol. 182 v.

21. Selden, *De Iure*, 545. "Bredani" is most likely the exegete al-Bayḍāwi.

22. Hottinger, *Historia Orientalis* (1651), the description of Mecca, 142–144.

23. Claudii Salmasius, *De vsvris liber* (Leiden, 1638), 666–673, where Salmasius discusses usury in Islamic law between Muslims and non-Muslims, both enemies and friends. In BL Sloane 1786, "he" is replaced by "any Christian," fol. 182v.

24. Profitable laziness.

25. Salmasius, *De vsvris liber*, 666–667.

26. Ibid, 667. The passage from Ambrose is on p. 666. "Since their resources lie open as though for plunder and the pillage of these is lawful on every road" is the same which St. Ambrose gives: "For one against whom arms are justly borne, against this man let interest be lawfully declared: he whom you are able to conquer in war, regarding him, you can swiftly avenge yourself with the one percent. Exact interest from him whom it would not be a crime to kill. The man who demands interest fights without a sword. Without a sword the man who is the exactor of his

enemy's interest avenges himself on the enemy. Therefore where there is a right to war, there is a right to interest."

27. BL Harleian 1876 continues with a quotation from the Qur'ān: "His words are these, they will aske you if you will drink wine or adventure upon any sort of Gaming in wch there is Lottery. But do you answer, yt there is in ym something yt is exceeding sinfull & also somewhat yt is beneficial to man: but the benefit yt accrues from thence is over ballanced much by ye evil yt accompanies ym," fol. 91. In the margin there is a reference to "Mahometes in Alcoran c. 2." See Q 2:219.

28. Pococke, *Specimen*, 327.

29. Hottinger, *Historia Orientalis* (1651), 249.

30. Pococke, *Specimen*, 322.

31. Ibid., 157.

32. Ḥafṣa.

33. Pococke, *Specimen*, 362.

34. "Publish" as in to "make public or generally known," "announce," *OED* entry, J. Davies, 1662.

35. Ibid., 190–191. See also Pococke's reference to al-Ghazāli as "cognomintu Hojjatol Eslam," 371.

36. An English translation of the Qur'ān had appeared in 1649: see my "A Note on Alexander Ross and the English Translation of the Qur'an," *Journal of Islamic Studies*, 23 (2011): 76–84. The French translation was made by André du Ryer in 1647.

37. James Windet, *Minhah belulah, sive, Stromateus epistolikos* (London, 1664), 223, where Windet also denounces the poor quality of the French and the English translations of the Qur'ān. Stubbe could be referring either to the 1543 Bibliander edition of the Latin translation of the Qur'ān by Robert of Ketton or to the Italian 1547 translation by Andrea Arrivabene who claimed to have translated from the Arabic, but actually used the Latin version: see *John Selden on Jewish Marriage Law: The "Uxor Hebraica,"* translated with a commentary by Jonathan R. Ziskind (Leiden, 1991), 82*n*185. See Levinus Warner, *Epistola valedectoria in qua inter alia de stylo hisotriæ Timuri* (Leiden, 1644), 9–10, where there is mention of the need for consulting Arabic, Turkish, and Persian interpretations of the Qur'ān.

38. See the discussion of miracles in Hottinger, *Historia Orientalis* (1651), 291ff.

39. BL Harleian 6189 has "great Test" instead of "greatest," fol. 303.

40. The whole section with the eight headings is taken from Pococke's notes, *Specimen*, 187–188, 190–194. It is interesting that in BL Sloane 1786 miracles 6, 7, and 8 are copied and then crossed out, fol. 185v.

41. All these "miracles" are listed by Abū al-Faraj in Pococke, *Specimen*, 17.

42. Mount Seir is specifically noted as the place that Esau made his home (Genesis 36:8). It was named for Seir the Horite, whose sons inhabited the land (Genesis 36:20). The children of Esau battled against the Horites and destroyed them (Deuteronomy 2:12). Mount Seir is also given as the location where the remnants "of the Amalekites that had escaped" were annihilated by five hundred Simeonites (1 Chronicles 4:42–43). The mountain is also mentioned in Ezekiel 35:10 ("A Prophecy Against Edom"). See also Pococke, *Specimen*, 183–186, and *Historia Compendiosa Dynastiarum* (Oxford, 1663), 103–104. A similar passage appears in the treatise

by Aḥmad ibn Abdallaḥ, inscribed after Stubbe's treatise in the University of London Senate House manuscript: "God had Said in the holy Scriptures that hee will come from Ierocina that he would Shine in Zagar & bee exalted in Paran which is Meccha where Mahomet our Most Holy Prophet & Messenger of God did appear from hence these three things are to be noted. 1st that Ierocina is Mount Sinai where God gave to Moses the tables of the Law, that by Zagar is Mount Jerusalem where this Law of God did shine by Jesus Christ our Lord, who was alwaies accounted a prophet of God, who also Said that hee came not to destroy the Law of Moses but to confirm it, & as a testimony thereof was himself circumcised, And lastely that by Paran is understood Meccha where this Law of United shall be exalted illustrated & magnified. And it is manifest that this is Spoken & understood of our most holy prophet Mahomet who is the fullness of the Law of God & the Paraclete or Comforter himself who was promised in the Gospel (fol. 2).

43. Stubbe borrows from Hottinger, *Historia Orientalis* (1660), 13–14, where the Qur'ānic verse from Sura 49 is discussed.

44. See the reference to the gospel mentioned by "Ahmed ben Edris, p. m. 305 . . . Evengelium quintum . . . vocatur Evangelium infantiæ, quia in eo commemorantur res à Messia , super quo pax, profecta in juventute. Ad scribitur autem is Petro, à Maria, super qua pax." Hottinger, *Historia Orientalis* (1660), 332.

45. This paragraph is crossed out in the manuscript and does not appear in any other manuscript.

BIBLIOGRAPHY OF HENRY STUBBE

Henry Stubbe published his first work when he was nineteen years old in 1651. A few years later, and s eager to show off his mastery of Greek, he translated, among others, Donne's' "A Valediction: Forbidding Mourning" and Herrick's "Upon Julia Weeping" (*Deliciae Poetarum*, Oxford, 1658). In the dedications to his subsequent publications, Stubbe remembered men whom he admired or who had advanced his career: Richard Busby (his teacher), Thomas Barlow (his superior at the Bodleian), and Sir Henry Vane (his patron). Because of his Independent leanings, he wrote against Presbyterian authors, such as William Prynne and Richard Baxter, but he ranged widely in his interests, from discussing church government and medical cures to chocolate and political theory. He admired Hobbes and was "much esteemed" by him, thought Harrigton's *Oceana* "light," praised Milton, corresponded with Locke (who signed his 1659 letter to him as "Admirer"), served John Owen, defended the Quakers, and attacked the Dutch. He was involved in a bitter exchange with supporters of the Royal Society, including Joseph Glanvill, and at one time caught the censorious eye of the Cambridge Platonist Henry More. He wrote pamphlets, treatises, and one-page broadsheets, original pieces as well as translations, rebuttals of other treatises and apologias for his actions. Many of his works proved popular and appeared in second and enlarged editions. After Stubbe's death, the physician James Cook found some of Stubbe's notes on the "Ars Cosmetica" and published them at the end of his book. Some of Stubbe's advice was on how to make gloves that whiten the hands and how to make teeth white. That Stubbe was writing his treatise on Islam while concocting cosmetic tricks highlights the intriguing paradoxes in the personality of the first English biographer of the Prophet Muḥammad.

Notwithstanding his attachment to the university and his voluminous output, the 1674 catalogue of books at the Bodleian included reference to only three of his many works: *Deliciæ Poëtarum Anglicanorum in Græcum versæ* (1658), *The Savilian Professors case stated* (1658), and *The Indian Nectar* (1662) in Thomas Hyde, *Catalogus impressorum librorum bibliothecæ Bodlejanæ in academia Oxoniensi* (Oxford, 1674), 184. In 1825 John Britton wrote that Stubbe's works were "now almost forgotten," *The History and Antiquities of Bath Abbey Church* (London, 1825), 196, but in 1829, Edmund Oldfield, made a list of all his publications, including those written against him, *A topographical and historical account of Wainfleet and the Wapentake* (London, 1829), 345–352.

Only three of his books have been published recently (2011): *A Censure Upon Certaine Passages Contained in the History of the Royal Society*, *Campanella Revived*, and *Rosemary & Bayes*, all by the United Methodist Publishing House.

MANUSCRIPT

Letters to Hobbes: BL MS 32553, fols. 5–25.

Nicastro, Onofrio. *Lettere di Henry Stubbe a Thomas Hobbes*. Sienna, 1973.

"An enquiry into the Supremacy spiritual of the Kings of England, occasioned by a proviso in the late Act of Parliament against conventicles," TNA: SP 29/275/fos 276–284.

Letters from Bath: BL MS 35835, fols. 269–276.

For the manuscripts of the "Originall & Progress," see the list in "The Printed and Manuscript Sources: Editorial Policy."

PRINT

Horae subsecivae, seu, Prophetiae Jonae et Historiae Susannae paraphrasis Graeca versibus heroicis. London, 1651.

Illustrissimo, summaeque spei juveni Henrico Vane Armigero, honoratissimi, & à me blurimùm observandi viri, Dni D.D. Henrici Vane de Raby, equitis aurati, filio primogenitor. London, 1656.

Clamor, rixa, joci, mendacia, furta, cachini, or A severe enquiry into the late oneirocritica published by John Wallis, grammar-reader in Oxon. London, 1657.

A Severe Enquiry into the late Oneirocritica: or, An Exact Accovnt of the Grammatical Part of the Controversy betwixt Mr. Hobbes and J. Wallis D.D. (London, 1657).

Deliciae poetarum Anglicanorum in Graecum versae quibus accedunt elogia Romae & Venetiarum / authore H. Stubbe. Oxford, 1658.

The Savilian professours case stated. Oxford, 1658.

A light shining out of darknes; or, Occasional queries submitted to the judgment of such as would enquire in to the true state of things in our times. London, 1659.

A vindication of that most prudent and honourable knight, Sir Henry Vane, from the lyes and calumnies of Mr. Richard Baxter, minister of Kidderminster: In a monitory letter to the said Mr. Baxter. / By a true friend and servant of the Commonwealth of England, &c. London, 1659.

The common-wealth of Israel; or, A brief account of Mr. Prynne's anatomy of the good old cause. By H.S. London, 1659.

An essay in defence of the good old cause; or, A discourse concerning the rise and extent of the power of the civil magistrate in reference to spiritual affairs. London, 1659.

The common-wealth of Oceana put into the ballance, and found too light; or, An account of the republick of Sparta with occasional animadversions upon Mr. James Harrington and the Oceanistical model / by Henry Stvbbe. London, 1659.

A letter to an officer of the Army concerning a select senate mentioned by them in their proposals to the late Parliament. London, 1659.
A vindication of that prudent and honourable knight, Sir Henry Vane, from the lyes and calumnies of Mr. Richard Baxter, minister of Kidderminster. London, 1659.
The common-wealth of Oceana put into the ballance, and found too light, or, An account of the republick of Sparta. London, 1660.
The Rota; or, News from the Common-wealths-mens club. London, 1660.
The Indian nectar; or, A discourse concerning chocolata the nature of cacao-nut. London, 1662.
The arts of grandeur and submission; or, A discourse concerning the behaviour of great men towards their inferiours, and of inferiour personages towards men of greater quality. London, 1665.
The miraculous conformist; or, An account of severall marvailous cures performed by the stroking of the hands of Mr. Valentine Greatarick with a physicall discourse thereupon. Oxford, 1666.
Legends no histories; or, A specimen of some animadversions upon the history of the Royal Society. London, 1670.
Lex talionis; sive, Vindiciae pharmacoporum. London, 1670.
Campanella revived; or, An enquiry into the history of the Royal Society. London, 1670.
A censure upon certain passages contained in the History of the Royall Society. Oxford, 1670, expanded ed. 1671.
An epistolary discourse concerning phlebotomy in opposition to G. Thomson pseudo-chymist, a pretended disciple of the Lord Verulam. Np, 1671.
The Lord Bacons relation to the sweating-sickness examined, in a reply to George Thomson, pretender to physick and chymistry. London, 1671.
Medice cura teipsum! or, The apothecaries plea. London, 1671.
A justification of the present war against the United Netherlands wherein the declaration of His Majesty is vindicated, and the war proved to be just. London, 1672.
Rosemary & Bayes; or, Animadversions upon a treatise called, The rehearsall transprosed [sic]. London, 1672.
A further iustification of the present war against the United Netherlands illustrated with several sculptures. London, 1673.
The Paris gazette. London? 1673.
The history of the United Provinces of Achaia. London, 1673.
Select observations on English bodies of eminent persons in desperate diseases . . . In the Close is added, Directions for drinking of the Bath-Water, and Ars Cosmetica, or Beautifying Art: By Henry Stubbe, Physitian at Warwick. London, 1679.

SECONDARY SOURCES

About Muhammad: The Other Western Perspective on the Prophet of Islam. Ed. Abdelwahab El-Affendi. Richmond, Surrey, 2010.
Birchwood, Matthew. "Vindicating the Prophet: Universal Monarchy and Henry Stubbe's Biography of Mohammed." *Prose Studies* 29 (2007): 59–72.

Bosworth, C. Edmund. "The Prophet Vindicated: A Restoration Treatise on Islam and Muhammad." *Religion* 6 (1976): 1–12.

Britton, John. *The History and Antiquities of Bath Abbey Church*. London, 1825.

Campos, Edmund Valentine. "Thomas Gage and the English Colonial Encounter with Chocolate." *Journal of Medieval and Early Modern Studies* 39, no. 1 (2009): 183–200.

Champion, J. A. I. "'I remember a Mahometan Story of Ahmed Ben Edris': Freethiking Uses of Islam from Stubbe to Toland." *Al-Qantara* 31 (2010): 443–480.

——. *John Toland: Nazarenus,* ed., Oxford, 1999.

——"Legislators, Imposters, and the Politic Origins of Religion: English Theories of 'Imposture' from Stubbe to Toland." In Sylvia Berti et al., eds., *Hetrodoxy, Spinozism, and Free Thought in Early Eighteenth-Century Europe*, 333–356. Dordrecht, 1996.

——. *The Pillars of Priestcraft Shaken*. Cambridge, 1992.

Collins, Jeffrey. *The Allegiance of Thomas Hobbes*. Oxford, 2005.

Cook, Harold J. "Physicians and the New Philosophy: Henry Stubbe and the Virtuosi-Physicians." In Roger French and Andrew Wear, eds., *The Medical Revolution of the Seventeenth Century*, 246–271. Cambridge, 1989.

Dimmock, Matthew. *Mythologies of the Prophet Muhammad in Early Modern English Culture*. Cambridge, 2013.

Elmarsafy, Ziad. *The Enlightenment Qur'an*. Oxford, 2009.

Feingold, Mordechai. "Stubbe, Henry (1632–1676)." In *Oxford Dictionary of National Biography*. 2008 [2004].

Garcia, Humberto. *Islam and the English Protestnat Imagination, 1660–1830."* Ph.D. diss., University of Illinois at Urbana-Champaign, 2007.

——. "A Hungarian Revolution in Restoration England: Henry Stubbe, Radical Islam, and the Rye House Plot." *Eighteenth Century* 51 (2010): 1–25.

——. *Islam and the English Enlightenment, 1670–1840*. Baltimore, 2012.

Gunny, Ahmad. *The Prophet Muhamad in French and English Literature, 1650 to the Present,* ch. 1. Markfield, 2010.

Hill, Christopher Hill. *The Experience of Defeat*. Harmondsworth, 1984.

Holt, P. M. *A Seventeenth-Century Defender of Islam, Henry Stubbe (1632–76) and His Book*. London, 1972.

Jacob, James R. "The Authorship of 'An Account of the Rise and Progress of Mahometanism.'" *Notes and Queries* (February 1979): 10–11.

——. *Henry Stubbe, Radical Protestantism, and the Early Enlightenment*. Cambridge, 1983.

Jordan, W. K. *The Development of Religious Toleration in England*, vol. 3. Cambridge, 1940.

Kaplan, Barbara Beigun. "Greatrakes the Stroker: The Interpretations of His Contemporaries." *Isis* 73 (1982): 178–185.

Khairallah, Shireen. "Arabic Studies in England in the Late Seventeenth and Early Eighteenth Centuries." Ph.D. dissertation, University of London, 1972.

Kontler, László. "'Mahometan Christianity': Islam and the English Deists." In Eszter Andor and István György Tóth, eds., *Frontiers of Faith: Religious Exchange and the Constitution of Religious Identities, 1400–1750,* 107–119. Budapest, 2001.

Locke, John. *Two Tracts on Government*. Ed. Philip Abrams. Cambridge, 1967.
Matar, Nabil. *Islam in Britain, 1558–1685*. Cambridge, 1998.
Minois, Georges. *The Atheist's Bible: The Most Dangerous Book that Never Existed*. Trans. Lynn Ann Weiss. Chicago, 2012.
Mulsow, Martin. "Henry Stubbe, Robert Boyle and the Idolatry of Nature." In Sarah Mortimer and John Robertson, eds., *The Intellectual Consequences of Religious Heterodoxy, 1600–1750*. Leiden, 2012.
Oldfield, Edmund. *A Topographical and Historical Account of Wainfleet and the Wapentake*. London, 1829.
Rose, Jacqueline. "Royal Ecclesiastical Supremacy and the Restoration Church." *Historical Research* 80 (2007): 324–345.
Rosenblatt, Jason P. *Renaissance England's Chief Rabbi: John Selden*. Oxford, 2006.
Shapin, Steven. "The House of Experiment in Seventeenth-Century England." *Isis* 79 (1988): 374–404.
Tolan, John. "European Accounts of Muhammad's Life." In Jonathan E. Brockopp, ed., *The Cambridge Companion to Muhammad*, 226–250. New York, 2010.
Toomer, G. J. *John Selden: A Life in Scholarship*. Oxford, 2009.
Westfall, Richard S. *Science and Religion in Seventeenth-Century England*. Ann Arbor, 1973 [1958].
Wood, Anthony à. *Athenae oxonienses: An exact history of all the writers and bishops who have had their education in the University of Oxford. To which are added the Fasti, or Annals of the said University*, 3:1067–1083. 4 vols. New York, 1967.

INDEX

GPSR Authorized Representative: Easy Access System Europe, Mustamäe tee 50, 10621 Tallinn, Estonia, gpsr.requests@easproject.com

www.ingramcontent.com/pod-product-compliance
Lightning Source LLC
Chambersburg PA
CBHW030825310726
48980CB00006B/645/J

* 9 7 8 0 2 3 1 1 5 6 6 4 6 *